What the Doctors
Don't Tell You

What the Doctors Don't Tell You

One Woman's Journey Through Hodgkin's Lymphoma

Kimberly Joy Beam

authorHOUSE®

AuthorHouse™
1663 Liberty Drive
Bloomington, IN 47403
www.authorhouse.com
Phone: 1 (800) 839-8640

Published by AuthorHouse   05/16/2016

ISBN: 978-1-4969-7161-6 (sc)
ISBN: 978-1-4969-7196-8 (hc)
ISBN: 978-1-4969-7160-9 (e)

Library of Congress Control Number: 2015902980

Print information available on the last page.

Acknowledgments

I thank my mother and father for giving me life—twice. I wouldn't have made it through this ordeal without their support, strength, perseverance, and unending love. Also to my mom for her endless patience, her reading of this book which were harder for her every time she read it and her unconditional love.

Jena and her daughter, GiGi, and son, Jay, thank you as well. I took so much of Jena's time away from her family while we were editing this book. They were so patient and willing to share her. Thank you for making me a member of your family.

I am grateful to Linda and Steve for making me one of your own. I am thankful to Erin and her family for their endless support and for Erin's presence throughout the entire process.

Thank you, Randy Wagner, the real editor of this book.

Thomas Leavy, thank you for starting this adventure we are on.

G. Flynn McCauley is the artist who created this book's cover. He is one of the most accommodating and insightful artists with whom I have ever worked.

I am appreciative to all those who made living through this time possible.

A Note to Readers

I have changed many names and descriptions of relationships to protect those I love. This account represents what I remember. It is possible that some of these details will be remembered differently by someone else.

My goal was to write an authentic account of what it is like to go through diagnosis, treatment, and recovery and not be the same person on the other end. I want to show what navigating the world of sickness and medicine looks like and how everyone has his or her own story to tell. I want to explain what it's like to rely on people who hold all of the information and only give you bits of it when they feel that it is necessary or good for you. I want to share how no one handles sickness well—not the patients or their families or even the doctors, who are used to seeing it all.

PREFACE

I stood with cold water washing up over my toes, going over the bridge of my foot, and slapping around my ankles. The cold water washed past me, licking the beach behind me.

Where I was standing, the water was clear. My toes were yellow, pale, and curling into the golden brown sand, sinking deeper and deeper with each wave that washed in.

When I first put my toes in this frigid water, it was like pinpricks of needles. It reminded me of sewing on a button, when, instead of going through the button, the needle comes around the side and bites deeply into one's thumb. Pinprick after pinprick deep down into the flesh, over and over. Slowly I grew numb and eventually my feet were completely submerged. The blood running up my legs from my toes was cool.

Flecks of red from the blinding sun stained my vision.

There were some cute boys up the beach playing football. They would yip, hoot, and shout at each other. Sometimes the ball would go too far, and one of them would dive, getting sand all over his chest and in his long, shaggy hair. I noticed but did not watch too closely. Those cute boys with the football—I heard them talking about me, in the corner of my thoughts. Mostly, I just stared down into the water where my feet should have been but were now covered by sand. My invisible toes were warmer than my upper foot and ankle where the cold water was piercing them.

I had been wondering about walking on water and whether I had enough faith to do it.

One of the sandy, muscled, lanky haired boys flew into my range of vision. He jumped into the water right in front of me, splashing. He screamed out in utter shock, jumped high into the air, and then landed knee deep. Then a wave washed back out to sea, so what was knee deep on him washed down to his calf.

My eyebrows arched in surprise.

He charged out of the water, ran back up the beach, and yelled to his friends, "I don't know how the hell she is doing that!"

It's not everyone who learns how to handle pain.

FINDING THE LUMP

I had put myself on a diet the previous June. Pushing out of my size 10 pants into size 12s, creeping past 159 pounds, was not acceptable. I was near Ithaca, staying with a dear friend, Jessica, when I decided it was time. I got serious and signed up with an online weight-loss system.

Over the next couple of months, my weight dropped gradually, two or three pounds a week. Then, as the fall approached winter, the weight dropped off faster: I could eat a giant meal at a restaurant—a cheeseburger, fries, and cheesecake for dessert—but on the scale the next morning, another pound would be gone.

On April 1, I was on the phone with my good friend Erin. We had been on the phone for some time, and as the conversation progressed, I grew bored of pacing and took my fingers and jabbed them into my collarbones.

My collarbones were now sticking out prominently like a model's, and I was rather fond of them. I raised my collarbones up and felt around their curve as deep into the hollow as my body would allow. My right hand was rooting around in the lower corner.

We were trying to end the conversation, doing the last mumbles before hanging up the phone. Instead of my usual, "I love you," I blurted out, "Oh, my God! I think I found a lump!"

Erin's father had been the president of the American Cancer Society on Long Island for almost her entire life. During her high-school summers, she worked at camps for kids who had cancer. When she replied, "Go to the doctor tomorrow," I took her seriously.

"I do have the day off, and I don't have any plans," I thought aloud.

"Good, let me know how it goes," she said as we hung up.

The next day, my doctor felt inside my collarbone and at a different lump I had found in my left breast a couple of months earlier. I wasn't concerned about either, until she said, "I don't think the lump in your chest is anything, but the lump here"—she was probing my collarbone—"I'm just not sure. I'm going to call for an ultrasound of the breast and a CT scan for this lump." She kept pressing her fingers in the lower corner of my collarbone. She would walk away and then come back, have me move my arm to create the hollow in my collarbone, and press her fingers in again, clearly thinking.

She ordered a CT scan for the following Friday, April 9, 2010, one week to the day after my appointment with her.

***

During the week between the doctor's visit and the CT scan appointment, I sought other people's opinions about the lump, including my landlords'. I lived in an apartment in Nottingham, Pennsylvania, above a garage at the end of a quarter-mile driveway. It was such a great spot. It was adjacent to the Herr Factory barren lands. Occasionally in early morning on a Saturday, like around 6:00 a.m., a foxhunt would go through with barking dogs and horse riders with red coats, which are apparently called "pinks." The property had a pond, a chicken coop, and cornfields at the top of the hill, and one day an escaped emu ran around at the top end of the driveway.

I walked into my landlord's kitchen and the female half of the couple leaned in and placed her fingers in the space behind my clavicle. "I'm sure it's nothing," she said.

I agreed. Of course it was nothing. I was God's chosen daughter; not only was I a Christian, but I came to faith from Judaism. Of course I would be just fine:

1. God had my back.
2. I had planned to go to graduate school for a master's in divinity. I had been accepted and was headed to school in Chicago. Nothing was going to stop that.

***

Jean, a dear friend of mine in her sixties, drove me to Syndersville Regional Hospital. We were both concerned about what the CT scan involved and whether my body might have some sort of reaction to the chemicals. She promised me eggs for breakfast afterward, since I had to fast before the test.

I wore my going-to-the-doctor clothes—a black tank top with a built in shelf bra and a little bit of lace at the top, a pair of athletic pants with no zippers or grommets, and a knitted gray cabled cotton hoodie sweater I'd bought in Philadelphia the previous Thanksgiving.

I went in for the CT scan first; an ultrasound would be next. The technicians put the IV into my vein. I didn't know the IV drip had to be turned on; I thought because the needle was in my arm and the curly tube was attached to the hanging drip bag, the liquid had to be going into my arm.

The tech looked to be about eighteen years old, as did her assistant. They were both white and ridiculously thin. The CT scanner had a scooped bed to lie on, where the sides were higher than the bottom. The techs told me to lie down on the curved bed with my head on a pillow and another pillow under my knees. They covered my legs with a blanket and told me, "Raise your hands up over your head."

The IV line pulled a little when I lifted my arms. The bed started to slide into the CT scanner.

A mechanical female voice told me to breathe and then not to breathe. I was instructed to follow the directions of the disembodied voice. They would do one scan without the contrast dye and then one scan with contrast. I didn't know what that meant.

When the voice said, "Take a deep breath, and hold it," I filled my lungs and held my breath as I rode the scanner bed in and out of the cream-colored, doughnut-shaped machine. There was a window of about six inches through which I could see a camera whirling around; it sounded like a large industrial fan and created a chilling air current. The room was cold to start with. The fan's blowing made me shiver, which made it almost impossible to keep still when the disembodied voice directed me to hold my breath.

"Okay," the tech said. "We got that one. Now we are going to start the dye."

There was another high-pitched whirring sound. I felt pressure in my arm as the liquid from the contrast dye forced itself into my body. All of a sudden, there was a cool liquid all over my neck.

The flighty tech came charging into the room and said, "Ugh! These new IV tubes do this all the time. It's beginning to really get on my nerves."

But I was laughing. It just struck me as funny—the sensation of cold liquid all over my neck and the tension of the whole procedure.

As the tech stood over me, trying to fix the problem, I realized that I was warm all over, crazy, crazy warm. It sort of felt like I had peed my pants.

A student of mine named Daisy had warned me that might happen. She'd had a CT scan just a couple of weeks earlier. At softball practice, the ball machine had chucked a ball going forty or fifty miles per hour at her, and she hit it with the wrong part of the bat. The ball nailed her right in her throat. The techs were concerned Daisy had shattered her windpipe. She hadn't, but her voice was gone for about a week or so.

When she found out I was going to have a CT scan, Daisy told me, "Don't worry, Beam. It will feel like you peed your pants, but you didn't. It will just feel like it."

I said to the tech who was mopping up the dye, "I feel all warm, like I just peed myself."

"You do?" the tech asked. Then she said, "Okay, let's put you through the scanner fast. Maybe there will be enough dye in there to get a good picture."

She left and, again, I followed the directions of the disembodied voice. At the end, though, I let out my breath too soon. I couldn't hold it any longer. I didn't know if it was from the laughing or from nerves. As it turned out, my exhaling didn't matter. They got the pictures they needed.

The tech helped me off the narrow scanner's bed, and I was escorted to another waiting room to await an ultrasound on my left breast. The room was dim, with an overhead light on low. It was such a contrast from the CT scan room, which was florescent and bright. I put on one of those gowns with the opening in the back and curled up on the bed under a blanket. The lighting in the ultrasound room was so low that I considered falling asleep.

I closed my eyes and saw two vague images of very tall beings with overly large wings hovering above the bed. They emitted a sense of white. A sense of comfort rushed over me; whether it was my imagination or real insight into the spiritual world didn't matter much. I wasn't alone.

As I focused on them, I felt their wings flapping slowly. Still comforted, I realized their heads were in the ceiling, looking into the room above me.

I thought about a bed and a surgery going on above me: doctors in blue face masks and gloves under bright lights and sterile blue sheets of paper fabric. I prayed for the surgery I imagined and the patient I couldn't see.

As the giant beings moved their wings with more power, I thought I felt the air currents in the room change. A warm air moved in. When the flapping stopped, the room's air turned cool once again.

Eventually, the ultrasound tech came in and sat down next to me. She was white and older. I felt comfortable with her instantly because she presented as experienced and confident. She picked up the ultrasound wand and told me, "This is going to be cold." She held up the ultrasound gel and with her eyes on the screen, she lifted the blanket and gown. With only a partial glance at my chest, she squeezed the freezing substance all over my left breast, and I shivered involuntarily.

"Sorry," she said.

"You don't have heated gel?" I asked.

"I wish. I feel so bad when I have to freeze patients." She moved the wand around my chest but couldn't locate the lump. "Can you point out where it is to me?" she asked.

"Sure," I said. I ran my hand over my breast and found it toward the southeast quadrant.

The tech took the wand and tried to find the lump on the computer screen, but it wouldn't appear on the screen. She asked if she could find the lump with her fingers. She hoped that once she felt it, she could pull it up on the screen.

"Go for it," I said.

Again, the lump didn't show.

She took images of what she couldn't see and said, "I'm going to go talk to the radiologist."

She left me in the room by myself and I looked around for what I had decided were angels, but I was no longer quiet enough to sense them.

The ultrasound tech eventually returned with the radiologist, who looked at the screen as she moved the ultrasound wand around. The radiologist said, "It's confusing. We are sending you to get a mammogram, just to be certain that nothing else is going on there."

"Okay," I replied. "So, what you are saying is that you don't think it's anything, but you aren't certain."

"Exactly," she said and left, allowing me to wipe off the ultrasound goo and get back into my clothes.

My friend Jean was married to Aubrey, and they were both a little younger than my parents but only by a year or two. They had been Christians since the 1970s. Aubrey and Jean were dear friends who gave me advice and were a sounding board for most of the decisions I had to make. They followed my belief system and shared my values, unlike my parents, who came at the world differently than I did.

My mother was a Reform Jew who took off from work for the High Holy Days in Judaism and celebrated Hanukkah. She never went to synagogue anymore, even though she lived less than three miles from the Reform Synagogue, which her parents had helped found. My father converted to Judaism to marry my mom, but when they divorced, he ended his commitment to organized religion. He said he wanted to put together a pamphlet on his secular humanistic beliefs, so that when the Jehovah's Witnesses came to the door, he could give them his reading material in exchange for theirs.

I met Jean and Aubrey at the local Vineyard Church, where I was also a member. It had become a tradition that we would go to lunch after church: the Olive Garden, Applebee's, Red Robin. Their only son called me the sister he never wanted.

The Sunday after my CT scan, April 11, we were at an Irish pub. In our company weren't just me, Aubrey, and Jean, but Aubrey and Jean's son and his wife, and their granddaughter, who was a strong softball player, along with another couple who were Aubrey and Jean's old friends. We'd been at her softball game earlier that afternoon. We had ordered the crab and artichoke dip and hot roast beef sandwiches.

In the middle of dinner, my phone rang. I looked at the caller ID and didn't recognize the number. Therefore, I let the call go to voicemail. I was in a noisy pub with people; I never answer my phone when I am eating with others, unless it is absolutely necessary. When the meal was over, I hopped into Aubrey's truck and listened to the voicemail.

It was from a doctor at the medical center, the place that had sent me for the ultrasound and CT scan. A doctor I had never met was calling at 5:30 on a Sunday evening. This could not be good.

Aubrey said, "I'm sure it's all going to be okay."

I called the number the doctor left and got the answering service, which said the doctor would call me back in ten minutes, and if he didn't to call them back.

Ten minutes was enough time to get home and settle in on Jean and Aubrey's back deck. Only moments after I sat down, my phone rang again.

The doctor introduced himself and then gave the results of my tests. He said, "The ultrasound looks okay, but the radiologist recommends that you get a mammogram just to be sure."

"Okay," I said. What else could I say? The radiologist had already told me that.

The doctor continued, "The doctor you see here at medical center is only part-time. She won't get these results until Tuesday. I want to get started right away."

I was listening carefully when he said, "The CT scan reads that there is a mass that is three by four by point four centimeters directly under your breastbone. The doctor who read your CT scan thinks it's either a thymoma or lymphoma."

"It's how big?" I asked.

"Three by four by point four centimeters, which means it's long and really thin."

Stunned, I tried to listen more carefully, but I was having a hard time concentrating on his words. I was going over what he said it might be—*lymphoma or … what was the other thing?*

"I want to get you an appointment with a surgeon as soon as possible to try to diagnose what we are seeing."

"Okay. What did you say it might be again?"

"Thymoma, cancer of the thymus gland, or lymphoma, cancer of the lymph nodes."

Silence. *Lymphoma—that's not good. That's never good, right?*

Then he added, "I'm going to have our scheduler make an appointment for a surgeon at a local hospital so that you can meet with them to discuss the next steps."

"Okay."

"If you have any further questions, feel free to call me back."

"Okay."

I hung up the phone.

The sky was a gray-purple, and Aubrey and Jean were sitting in Adirondack chairs in the fading light. Their jackets were blurring into the woods behind them. Night was erasing sharp lines and it was beginning to cool.

"He thinks I have one of two possible types of cancer," I said.

"What types?" Aubrey said.

"I don't know. Lymphoma or something else, a cancer of some gland."

"What did he say?" Jean asked.

Looking back on it, as the doctor and I talked, I should have put him on speakerphone so that Jean and Aubrey could have heard him for themselves. Then all of us could have listened at once and maybe heard all of the pieces together. Instead, my numb brain wasn't able to process much of what was said.

I told Jean, "He said he's going to get some surgeon at the local trauma hospital."

Birds chirped. The peepers in the pond out back were starting to sing.

"You going to call your mom?" Jean asked.

I shrugged. *Yes. Of course.* But I knew my mom. She was going to ask all these questions, and I just didn't know the answers. I decided to procrastinate by watching a reality TV contest show and call my parental units after it was over. My parents had divorced when I was two, which meant I had to report any news twice.

I called my dad and stepmom first and did something I have never done before or since: I asked to be put on speakerphone.

"I just got a call from the doctor about the CT scan on Friday. I did tell you I was getting a CT scan, right?"

"Right," Dad said.

"The doctor called on a Sunday night?" my stepmom, Giselle, asked.

"Never good, right?" I replied. After a pause, I said, "He thinks, based on the CT scan, that I might have cancer."

More silence.

Then my stepmom said, "Oh man," soft and slow.

"Right," I said. "Oh man."

Then Dad changed into dad mode. "You are the one of the kindest, most caring people I know."

"Thanks, Dad," I replied.

We talked for about a half an hour or more, and they both insisted on being informed of every move from here forward. They both wanted to be very much involved in the process and know how I was doing.

A little weepy, I hung up the phone and called Mom. We were on the phone for maybe ten minutes. I said, "I got a call from the doctor, and he's thinking cancer."

She got quiet and asked basically the same questions as Aubrey and Jean. Then she asked if I had told anyone else, like Wendy, my mom's niece and practically her best friend.

"I'm going to call her right after this," I said.

Mom replied, "Well, go call her. I have the Japanese student who's staying with me moving in right now, and I can't talk. Can I call you back later?"

"Fine," and we hung up.

Did I just get passed over for a Japanese stranger? Did I not just say, "I might have cancer?" What does it take to get some attention around here?

I called Wendy, and her advice was to go to the Hospital of the University of Benjamin Franklin instead of a local hospital. She'd had a tumor growing in the roof of her mouth and went for a second opinion at UBF. She said the difference between her local hospital and UBF was striking. She thought it would be good to work with someone who coped with this type of thing every day.

I hung up with Wendy and called the doctor back, going through the answering service. Less than five minutes later, we were on the phone.

"I'm glad you called back. I was hoping you would," the doctor said. "What are your questions?"

"Can we start at UBF?" I asked.

"I'm glad you want to take this so seriously," he said. "I was going to recommend you get the diagnosis from the local hospital but move on to the University of Benjamin Franklin from there. It's great that you want to start at UBF."

When I'm on the phone, I pace. That night, I paced around the kitchen island but stopped at the backdoor overlooking the deck. The lights were dim in the living room, and the kitchen lights were off, so I was able to make out a few of the floorboards out on the deck, which was now cloaked in total darkness.

I spoke softly, "How serious is this? Should I be worried?"

The doctor cleared his throat. "I know this is awkward since we've never met. This isn't the way to do this, but I want to get you started as soon as possible. I do think you have a challenge in front of you. I think you're going to be okay, but it's going to be a rough road for a little while."

He said that there were some kinds of lymphoma that he would want to get if he were to get cancer. He said there are some kinds of lymphoma that are curable. He also said the surgeon would be able to answer a lot more of my questions, since all he had to go on was the CT scan, and it was pretty inconclusive.

***

Later that night, I was sitting on the floor next to Aubrey's plaid armchair. I had my knees pulled up to my chest and I was rocked back on my tailbone. Jean had the TV on low, and we were all sitting in silence; none of us were watching the screen.

Even though I lived in an adorable apartment about forty-five minutes away, they didn't want me to be alone that night. They sent me upstairs to bed in their guestroom. The next morning, I got up from an okay sleep and headed off to the high school where I taught. I got ready to go and headed out the door with my normal cup of tea in hand. But I felt heavy, like everything took effort, and nothing seemed quite real.

Telling Mr. Trebuchet, Berry, Zern, and the English Department

I drove to school with my iPod playing through my Honda's radio. David Crowder. "All I Can Say." Acoustic guitar. Haunting vocals. "Lord, I'm tired, so tired from walking … And Lord, the dark is creeping in …"

On repeat, over and over, playing loud enough drown out any thoughts that might try to sweep me down and under.

***

My way to school took me down Route 40 from Newark, Delaware, to the town in Maryland where I taught. As I listened, tears I didn't even know were hidden started to drop.

Couldn't it be possible that someone from little podunk Syndersville Hospital got it wrong? What did their radiologists know?

"This is all I can give; that's my everything," was the chorus playing as I drove into the school's parking lot and parked my car in the illegal spot I used every day. I quickly got out of my car. My principal, Mr. Trebuchet, was on the sidewalk in front of the cafeteria, walking from his truck into the building.

One of my colleagues, Doug, saw me getting out of the car. "Kim, are you okay?" he called after me as I closed my car door and started to power walk toward Mr. Trebuchet.

"No!" I yelled back to Doug and hightailed it to catch up with Mr. Trebuchet. I hurried so I would only have to say it once and fast.

As I closed in, I called his name. He stopped and turned toward me. He's a bear of a man; I have said many times, if I ever have the privilege to cast a giant in a movie, Mr. Trebuchet would be my first choice for the role. He's very tall, white, with a round, lightly freckled face, a shaved head, and intense blue eyes.

He looked at me expectantly. When I caught up, I continued walking, looking down. We matched pace and walked toward the building.

I mumbled, "I got a call from the doctor last night. They're saying cancer, so if I get a call that says the doctor can see me as soon as this afternoon, then please know I'm dropping everything to go to Philadelphia."

He held the door open for me and said, "Do what you need to do."

Still not making eye contact, I turned into the office to check my mailbox and sign in. Relief coursed through me. My job could come second. I had been so worried about how to juggle both teaching and diagnosis. But I also knew I would feel really dumb if this big scare came to nothing.

This whole thing had to be some sort of joke. I'm God's beloved, His chosen daughter. I'm a sister of Christ and married to Him at the same time. Don't ask me how that works, but it does. Since I am sold out for Him, solely and soully dependent on Him, of course there has been a mistake. There's no way I will be diagnosed with cancer. There just isn't any way.

Here I am telling people the doctors are saying cancer, and how dumb will we all feel when it's proven to be nothing? Those radiologists have it wrong. Everyone will see there's no way I can have cancer. I'm thirty-three. This is one big mistake.

Mr. Trebuchet turned into the office behind me, but when I turned to go to my mailbox, he continued down to his office.

I walked out of the office, down the hall, past the gym, and around the corner by the guidance office. As I rounded the corner, my lead teacher, Josephine Poppy, was walking ahead of me.

"Josephine!" I called.

At the same time there was an all-call on the PA system. It sounded like Mr. Trebuchet's voice, only thicker and sad. He was calling someone to the office.

"Did you hear who he wanted?" I asked.

She shook her head no.

"I have to tell you something," I said, and we walked up the stairs together.

***

When we got to the top of the stairs, I asked Dave to come out of his classroom, and Rob stood in the hall with me and Josephine. I gave more details: *three by four by point four centimeters right behind my breastbone. No, the doctors didn't know what it was. They were making an appointment for me at BFU and I didn't know much beyond that.* I looked at them and said, "I don't know when the appointment is going to be, and you may have to cover for me. I'm really sorry."

Josephine looked at me and said, "Don't even worry about that. Take care of what you need to."

As I was speaking, I felt a large presence behind me and immediately knew it was Mr. Trebuchet without even having to turn around. After I'd finished talking about what the doctors had said, I turned to Mr. Trebuchet.

"Yes, sir?" I asked in all sincerity.

"Do you want to go home?" he asked.

"What? Why?"

He just looked at me.

"What am I going to do at home? Sit around and think? No. That won't do me any good," I replied.

"Are you going to be able to do this today?" he asked.

I shrugged and tried to smile. "We'll find out."

***

There were four main building areas in our high school, each labeled with a letter. The English department was in the upstairs of B Building, making it "Upper B." During the switch for classes, Ms. Berry, Mr. Zern, and I were in the Bat Cave, our affectionate term for the Upper B workroom. It was a dingy room, with cubicles for people to work, bad light, a printer for the whole English department, and an extremely slow computer.

Berry, a special-education teacher, was freaking out about one of her students.

"They are going to make me pass him! He doesn't deserve it. I give him chance after chance to retake stuff, and he doesn't even care! I work harder than he does. I do more by carrying my pencil behind my ear from class to class than he does in a whole day!"

I was listening to her, but not really. Hers was the usual rant that could be heard pretty much anywhere in our building at any given time. Except the pencil bit—that was Berry's own special flare to the rant.

"So," I said, waiting for her to pause so I could get into the conversation. Zern looked at me, and Berry paused.

"I think I might have cancer," I blurted.

Berry stopped speaking, and Zern just stared at me. I guess the look on my face told them I was serious.

"What? Why?" Berry asked. Zern just stood there, quiet.

I explained the lump and talked about how tired I was; maybe my exhaustion had nothing to do with being on a diet or the fact that I was now over thirty years old.

"What do you mean 'tired'?" Zern asked.

"Remember when we moved the couch into your classroom from the truck?" I asked. A few months earlier, a colleague had garbage-picked a couch, put it in his truck, and gave it to Zern. After school one day, Zern and I hauled the couch up to his classroom and put it in front of his floor-to-ceiling windows.

"Yeah?"

"It was exhausting. Exhausting. I thought I would die I was so tired. I seriously thought about a nap afterward."

Zern was a couple of years older than I. He hadn't been exhausted after moving the couch up one flight of stairs and down a couple hallways.

"That's not normal," he said.

"I know. Neither is this," I said, inviting them to feel the lump in my neck.

From there, we all went to class, Berry and me to my ninth-grade English class and Zern to his third-period creative writing class.

***

Most of the English department ate lunch in the Upper B planning room, which should not be confused with the Bat Cave, the department's workroom. Every department had its own workroom, but the planning room was used by the whole faculty. It just happened to be in Upper B. The planning room had a large white table with swears written on the sides and uncomfortable plastic chairs. It contained two couches and two rolling chairs that reclined so far the people on them were practically lying on their backs. One of the recliners was nicknamed the penis chair because of the drawing on its right armrest. The planning room also held two copy machines that were always jamming, eating papers, or melting transparencies. These copiers often demanded the furtive repair man to come with his little suitcase and spend quality time with them.

Cell phones were taboo for teachers. If students were not allowed to use their phones, then teachers were not allowed to either.[1] That day, my phone was in my back pocket, and I told each of my classes that if my phone rang and it was a doctor, I would have to take the call.

---

[1] Boon Win High School changed its policy about cell phones in the 2013–14 school year. Administrators stated that students were allowed to use their cell phones, but at the discretion of their teachers. The new policy stated teachers were allowed to have their cell phones on their persons, but they could not take them out or use them in front of students; however, students could text, tweet, Facebook, or engage in any online activity, as long as they did not hook into the school's nonsecure Wi-Fi network. As a teacher waiting to hear if I had been diagnosed with cancer, I wasn't allowed to have my phone. If I had been diagnosed in the 2013–14 school year, my students conceivably could have had the news before I did.

At the end of lunch, my phone rang. It was the surgeon's nurse practitioner calling to answer some of my questions. The bell was ringing to go back to class, and teachers started to file out of the planning room to go to class. Ms. Berry said, "I will cover your class. Take as long as you need."

The nurse practitioner told me that I would meet with the doctor the following Tuesday. I had to wait a whole week and a day before I could discuss all the scenarios and find out the next steps. Afterward, I called my mom and then my dad to tell them what I'd just learned. Whenever I talked with the doctors' offices or the nurse practitioner or the actual doctor, I had to report back to my parental units and report the news twice, because they both wanted to know all that was happening.

That day, especially, as I talked with one parent and then the other, I found the details were just too much. The idea of going to a surgeon, having to wait a whole week before I could even see him, and there weren't any immediate answers made my eyes teary and my body shake, full of adrenaline and exhausted at the same time.

One of the women at the local doctor's office said that the waiting for the appointment to come was the hardest part but that the appointment would come. She also said that not too much would change in the week of waiting. She was speaking from the experience of having breast cancer, and I wanted her words to bring me comfort. But the truth was, I was the one waiting and I don't wait very well.

By the time I got back to class, I was trying to hold it together. My eyes were red, I knew that. I walked in boldly, doing my job, going over vocabulary with all the fake energy I could muster. No one seemed to notice, until about seven minutes in. One of the female students in the middle of the room stopped class by saying, "Beam, are you about to cry?"

I paused and looked at her. "Don't ask me that."

"You are, aren't you? What's wrong?"

I looked up at the ceiling. "I don't know."

"You are getting calls from doctors," she thought aloud, looking at me. "What's going on?"

"I don't know." I paused when I saw that wouldn't satisfy her. "But they are saying cancer."

Faith

I went back to Aubrey and Jean's that night to eat dinner. I don't remember if I spent the night there, but I do remember a dinner conversation clearly. I might say that I remembered dinner clearly, but that would be silly, since I don't know what we ate that night.

I felt trapped. I felt pressed under a weight; I know that's probably cliché, but it's really how I physically felt. I felt there was incredible pressure on my shoulders and back coming down from an invisible force above. Fear lurked in my insides. If I turned my attention inward for too long, I would physically shake. My strength crumbled, and tears pushed at the corners of my eyes. If I held myself strong, my stomach tight, my back upright, I forgot to breathe.

Jean was doing the dishes, and I was at the table with a cup of tea. I looked at Aubrey, sitting across from me, and something in me just snapped. I picked my hand up and brought it forcefully down on the table, making a loud thumping crack when my rings hit the wood. Jean jumped and turned. Aubrey's eyes got wide. I spoke with all the force of my being.

"Satan is a liar. He comes to steal, kill, and destroy."

Aubrey nodded, and Jean agreed with me.

"If that's the case, I'm fine. I'm fine," I repeated. "Satan is a liar, and I choose not to stand with his pronouncement of my death. I also declare that my family will come to see God based on what He does in my life as a result of this false pronouncement over me. The doctors are not God, and God is the One who defines who I am and what happens to me."

"Amen," they said, and I felt that weight on my shoulders and back lift.

I am not exaggerating about that weight. I did feel something different after this declaration. The fear left. The cloud lifted. I felt much better. Aubrey, Jean, and I knew the diagnosis would not be cancer. It couldn't be. Satan was a liar, and I was God's daughter and beloved.

Interactions with Colleagues

I was on hall duty, watching kids pass down the main corridor not too far from my classroom. One of my colleagues in the English department had to walk past me to get to the printer in the Bat Cave. He came up and stood close, so close I could smell the coffee on his breath. I wanted to take a step back, away from him, but previous experience taught me he would close the gap I created. I had learned not to back up, especially with a bank of lockers not far behind me; I didn't want to get pinned. Instead, I stood tall as he approached, waiting for whatever it was he was going to whisper.

He mumbled, "Are you dying?"

I shrugged, "I don't know."

He nodded and continued his walk to the printer.

***

I was in the hallway where the Upper D building met Upper A. Maeve, the art teacher, and Emma, the math teacher, were in the hallway with me. We all attended the same church. We were discussing my diagnosis and all of my questions at that point.

Maeve asked what I was going to do. Kids started to pass to their classes, making the hallways grow louder and louder. I got louder and louder too. The answer was: whatever the doctors said. Soon I was yelling over the student's din, telling Maeve and Emma that no matter what happened, I'd win. "If I get sick and get better, then it all works out," I said. "If God heals me, then my family will see Him. And I if I die? How great would that be? It would be so cool to be in heaven! I can't lose on this one."

Maeve and Emma had worried looks on their faces as we turned to walk to our respective classrooms. Emma told me later that she went to her classroom and wept. Emma is not a weeper, either.

To: Important Contacts
From: Me
Subject: Crazy talk
Date: April 14, 2010

Okay, I have had this thought for a number of you: "I have to call them and talk to them and tell them what's up." But, in reality, how do you call people over and over and say what I've had to say too many times already? I'm going to say it here, once. Whoever wants to call and ask more questions or just laugh with me, please don't hesitate. I want to talk to you. I just don't want to have to say this a ton of times.

I found a lump behind my collarbone on Thursday, April 1. I was on the phone with Erin at the time, and she made me promise to go to the doctor. I took the health form that the graduate school I am planning on attending wanted filled out and went to the doctor the next day. I got checked out for a lump on my breast (sorry, but it's true), the lump behind my collarbone on the right side, and that form. The doctor was flummoxed about what to do about the lumps and called for tests just to be sure. Both tests showed nothing as far as the CT scan tech (for my collarbone) could tell. A doctor came in on the ultrasound, and said she would call up a mammogram to make sure all was fine.

On Sunday I got a call from the doctor about the CT scan. You know, it's never good when the doctor wants to talk results at 6:30 p.m. on a Sunday night.

They found this mass growing behind my breastbone, in front of my lungs in the area where the ventricles are. Lymph nodes are there and the mass is between the lungs. They have labeled it one of two types of cancer.

A close family relation, for those of you who don't know, had a tumor in the soft palette of her mouth going up into her head (eew). She told me she wished she started at UBF instead of monkeying around at her local hospital. I talked to my doctor and he agreed. By 4:00 p.m. on Monday I had an appointment on Tuesday, April 20, 2010, at UBF to meet with a surgeon to talk about my neck and the mass in my chest (which is about three by four by point four centimeters).

Okay, those are the hard tangible facts, the stuff of science. Now faith. I have crazy peace, for the most part. I see this as an opportunity to derail me from what God has been trying to accomplish. He's been working on my trusting Him in going out to Chicago for graduate school. I sometimes even wonder what I am thinking or why I'm going to Chicago, but I know what He is saying and what He is asking, and I will go where He sends me. Anyway, there have been a lot of crazy prophetic words recently about what God is going to do with me. The enemy clearly wants to derail me, and how best than to attack my body, use one of the scariest labels in our vocabulary, and make me know that I'm going to have to be cut open in order to get healthy? But if you look at the other side, it was revealed and revealed early. The truth shone through, and He will be able to heal me, both spiritually and medicinally.

The encouragement I have received since my church sent out the prayer announcement has been so uplifting. The love of Aubrey and Jean—letting me cry on their living floor the night I found out and standing with me on Monday night when I pounded on the table in the middle of dinner and announced, "Satan is such a big fat liar!" At that moment, everything changed. Seriously, that's when the peace came in. Sunday, I couldn't sleep. Monday, less than twenty-four hours later, I was in bed, eyes closed, and asleep with no fear, tears, or torment. I will say, the prayer meeting at church on Monday night helped a whole ton as well. I've been able to laugh, make jokes at work, and be almost okay. I am a little short with my students when they ask too many questions about what I see as insignificant things (their papers, grades, etc.). But I'm going to work on being gracious and understanding, because their concerns are just as important as mine.

Thank you for reading all of that and standing in faith with me. What is hidden is always revealed. I'm a little scared and make sick, morbid jokes. Whatever my future holds, God is there with either His presence here on earth or His presence in heaven. I received a prophetic word that I will be fine, and this is a bump in the road. I am more than a conqueror who sees this momentary struggle as means for creating eternal glory for God.

I will keep you posted. And again, don't hesitate to write or call.

Love,
Kim

"Not all those who wander are lost." ~ J. R. R. Tolkien

Meeting the Surgeon

My first appointment with Dr. K was on April 20, 2010, a Tuesday morning. April 20 is not a day I love.

I have a teacher friend who used to say, "We should erase April 20 from the calendar."

April 20 is Hitler's birthday, and many bad things have happened on this date in history, intentionally and unintentionally:

- Columbine.
- The Gulf oil spill.
- An earthquake in China that killed 150 people.
- Our country's unofficial annual celebration of marijuana

One year, the high school held the prom on April 20. My first reaction was, "Who planned this one?"

This April 20 was no exception.

Dr. K's office was on the first floor of UBF's medical building adjacent to the UBF hospital. This medical building would become a building I know well. But on that day, I found it very confusing. The ground floor is the lobby floor—street level—but also home to the major testing sites: radiology, pulmonary, mammography, and the like. The second floor was labeled the first floor; it's also Dr. K's home. The third floor was really the second floor, according to the elevator panel and is home to UBF's Cancer Center. "CN floor" was listed on the elevator panel, where they do proton therapy. It was below the ground floor, but above the parking levels, P1, P2, and P3. It took us forever to find out what CN stood for—"Concourse," not any of the silly names we gave it: Crazy Nurses, Computer Nerds, Company Noshes.

My appointment was in the late morning, and the people who felt it was important to be present were there: Mom; Dad; Giselle, my stepmom; Wendy, my cousin, and her baby. Aubrey and Jean were there too, but they waited in the lobby. I went in solo, at first, and met the nurse practitioner, Claire. She took vital stats and left me alone for a little while.

While I waited in that ochre-colored room with the traditional "doctor's office" beige linoleum flooring, I thought back to my previous couple of days. Like Jean, Aubrey and I believed that the radiologists and techs in the hospital in the "sticks" of Pennsylvania didn't know at what they were looking. We were all hoping that maybe, maybe, the "readers" in the little hospital got it wrong. Those little, out of the way hospitals didn't see what the "big serious" hospitals saw every day. It would be so simple to make a mistake like that and say, "Looks a little weird. Let's call it cancer."

When Claire, Dr. K's nurse practitioner, came back, I said to her, "Did you see the mass they said was on the scan?"

"Oh yeah," she said. "It's clear."

There was no mistake. Her words stung on several levels: 1) the lumps were there, 2) I was insulting completely competent doctors I didn't even know, and 3) I believed God would have healed me with all the prayers I had received.

Claire asked questions about my and my family's medical history. We talked for some time as she took notes in the computer. Eventually, she said she would get my family, and the doctor would come in to see us.

The room was small to begin with, but when we added Mom, Dad, Giselle, Wendy, and the baby on her lap, it became absolutely tiny. (Aubrey and Jean said they would wait in the waiting room. Just being there for me was enough for them. Looking back on this, a part of me hurts that they drove all the way up into Philly to be a part of what was going on, and had to hold back from the main event of seeing the doctor.) When Dr. K entered, he looked at all of the people sitting in the room waiting for him, and he turned to me. "You must be Kim. Only the patient willingly takes a seat on that," he said, indicating the examination table.

He sat in the rolling chair in front of the computer and began to discuss options. He was white and of thick stature. His hands and girth were large—not in a fat way, just in a broad, sturdy way. As he spoke, Giselle took notes. Dr. K said, based on the scans, there were two possibilities: one was lymphoma, cancer of the lymph nodes; the other was thymoma, cancer of the thymus gland, which one needs when one is young and helps the transition into adolescence. The thymus gland tends to shrink and become unimportant when one is an adult.

"If it is thymoma," he said, "the treatment is we crack open the breast bone, take it out and that's it." The other option wasn't so easy to treat. Lymphoma would require chemotherapy and radiation, six months of treatment.

Whenever he said the word *treatment*, I found myself shrinking away from him a little. I feared and cringed and swam away from what that meant. It wouldn't come to *treatment*.

At one point I looked at him, shoved my right hand into my right collarbone, and said, "It's right here. Can't you just take it?"

"I know you think you can feel it," he said. "I cannot take the mass out if it's lymphoma. It's illegal. The only way I can take a lymph node out is for diagnosis. But if I 'treat' lymphoma by removing the lymph nodes, it will just spread to other lymph nodes."

His line, "I know you think you can feel it," rankled. Damn straight I knew I could feel it. That's what sent me to the doctor in the first place. I felt the lump.

I was vindicated later when he eventually got off of his stool, shoved his meaty hand into my collarbone, and said, "I think I can get this."

"Told you."

He poked around in my neck some more. Then he asked, "How does your hand feel?" as he applied pressure on my collarbone.

After a pause, I said, "It's a little tingly."

He nodded, "That's a major artery. I'm not going after it. It's too risky."

Instead, he sent me for a needle biopsy the next day, which required labs to be drawn across the lobby before we could all go to eat.

Flower Panda for Lunch

We headed off for lunch at Flower Panda, a Chinese restaurant a couple of blocks away from the medical building. We were seated at a large round table in the back corner, and there were black plastic chopsticks at every person's place setting.

I took a seat in the back corner. I really do prefer the back corners of tables. It allows one the ability to see not only one's companion but also all the other activities in the room. But more than that, being in the corner means that it is hard for anyone to sneak up on you, freak you out, and make you spill your tea everywhere. This is an important consideration, since I flinch at the slightest provocation.

As we were escorted through the restaurant, I found myself eyeing the chopsticks at every place setting. When we got to our seats and the waiter left us, I announced, "I'm taking a set of chopsticks for my hair. I might have cancer," as if this explained why stealing chopsticks made sense. If I were to be diagnosed with cancer and I had to have chemotherapy, it would be possible that I would lose all of my hair. A bald person wouldn't be able to use the chopsticks as hair accessories. As the comedian Gallagher says, "Don't steal shit you can't use."

I picked up a set and shoved them in my bag. Some of the people at my table raised their eyebrows, but nobody tried to stop me.

For the record, never once did I wear them in my hair. But now that I think about it, I will start eating with them.

Ultrasound Biopsy

Because I knew I was fine, I didn't take the ultrasound biopsy for the lymph node in my neck too seriously. I didn't have cancer, and this was just an experience I would write about one day. I simply took it all in.

I went to the biopsy in my usual testing outfit: a black tank top with a shelf bra (no underwire or metal clasps) and a bit of lace at the top; a pair of brown athletic pants; and my zippered, gray hoodie sweater that I could take off quickly.

The biopsy was at the Hospital of the University of Benjamin Franklin, what I call the mothership. It's across the street from the medical building. The mothership is where my surgeries happened.

After checking in with radiology, I went to the examination rooms. My mom went with me. Jean and one of Mom's friends hung out in one of the waiting rooms talking, waiting for us to reemerge.

The nurse did not give me a gown, for I had dressed perfectly for the exam. She asked me to take my sweater off, and she left the room. I was soon shivering and miserably cold, so I put my sweater back on. When the ultrasound tech came in, he took one look at me and walked over to a cabinet behind me. When he opened the doors, I saw gowns filling the shelves. He turned to the closet and said, "I'm going to need you to …"

Knowing what he was going to say, while his back was turned, I unzipped my gray sweater and threw it at my mom, who, surprisingly, caught it. By the time the tech turned around, I was sitting on the bed in just a tank top. He was holding a gown in his hand and said, "… do absolutely nothing."

I smiled at him and said, "I got cold, so I put my sweater back on."

He picked up a bottle of ultrasound gel and asked me to lie back. I did and he squirted it on my neck. I was surprised but happy to find that it was warm. When I commented on how I liked that the gel was warm, the tech offered to refrigerate it for me. As he was pushing the ultrasound wand around on my neck, he asked, "How did you find this?"

"Honestly? I like my collarbones, and I was just feeling around in them," I replied.

The tech put down his wand for a moment and shoved his white fingers in his own clavicles, pushing around and feeling about. With his hands still feeling around his collarbones, his elbows pointing out to his sides, he turned his gray-haired head to my mom and asked, "Is this your only daughter?"

My mom said, "No."

He replied, "Is this one your youngest?"

"Yes," Mom said.

"Good thing," the tech replied. Then he smiled, saying, "This one's weird."

Mom and I both smiled at this.

Neville, the nurse, came in; he was shorter than the tech, white, and not as thin as the tech either. Neville also wanted to know why I was there. I explained how I found the mass in my neck.

Neville asked, "Do you know what they are thinking?"

"Thymoma or lymphoma."

He let out a deep sigh and said, "That's not good."

At the time, I thought he said that because I was being laissez-faire about the whole thing, joking and picking on the nurse and tech. Now, I see that he was just making a comment on how rough such a diagnosis would be if it were true.

Eventually they gave me two blankets, double layered on top of my shivering body. Neville told me they would numb me up and put cold spray on my neck. He said that once the doctor's needle was in my neck, I shouldn't move or talk, but I could breathe.

"Good thing. One needs air," I replied.

"Here," he said, "let me see your hand."

I stuck my arm out from under my blanket, and he sprayed me with his cold spray. The cold went deep into my hand and up my arm.

He walked out the door, but before the door was completely shut, I said, "Nice. Nice. I'm freezing already and what does he do? He sprays me with his freezing spray and turns my body to ice."

Neville reopened the door and said, "Are you sure you are an English teacher and not a comedian?"

The doctor came in. She asked, "How did you find the lump?" in an accent I didn't recognize.

I turned to the ultrasound tech before I answered her, saying, "Any snide comments before I tell her the truth?"

He stood next to my bed with a blank look on his face and stared at nothing over the top of my bed and toward the door of the room.

The doctor looked back and forth at me and the tech and said dryly, "Oh good. We've established rapport."

I explained to the doctor how I found the lump, and the tech did make little snarky comments here and there. I retorted back. Neville came in again and helped to prop me up a little higher using more pillows. The doctor stopped him, saying, "I hate seeing patients on exposed pillows," and had Neville cover the pillows in towels.

We bantered about as the doctor took the ultrasound wand and moved it around my collarbone. She had me turn my neck in one direction, then a little more in the other.

The doctor got to work numbing my neck. She had me lie on the pillows with my head turned to the left, which gave her a good view of my right collarbone.

Neville asked how long I'd been teaching. "Ten years" was my answer.

"What?" he responded, "Are you some kind of prodigy? Start teaching when you were 16?"

"I'm ancient," I replied.

Mom said from her seat at the end of my bed, "Oh yeah, thirty-three is ancient."

"When you work with fourteen-year-olds all day, thirty-three is ancient," was my response.

In the middle of the procedure—I could tell there was a needle stuck in my neck not because of pain but because of tension and movement—my phone rang. "Hava Nagila" sounded through the dimly lit room.

"What is that I am hearing?" the doctor asked.

"My ringtone. It's my mom or dad calling."

Mom piped up from her seat and said, "It's not me. I'm right down here."

The doctor said, "Only at UBF can you be doing a biopsy to 'Hava Nagila' as the background music." She paused, adding, "I was born in Israel," which then explained her accent, which I couldn't place.

The doctor took a number of samples and asked for a couple of different things in the middle of the biopsy. At one point, I saw Neville holding a needle in front of my face. The doctor then asked for a 12-gauge.

I looked at the needle. "Do you mean that needle or a shotgun?" I asked.

The doctor said, "Guns and pistols come in calibers."

The tech then said, "And shotguns come in gauges."

Neville said, "Looks like she knows more than you do, doctor."

The doctor said a little seriously, "I'm normally way more stoic and professional than this. It's all you people bantering around like this that is making me act this way."

Later, after the procedure, I talked to one of my oldest friends and told her the 12-gauge story, and she burst out laughing, saying, "Oh my God!"

"What?" I asked.

"That is one huge needle. The smaller the needle, the higher the number," she said. "I work with needles that are like 26 and 28. I can't even imagine how huge a 12-gauge is!"

Well, that explained why that needle hurt so much going in. It was a deep, aching pain. The doctor was upset that I could feel what she was doing, but at that point, there wasn't too much they could do for me.

After the needles were filled with lymph fluid, the doctor left the room to talk to pathology. She wanted to find out if they had enough of a sample to make a diagnosis. The doctor was gone for some time, but the tech and Neville didn't help me get up. The doctor might have to go back in and stab me with the 12-gauge again.

She came back and said, "It looks like I have enough lymph cells, but the pathologist doesn't know if any them show what is causing your lymph nodes to be so enlarged." She paused, then stuck out her hand for me to shake. "It was lovely meeting you. I haven't enjoyed a biopsy this much in a long time. Thank you for that."

I was surprised by her words, but said, "Thank you."

Later, as Neville was helping me get ready to leave, I asked him about it. He said, "Most people who come in here are scared, overwhelmed, and even angry. You made this one a good time."

Neville helped me to my feet, but after that needle event, my body reacted. It got dizzy. My stomach felt wiggidy, and I didn't trust my center of balance. I was unhappy and not myself. I got quiet and didn't trust my own footing.

***

That night I dreamt I was at Boon Win High school as some weird combination of teacher and student, as can only happen in dreams. I was supposed to take a test on *The Grapes of Wrath* in a class of one of the other English teachers, one about whom many of my students complained.

I hadn't read *The Grapes of Wrath* since I was a junior in high school, and even then, in Mrs. Potter's class, I never really finished it. The interstitial chapters killed me, and I couldn't get through it.

In my dream, I had to take this test for Ms. Barmy. In the dream, I had to sit away from my friends because I was "the bad kid." In real life, this teacher had come into my classroom on a couple of occasions and told me what she thought of me and my teaching style. In the dream, Ms. Barmy showed a video clip for three seconds, and we had to answer questions that flashed on the screen in thirty-second intervals. One of them was about theme, so I made up some answer about the turtle that walks down the road in the first couple of lines (and I think the last couple of lines) in the book. But the other questions weren't on the screen long enough to catch.

This classroom wasn't set up like it was in reality. It was in the actual location in Boon Win, but in the dream, the classroom turned into a lecture hall, with a sloped floor, cushioned seats, and brown carpeting.

I went down front with a bunch of other students to ask what the questions were. Ms. Barmy then turned on me and said I wasn't being a team player and that we were supposed to be on the same team, supporting each other and blah, blah, blah. She sent me out of the room to the principal's office and I left, with my shoulders hunched and my proverbial tail between my legs. Then I turned back and looked at Ms. Barmy in the front of the classroom. My anger flared, and I took my red Pilot pen, the kind with a fine tip and flowing red ink, and I threw it at her. The cap broke off, and red ink flowed all over.

In the dream, I failed that test. I got 40 percent.

The way I saw it when I woke up was that when I called the doctor on Friday to find out the biopsy results, I would fail that test too.

***

The next day was April 22, 2010. I was back at school. I still felt a little woozy, a little slow, but I was doing okay. Neville and the tech had told me not to do anything too strenuous for twenty-four hours after the biopsy. However, just about everything regarding teaching was exhausting, even for a healthy person.

Before school started, I was walking around the hallways, but don't ask me what I was doing. It was possible I was socializing, or going to or coming back from photocopying, or monitoring the hallway. I do know I bumped into Mr. Trebuchet as I was making my way back to my classroom. He pulled me aside, out of the migrating streams of students in the hallway, to talk to him next to the lockers between Dave and Josephine's rooms. I faced the hordes of students moving to their first-period classes, not wanting to make eye contact with Mr. Trebuchet.

He wanted to know what the doctor had said two days before, and I told him. He asked about my test the day before.

"How are you?" he asked.

"I'm okay," I said. I felt okay. I was weak, but had been weak for months. This was just a different kind of weak. "According to the doctors, I can't lift anything heavier than ten pounds."

His eyebrows came together in concern. "I didn't expect you to come in today," he said. "I want you to take it easy."

I turned and looked at him steadily. Right. How, as a teacher, was I supposed to take it easy? Students, especially mine, were demanding. "Okay," I said, "I promise not to stand on any chairs, desks, or tables today."

He frowned, furrowed his forehead at me, and we walked away from each other.[2]

---

[2]   Later, when I had left Boon Win and was getting a master's in social work, I stopped by the head office, where Mr. Trebuchet now worked. I told him that I'd been doing some writing about the cancer stuff. I talked with him about this conversation and said that I probably didn't make him feel any better. He smiled and shook his head, saying, "I wasn't up there to make me feel better."

Needle Biopsy Results

I didn't fail the biopsy. The truth is, they didn't find any sick cells. Claire, Dr. K's nurse practitioner, made it clear that my diagnosis was still undetermined. They wanted to find out why the lymph nodes in my chest were so large.

I found out later from Dr. K that when one has Hodgkin's lymphoma, only 10 percent of the cells are "sick." The rest are normal. It is the sick ones that make the lymph nodes larger, and some people find it hard to breathe. He said that not everyone with enlarged lymph nodes experiences pain, because there aren't many nerve receptors in one's chest. Dr. K also said that Hodgkin's doesn't show up on blood tests, which also makes diagnosis difficult.

At one point, I asked Claire if Dr. K had discussed my case with other doctors, since he said I was proving difficult.

"You are proving difficult to diagnose, but that doesn't mean your case is unusual," she said. "Your scans and situation look like things we see all the time. In that way, you are not difficult."

I repeated what I'd just heard. "I look like everyone else?"

She laughed. "You look like everyone else we see, but that does not make you normal. It makes you normal for us."

Kimberly Joy Beam

To: Important Contacts
From: Me
Subject: Can't believe this
Date: April 23, 2010

Okay, so inquiring minds want to know. I'm in school and typing this illegally on my laptop. I hope you all appreciate my breaking the rules.

So here it is. I saw Dr. K on Tuesday at UBF. I was scheduled for an ultrasound biopsy on Wednesday, where they attacked the lymph node with a number of needles. We all thought that the lymph node in my neck was connected to the mass in my chest. If the biopsy came back malignant, then they were going to go forward with chemo and radiation for six months.

Claire, Dr. K's nurse, called. She said that the lab results showed that the lymphocytes in the lymph node are normal. There are no bizarre cells, and it appears to be benign.

This means that the mass in my chest could be either malignant or benign. They don't know. If the lymph node in my neck was malignant, then it all would have been malignant. However, there is still the question of what is in my chest.

They are going to schedule another needle biopsy for the lump in my chest. From there, we will talk. If it's malignant, they are going to crack open my breastbone and remove the lump. There is also another cloudy lymph node in there, which he said he would probably take out while he was at it. (This will entail three days in the hospital and six weeks of recovery—if it's a contained mass.) He also mentioned at one point he may remove the pissed-off lymph node in my neck, just to do it. If the mass in my chest is benign, they said Dr. K and my whole family will have a powwow to discuss next steps.

It is hard for me to believe that the lymph node in my neck is clean. It's big, which means it must be angry about something. Even with that, I am at incredible peace. I have been all along, really, which makes me happy.

I appreciate and love you all. All of your words were really encouraging, and knowing you all stand behind me and with me makes me feel really loved. Thank you.

Much love,
Kim

"Not all those who wander are lost." ~ J. R. R. Tolkien

Thoracic Biopsy

Dr. K called for another biopsy, a thoracic biopsy, a test that proved the methods of diagnosis are not for the faint of heart.

***

Before this test, I went to church and received prayer. One couple in church has seen miraculous healing after miraculous healing. When the wife said, "The mass that was on the CT scans won't be there," I believed her. She said that when I slammed my hand on the kitchen table and declared Satan a liar, I broke his power. Both she and her husband stood in total faith that when I went in for the next biopsy, which involved both needles and a CT scan, the scan would be clean.

In my journal on April 27, 2010, I wrote:

> I have been thinking all along that if I go through chemo, I will have compassion and passion for others going through it; that will be the only way to minister to people suffering under chemo, radiation, and cancer.
>
> God, I ask for the miraculous. I ask for the BIG. I ask that my family will not be able to give the glory of my healing to doctors, science, and medicine, but that they will only be able to look to you and say, "I don't know you, God, but I know you did it. You healed my Kim."

What passion and surety that would give me when I prayed for others. If He did it for me, then He certainly will do it for them.

***

The physician Dr. K chose to do the thoracic biopsy was his personal favorite for my scenario. Before I went into surgery, this doctor (also a Dr. K) sat down with Mom, Jean, and me. She was older, blond, and had an accent—not the same accent as the doctor who did my lymph node biopsy, but just as unidentifiable. She said that she would have to go through my lung with her needle to reach the mass in my chest. The aim was to get the needle into the mass under my breastbone; to get there, she had to break through the cartilage between my ribs, aiming her needle as best she could. She said that there was the risk that my lung could collapse, but that was rare, and if it did happen we were already in the hospital to take care of it. She said she did this every day, all the time, and she would do her best for me.

Jean looked at me, grabbed my hand before I went in, and whispered, "It's not there. You will get in there, and the lumps—they will be gone."

***

This time I did have to wear a hospital gown. In the room, there was a CT scanner and the lights were dimmed. I had an IV placed on the back of my hand before entering this room. They hooked the IV port to a drip. But to be honest, I don't remember seeing many nurses in there with us. I just remember sweet, kind Dr. K explaining everything as she did it.

She slid me into the CT scan. As the giant yellow doughnut of the CT scanner whirred and hummed, blowing cold air everywhere, I lay on the bed and breathed in and out slowly, over and over, focusing on God and His promises. The mass would be gone. I found myself anticipating Dr. K's confirmation of God's reality.

The doctor came back from behind the window between us and took out a felt pen. There was a red, glowing grid on my chest shining down from the CT scan, and she started to draw inside the grid marks on my chest.

She said, "We're just going to mark you up, right here. And here." Her pen traveled across the top of my chest, well above my breasts.

"Did you see it?" I asked.

"Oh yeah, it's there," she said, not at all aware of the weight of her words. "Now," the doctor said to those around her and called for twenty-five milligrams of Fentanyl.

As the opioid entered my body, I felt the bottom fall out of everyone's faith for me. I felt alone there on the table. I knew Mom and Jean; Aubrey and my dad; my colleagues, Mr. Zern, Ms. Whitherspoon, and Ms. Berry; people at church; and my friends were there for me, but there in that dark room, with a mass still inside my chest, I was alone.

Tears rolled out of my eyes, down my temples, and into my long, curly hair. They had nothing to do with the four-inch needles the doctor was pounding on my chest as she tried to break through the cartilage. The tears had nothing to do with my fear that came after she shoved the needle into my chest, she said, "Okay, let's see where we're at," as she slid me into the CT scanner. The tears had nothing to do with the pain that came when she pulled blood out from under my breast bone.

If my faith wasn't enough to heal me, then was it possible that living for God wasn't the reality the Bible says it is? What about the desire to study theology in Chicago? What about living off my writing? What about holding out for years and years for God to come through with my husband? What about the reality of God and His love—were those things false too?

Eventually the Fentanyl kicked in, and the world went shiny. I was floating and hazy. I watched the doctor pound the hell out of my chest with the long hollow needles, and my cartilage fought her off. I commented on how hard her task was and how well my body was doing its job, protecting my heart and organs. She laughed at my joke but continued to shove her needles in and slide me into the CT scanner to see where her needle rested deep inside my chest cavity.

A little while in, this process started to hurt, and I started to squeak as she pushed her needle at my cartilage. Concerned about my pain, the doctor immediately asked for twenty-five milligrams more of the Fentanyl. As it flowed in and the world floated, I didn't care about her needles or her jabbing.

At one point, she thought she was in the mass and said that I would feel this enormous pressure as she tried to extract material from it into her needle. Through the Fentanyl haze, it didn't feel like just pressure and bit of pain. It felt like someone was stepping on my breastbone making breathing almost impossible. To be honest, it was a sensation that I have a hard time describing. It's nothing like a broken heart. It's nothing like acid reflux or heartburn.

The doctor told me that even with all of the jabbing and all of the work she did, even with that moment of incredible pressure inside my chest as she filled her needle, she thought that all she collected was blood. She didn't think that she got any of the material from the mass in her samples.

Later, this Dr. K told my mom and Jean how sweet I was, that I had done a really good job with diagnosis and the crap the doctors poured out. She said I was beautiful, not something that's said about me very often. She also said I was wonderful.

She reported she did go through my lung. She said that her needles were within two millimeters of my aorta. Let me put that in perspective. According to Reference.com, two millimeters is larger than the thickness of one dime, but not thicker than two dimes together. That means she was less than two dimes' width from my aorta. The doctor also said that she was closer than she was "comfortable with" to my pericardial sac. That means, by process of deduction, she was probably closer than two millimeters to rupturing the sac that holds one's heart; if that sac is ruptured, it will cause one to bleed internally and possibly die.

She said I should keep an eye on my pain level as I recuperated. Strong pain was a sign of internal bleeding. I was having quite a bit of pain and asked about the difference between pain from the needles and pain from internal bleeding. Her response was to give me twenty-five milligrams more of the Fentanyl. I stopped worrying about such things.

They gave me an X-ray a couple of hours later to make sure all looked good inside my chest, and then I was released to go home.

The results of this procedure showed that I had blood inside my chest cavity. She didn't get any lymph material in her needles. I'd have to have surgery to diagnose what was causing my lymph nodes to be enlarged.

To: Important Contacts
From: Me
Subject: Events of April 28
Date: April 28, 2010

To say today was easy would be impossible.

The mass is high up behind my breastbone. I thought it was low, but I think what made me think that was feeling my xiphoid process, if I have the name of that right. I've been feeling the little diphthong that hangs between where the ribs meet at the bottom of the sternum. That is not where the mass is.

So the mass was really, really hard to get to. She used needles that were about four inches long, went through my lung, missed my aorta by two millimeters, and she still isn't sure she got enough for pathology to make a diagnosis. If that's the case, we're probably talking surgery here.

To be honest, I am weepy about the eyes, but not weepy in my soul/spirit.

I hear Friday what the pathologists have to say, most likely. And my upper chest is mad. She tried to go through cartilage but my bones and sinew wouldn't let her in. As she was jabbing me with needles, we actually joked my body was fighting her. Now, it seems my bones might be bruised.

I meet with the doctor on Tuesday. I'll know more then.

Thanks for all of the love and prayers. I have been so supported and loved. Your love means everything.

Kim

"Not all those who wander are lost." ~ J. R. R. Tolkien

***

I took the next day off of work. I was weak, and my body wasn't handling the trauma well.

I convinced my brain that I was doing fine, though. God was big, bigger than my doubts, and He could handle whatever was coming my way.

I went into Boon Win two days later wearing a V-neck shirt with a scarf around my neck.

I walked down the hallway to Mr. Trebuchet's office, where he was meeting with Joe, one of the assistant principals. Once I was in the doorway, and the two men weren't talking about school, I pulled at my collar, showing the flaming yellow and blue and black that was my upper chest.

"Isn't it pretty?" I asked.

Trebuchet looked a little horror-struck, and Joe smiled, but I could see the pain in his light-colored eyes. One of the other assistant principals came into the hallway where I was standing and looked at the master calendar on the wall next to me. He really was not looking at the calendar, but eavesdropping on my conversation. I appreciated his desire to be nonintrusive.

Trebuchet shook his head, averting his eyes from my upper chest. He asked, "What do they know?"

"Nothing," I responded. I kicked my right leg high in the air and said, "I want this to be over."

Trebuchet grunted, and the eavesdropping assistant principal snorted out a laugh.

"I've got stuff to do," I said and walked out of the office and toward my classroom.

"Take it easy!" Mr. Trebuchet yelled after me.

"Yeah, whatever!" I hollered back.

***

A couple of days later, as plans for the next steps were put in place, and surgery became the word on everyone's mouth—even mine—the student who noticed I was crying that first day interrupted me in the middle of class.

"Ms. Beam?"

"Yes?" I asked.

"Can you do me a favor?" she asked.

"I can try. What's up?"

"When you come back from surgery, can you cover up your chest more than you are now?"

I looked down, still in a V-neck shirt with a scarf around my neck. The bruise was up high, and I couldn't see it just by looking down.

"What? This bothers you?" I asked, pointing to what I couldn't see right below my chin.

She nodded. "The bruising. It's hard to look at."

I hadn't even thought about that. After a day or two, I barely saw it. I didn't think the bruising was that noticeable, though Doug, the science teacher, said it was chartreuse, a nice, deep, sick pea green.

"I can do that for you," I said to her. "I can cover up whatever they do in surgery if that will make you feel better."

"Thank you," she said, and we kept reading *To Kill a Mockingbird*.

Tuesday Before Surgery

Dr. K met with patients only on Tuesdays and operated the rest of the week. Anyone whose patience had failed, anyone who was having panic attacks and needed to see him, had to wait until the following Tuesday. There were no exceptions. Even when my thoracic biopsy reported that I had blood in my chest but didn't explain what was going on with the mass, I still had to wait until the next Tuesday to meet with Dr. K and find out what was next.

The morning of my appointment, my dad, my mom, my aunt (Mom's sister), and I were in the waiting room, well past the scheduled time I was supposed to meet with Dr. K. To be honest, I had lost my patience with waiting. All I wanted was for Dr. K to open up my chest, remove what had to be removed, and let me live my life.

I had to hold myself back from opening the door to his offices and demanding, "Isn't it time for you to talk to me now? Isn't it time for us to talk about what you are going to do about the mass in the center of my chest?"

Dad patiently worked on a Sudoku puzzle as my aunt asked him questions about his life as a college professor. My mom was knitting a scarf out of teal ribbon yarn—which I now call the resurrection scarf—and trying hard not to make silly mistakes.

A man came out of the door that I wanted to enter so desperately. He sat across from us, his olive skin pale, and his eyes unable to focus. He looked like he was seconds from a panic attack. He had that all-too-familiar spacey, pale, and overwhelmed look. A woman came out shortly after he did. She was tall, thin, and had short blond hair. She carried a worried expression on her face that made her pale as well. She said that they had to go for labs and that Dr. K said there were a couple of other things they had to accomplish that day. She took him by the arm and helped him out of the waiting room.

Shortly afterward, we were asked to go back and see Dr. K. Once we were all in his office, he said he was ready to do surgery the next day. There was time in the schedule, and they had an operating room—but my insurance company wouldn't let them. The insurance company was asking for more time, so the surgery had been scheduled for Monday, May 10, 2010, six days later.

As we talked about the challenges he'd had diagnosing me, Dr. K asked, "Are you always this difficult?"

My dad responded, "Yes. Even at birth, she wouldn't do what the doctors wanted. She's always been difficult."

I smiled and said, "It's part of my charm."

As we talked, the frustration coming from Dr. K was palpable. I could tell that he was upset that he couldn't do the surgery the next day. He said something like, "I hate that insurance companies have so much power on how I work, but I need to get paid."

I spent most of my time in the next week thinking about having cartilage removed from between my ribs so the doctor could have access to the mass behind my breastbone.

In all of this, waiting was the hardest.

Telling the Office Secretary and an Assistant Principal

A day or two after seeing Dr. K, I was up in Upper D teaching my class of non-readers, mostly freshmen whose reading levels were well below ninth grade. Two colleagues were asking me what would happen next.

If this surgery revealed the mass was a thymoma, the doctor would break open my sternum and remove the gland, leaving me six weeks' recovery time. Or they would diagnose me with lymphoma and send me to oncology. The treatment with the oncologists would take somewhere between four and six months.

"Have you talked to the office about this?" one of them asked.

I shook my head no. *Why would I?*

"I think you should go talk to Tiff," the other one said, referring to the principal's secretary.

They covered my class as I ran downstairs to the main office. I walked up to Tiff's desk. Thankfully, she was sitting there and seemed approachable. She was often away from her desk or swamped. I asked if I could talk to her about what was happening with me. She said in a lighthearted tone, "Of course."

"On Monday, they are going to do one of two things," I said, realizing the whole office was listening to what I was saying. "They are going to cut open my chest and my breastbone. That will have a six-week recovery period."

"Right," she said matter-of-factly. "That's what happened to my father. It took about six weeks."

"Right," I continued. "Or they are going to find out that it's lymphoma, and I will be sent to oncology." I paused and let that sink in for a second. "That means Friday may be my last day of school for the year."

She sat in stunned silence for a few moments and then said, "I'm beginning to get that."

"Good," I smiled at her, "just so long as you and I are on the same page." I bounced out of the office in a somewhat jovial mood.

Everyone else in the office was silent, and I could feel them watching me as I walked away.

***

As I got closer and closer to surgery, I became more and more impatient with normal student antics.

I was talking to one of my students. Her eyes were watery and red, and she was having a hard time articulating herself. I looked at her and, right in front of everyone, said, "What did you do to yourself?"

"What?" she asked.

"What did you take?" I pressed.

"Nothing," she retorted.

"This is not nothing. What are you on?"

The student huffed out of my classroom without permission, and all of the students looked at me, horror-struck.

One of them said, "Ms. Beam, she's scary. Aren't you afraid she's going to hurt you?"

I thought about it for a second. "Not really," I replied. At that moment I was more scared of cancer than of an edgy, teenage girl.

As a result of my confrontation with this girl, I was called into one of the assistant principal's offices. Let me explain something about the hierarchy of the bureaucracy of Boon Win High School. There was the head principal, Mr. Trebuchet, whom I kept in the loop at all times. Then there were three assistant principals (APs) under him. Each one was responsible for a different grade—sophomores, juniors, seniors, and they broke the freshman class into thirds, with each AP getting roughly eight letters of the alphabet. The APs were responsible for different areas of leadership. Two of them were present around the building and during lunchtime, and were available for random questions. The third one I called the nonexistent AP. She was never in the halls and never in the lunchroom. When one did catch up with this AP and ask a question, her response was usually, "I'll have to get back to you on that."

I was summoned to the nonexistent AP's office. She confronted me about my exchange with the girl in front of the whole class. She demanded to know why I had belittled and humiliated the girl. Apparently this student had gone to her office, crying; she explained that she'd taken two allergy pills instead of one because her allergies were kicking her butt. She had not realized how two pills would make her feel, and I'd made her feel worse.

The AP was right; I was in the wrong. But instead of acknowledging my mistake right away, I said, "Do you know what's going on with me?"

"No," she said. "What are you talking about?"

Let me put this in perspective. I first found the lump on April 1 and went for a CT scan on the ninth. I told Mr. Trebuchet about the doctor's preliminary findings on April 12. The other APs knew what was going on; they supported me and my need for substitutes, since I was often absent. This conversation in the nonexistent AP's office occurred a full month later, on May 6. I still had the bruising from the needles all over the top of my chest. Every other person in the office, including the school's assigned police officer, was aware that I was being diagnosed with cancer, but this third AP had no idea.

I told her, "Friday might be my last day for the year." This was Thursday, the day before. I described what had been going on, how they were trying to diagnose me but didn't know what kind of cancer it was. The nonexistent AP asked a couple of questions and wanted to hug me.

At one point, she said, "I knew it had to be something. That kind of behavior is not normally like you. You are normally way more sensitive than that."

I left my thoughts unstated: *Why didn't you ask me what was going on instead of accusing me of intentionally insulting a student? How could you not know what was going on?*

Later that day I bumped into the student in the hallway. I apologized and said I'd been out of line. I asked if she wanted me to apologize in front of the whole class; she said that was not necessary. I said I would apologize out in the hall and say it loud enough for others to hear, and she couldn't argue with me on that one.

The next day was Friday; it did turn out to be my last day for the school year. As the student walked into my classroom, I called her over and apologized, and every student in the class watched as I said my intent had not been to humiliate her and that I was truly sorry. Later in class, she announced loudly that I had become her favorite teacher.

To:	Important Contacts
From:	Me
Subject:	Surgery in three days
Date:	May 7, 2010

I have held off on writing this until I had more answers than questions. Now, I don't know if I want the answers. Wouldn't it just be easier to shove my head in the ground and leave my body sticking out to be destroyed?

I met with the doctor on Tuesday. I kept asking him to take out the lymph node in my neck. Kind of bending my head over to really expose my neck and pointing at the mad node saying, "You want to take it out. Come on, just take it out." He just kept saying no the whole time.

Something funny happened. He looked at me and said that I was being difficult. Mom and Dad, who were both in the room, laughed. Might be the first time they both found the same thing funny in thirty-three years. They both agreed, again not a small thing, I was difficult, and the fact that he's having trouble diagnosing me is right in line with whom I've always been.

He said that just because the lymph node didn't reveal sick cells didn't mean they aren't there. There just weren't many of them. He said that the ultrasound biopsy of my lymph node yielded scar tissue and lymphocytes. He also said that the biopsy with the five-inch, life-sucking needles contained blood, but they didn't yield a sick cell. He said the lymph nodes that are enlarged inside my chest, the mass they've been trying to get at, and the enlarged lymph node on my neck are connected. With someone my age, they are always connected. He also said you don't have a three-centimeter lymph node in your neck and have it mean nothing.

He is going to do the surgery Monday, and I'm to be at the hospital to start admittance at 8:15 a.m. He is going to remove the cartilage between my ribs very high up on my sternum, just a little below my collarbones. He said it's going to reap a really pretty scar, and I will be able to feel the divot between the two ribs, but people shouldn't be able to see it. Once in my chest cavity, he's going to use a knife to slice off pieces of the main mass to send to pathology. When pathology says they have enough material to find a sick cell, they will tell Dr. K to stitch me back up. Monday's surgery reaps an 85 percent diagnosis rate.

Apparently they think the recovery time for this will be two weeks. I say I'll be better by the end of the week, but we'll have to see.

If pathology isn't able to reap a sick cell to discern what is going on, Dr. K says he will do a second surgery, break my breastbone and remove the whole mass. He really, really doesn't want to crack my breastbone because it takes six weeks to recover. I talked to his nurse yesterday, and she said that before he breaks my breastbone, I can certainly get a second opinion and, yes, I promise to do that.

Okay, so here's the thing. I'm going to be blunt about what they are saying and what it means. They are saying lymphoma. That's what they think. If pathology is able to find sick cells and diagnose, then I could move on to oncology next week. If they don't find what they are looking for, it will take a little while to get that second opinion. And then, if they crack my breastbone, it will take six weeks before "treatment" can start.

All of this being stated, please pray not only that the surgery rocks on Monday—goes smoothly and perfectly—but that it reaps all the right cells. I've been praying that when Dr. K goes in and stabs the mass with his knife, the whole mass just pops right out for him, that God just expels it from my body without all the cracking of my bones; if not, that God will allow the pathologists to see what they need to see.

I'm still praying for a healing miracle. God can change anything at any time. God doesn't need doctors, but He uses them.

I finished moving out of my apartment tonight. The walls are bare, the furniture gone, the carpets completely exposed. It's a bittersweet moment. I loved that apartment, on its eighty acres and quarter-mile driveway. I have moved in with Jean and Aubrey, friends of mine, who have been mind-blowingly amazing. I'm humbled and amazed by them daily. They have promised to walk this journey with me. And they know that this journey most probably includes chemo and some serious side effects.

I'm sure I missed something. But Monday, May 10, is the day, and the actual time of surgery, ten-ish, but that's a guess. Like I said, check-in is at 8:15 a.m.

So there it is.

Much love,
Kim

"Not all those who wander are lost." ~ J. R. R. Tolkien

Diagnosis

Meeting Serge

On May 8, the Saturday before the surgery, Wendy threw an annual spring party at her house. I attended. Everyone skirted the word lymphoma. Some asked me what was next. The answer was "surgery in less than forty-eight hours." It was odd, because not everyone there knew that I was in the middle of finding out if I had cancer. It was Wendy's party with Wendy's friends; how many of them needed to know I might be dying?

I left the party a little early and went to church, where there was a healing meeting. I walked through the two sets of double glass doors and across the stone floor in the vestibule. My friend Eliza was talking to Aubrey and some other friends at the other end of the room. As I walked across the room to fall into Eliza's hug, I heard a man behind me say, "She was in the BFU medical building this week."

I finished hugging Eliza, smiled at everyone, and went to grab a little spaghetti and hot tea. As I walked back to my friends, the man said, "You were at the BFU Lung Center on Tuesday."

I studied his long olive face, curly black hair and came up with nothing. "Yes. Yes, I was …"

I tried to place him. Where could I have bumped into him? When had I been there? With all that had been going on, I couldn't really remember the day of the week I'd had been in the medical building, which was always a Tuesday.

"Obviously, you were too," I said.

"You were in the lobby with your family," he said. "You were sitting there and your mother was scared and knitting. Your father, a professor, was working on a puzzle book, and your aunt was between them."

And then I remembered, "You were the guy that flew out the door and landed in the seat across from us. How are you doing?"

He shrugged. "They don't know. Some say lung cancer, some say kidney cancer. They can't figure it out. What about you?"

"They are saying lymphoma," I replied.

We formally introduced ourselves—Serge and Kim. Bruce, my pastor, walked up and said it was time to get started.

"This is Serge," I said to Bruce. "This is the second time we've met this week, though we didn't introduce ourselves the first time."

In the healing meeting, they put us both in chairs up front. One group prayed for him, another for me.

As they were praying for Serge, Bruce leaned toward me and said he could see this golden spinning ball inside my belly that was radiating light. That light was God, His power and glory spinning. As the ball spun and radiated, all that was sickness and darkness fled because it could not stay in that bright light and power of God. Bruce said that when I sat down he saw the word *lymphoma* in big letters going down my back, but as I prayed with the others, the word fell off and landed powerless and useless on the ground.

I recorded the words they prayed over Serge and burned them onto a CD for him and his wife.

Serge opted for a new type of treatment that was offered in the Poconos area. The treatment was interleukin, and he had to be hospitalized for a week while it was going into his system. He would come home for short visits, but most of his time was spent in the hospital. I didn't hear much about him as I had my own stuff going on, but I thought about Serge and his wife often and prayed for them.

The Tree on the Road to Turntown

I couldn't sleep. I was awake, staring at the sloped, white ceiling above my bed.

I can always sleep. Sleeping is never a problem for me. I normally lie down, and thirty seconds later I'm asleep.

But that was not the case on those nights leading up to the diagnosis. I would lie there until I couldn't anymore. One morning, I got out of bed at 2:00 a.m., wandered into my living room, pulled my favorite pen out of my bag, went back into my bedroom, and grabbed the journal my stepbrother had given to me for Christmas a number of years before.

It was an old-fashioned children's book whose innards had been ripped out and replaced with thick, sturdy, deep cream, almost gray, card stock. The cover was a worn, slate gray illustrated with a brown tree and fence and peachy-pink clouds. The original title was scrawled at the top in a flowing but ominous font: *The Tree on the Road to Turntown* by Glenn O. Blough.

I opened to the first page and wrote at the top "The Malignant Journal."

I stared at the reality of the word *malignant.* And then I drew a line under malignant and wrote "Benign," so it sort of looked like this at the center of the first page:

The <u>Malignant</u> Journal
Benign

Written that way, I could circle the one that applied and cross out the other.

I wrote down what had been happening so far: finding the lump, getting the first CT scan, the bad news that came on a Sunday evening.

The Tree on the Road to Turntown remained *The Malignant Journal* in my head. Despite my outward verbal denials, in my gut, I knew I was on the road to Turntown.

Admittance and a Living Will

As we sat and waited in BFU's admissions area to be called for surgery, I asked Dad for a pen and index card.

"Anything else you want?" he asked.

"Breakfast," I replied. "Eggs and bacon. Green tea. Toast with butter and honey. That would be great."

He scrunched up his lips into a duck face and said, "I wish I could do that for you, but I can't."

Mom was sitting next to him, knitting.

A little down from us, another white couple sat under the windows. They laughed, and the woman said, "I know just how you feel. I really want to eat too."

We talked a little as I wrote out my living will on the index card; then I handed it back to Dad. He put it in the book he was reading, *The Golden Notebook* by Doris Lessing, a selection for Great Books Week at Colby College in Maine. Mom got all nosy and said, "What was that?"

Dad replied, "It's not necessary. Just let me hold onto it."

We both knew that if Mom found out that I had just given away all of my earthly possessions and had given an order that if I wasn't the same person at the other end of surgery, they should not fight to keep me alive, she might have lost it right there.

Presurgery Joking

I was called to go up into the presurgery ward to prep by changing my clothes and getting an IV, plus the other medical things "they" needed to do before my family was allowed to come up. I was walked to a large room that had gurneys parked with their heads to the wall and their feet jutting into the room. Each bed was parked in such a way to allow the curtain tracks on the ceiling to give each bed privacy when the curtain was pulled. Some beds were vacant, some were occupied, and some were hidden from view by the curtains.

They took me to the last bed on the left by the window. The nurse pulled the curtain around the track so the fabric enclosed me. She said, "I want you take off all of your clothes and put them in this." She handed me a blue garment bag that had "University of Benjamin Franklin" written in white letters to the right of the zipper. "I also want you to put this on," and she handed me one of those hospital gowns that don't close in the back. "When you are done," she said, "pull the curtain open so we know you're ready."

I took off my sandals and dropped them into the garment bag. I pulled off my pants, sherbet-orange fleece, and tank top and put them on the hanger in the garment bag. I hung the garment bag where she told me to, on a hook attached to the gurney I was about to get onto, and pulled the curtain open. She came into my space as I was hopping up onto the bed.

She said, "Naked is naked."

"I *am* naked," I replied, a little hurt.

"You have on your underwear," she said.

"You want my underwear too?" I whined. "Why my underwear?"

The anesthesiologist walked up, and the nurse shooed him away, saying I wasn't ready yet. She turned to me and said, "If you don't take your underwear off, I'm going to send Fred in there to get them."

I quickly figured out that Fred was the anesthesiologist, because he was standing on the other side of the curtain saying, "Why is this a problem? I don't mind going in for them. This is not a big deal."

The nurse kept saying that he would take off my underwear if I didn't, so I quickly whipped off my undies, put them in the garment bag, and told the nurse. Fred came in as I was hopping on the gurney again. I was asked, for the first time that day, what the plan for the surgery was.

My response: remove cartilage from between my ribs, and use a knife to cut away slivers of the mass under my breastbone until pathology said they had enough, and the doctor could stop.

Fred said that I would feel a little pinch as the nurse put in the IV. It felt as though I'd been stabbed sharply in the arm, and I was unable to focus on the day's plan. I turned to Fred and asked, "You call that a little pinch?"

"It was just a little pinch," he said. With a playful smile, he added, "I'll see you in the OR," and he walked away.

This was my first experience with a messy IV. I saw the blood in the cap and on the sheet and worried there would be blood everywhere. The nurse was kind; she cleaned up some of the cap and put a towel over the blood on the sheet. I would come to learn how IVs really worked. Looking back, I realize that the IV was fine, and I was flipping out over nothing.

Mom and Dad came in and sat with me. Dr. Steel, Dr. K's fellow, came in at the same time. Dr. Steel explained he had all of the schooling and residencies completed. Now, he was specializing. He hoped to be as good a doctor as Dr. K, and he was spending time learning from Dr. K, refining his abilities and honing his skills.

I had to tell Dr. Steel the day's OR plan, just as the anesthesiologist had asked. As I did so, he pulled on my hospital gown and wrote on my chest, signing his name on the location where they would do the surgery and putting a NO on the other side of my chest

After Dr. Steel walked away, the nurse returned with a young guy, Tony, who said, "I'm an undergrad here and excited to observe your surgery. If it is okay with you, I will be in the OR too."

I looked at him and said, "You aren't going to do anything to me, are you?"

"Nothing they think I can't handle," he replied.

I nodded and asked, "You have seen the inside of a corpse?"

That's when Dad mentioned the book *Stiff: The Curious Lives of Human Cadavers* by Mary Roach, in which she discusses all of the lives bodies can have once they become corpses. The nurse and Tony said they wanted to read it.

Dr. K walked up. He too asked for the day's OR plan, and he too wrote on my chest. As he walked away, I turned to Mom and Dad and said, "Geesh. It's like they're dogs, and I'm a fire hydrant being marked."

They prepared to roll me down to the OR. I had to hand my glasses to my parents, which meant I couldn't see a thing as they wheeled me down the hall. Tony walked next to me as we went to the OR, and he kept talking about *Stiff*. I think that was so I wouldn't get even more nervous.

The OR was bright, really bright. White light made the operating table glow, and it made it hard to focus on just one thing.

They pushed my gurney parallel to the operating room table. I looked at the table and said, "You are going to move me from here to there?"

"No," they said. "You are going to move you."

"But I'm not wearing any underwear," I blurted out.

Fred, now seated at the head of the table, said, "This is not a problem. I will just watch your backside as you get onto the table."

With one swift movement, I got off the gurney and landed on the cold, hard white table. As I did so, the hospital gown floated up and completely open in the back. Yup. Fred got to see the whole lunar view of my backside as I landed on the table.

I looked back at the gurney and saw, in horror, that the sheets were wet, like I had peed on them. I knew I hadn't. But they were soaked. I realize now, they weren't really that soaked. They were wet, yes, but with sweat. Embarrassed, I quickly looked away. Someone told me to lie down, so I did.

Each person in there introduced himself or herself: nurses, fellows, and Fred, whom I already knew. One of the people said they would give me something to help me relax.

I inhaled, all excited. "Are you going to give me Fentanyl?"

He looked at me. "How do you know about Fentanyl?"

"I had some for this test last week," and I indicated the bruising on my upper chest from the needle biopsy. "I *love* Fentanyl."

Everyone in the room laughed, and someone said, "What happens in the OR stays in the OR."

Fred put an oxygen mask on me and told me to take deep breaths … again and again. I began to feel loopy, like the table was floating, or like I was floating and the table was turning. "Are you sure this is just oxygen?" I asked.

"Yup, keep breathing," Fred said, and that's the last thing I remember before I woke up in the recovery room.

Mom's Side of the Surgery Story

Some of this I found out almost right away. Some of this I found out four years after the surgery. But this is the whole story as I know it now.

I was out-out, given enough anesthesia to keep a person asleep while her chest is cracked open. Dr. K came out of the OR to find Mom alone in the surgery waiting room. Dad had left to teach a class. She was knitting, and the doctor sat next to her.

According to Mom, he said, "Damn, if she wasn't right. I think I can get that lymph node she wants me to take."

My knocked-out body had raised up the lymph node I had been begging him to remove. It was sticking out of my collarbone. He thought it would be an easy surgery to take the lymph node out so the biopsy could be done. He asked Mom for permission to go after it. He said they would only go through the cartilage in my breastbone if pathology needed more than the lymph node.

Mom gave him permission, and he told her she'd made the right decision.

Surgery

As I lay on the gurney after surgery, I tried to force my eyelids open. The cream-colored curtain was pulled closed and Dr. K stood over me.

"My neck hurts," I said to him.

"I know," he said.

"Not my chest," I slurred.

"I know," he repeated. "I'll explain that in a second."

My eyes slammed shut even though I was trying to keep them open. I tried to open them again, but I couldn't. My hand worked outside of my conscious mind; it found its way up to my hospital gown and clumsily poked and flopped around my chest, feeling around for missing cartilage, a gaping hole, an angry spot. There was nothing. But something higher up was mad and hurting. I moved my hand up toward my collarbone. I poked my neck, and the pain registered all over, deep into my unconscious mind.

Don't do that again, I thought.

A while later, Dr. K was back, standing on my left again. The curtain was still pulled closed. My eyes would barely open; they were just slits staring at him through my eyelashes. He was giddy. I understood that better than anything else.

"I took that lymph node you've been asking me to take," he said. "We got what we needed without going into your chest. It's Hodgkin's. We won't know that for certain until the end of the week, but we're talking Hodgkin's. I've already made an appointment for you with oncology for next Tuesday."

I opened my eyes again, and he was gone.

The time I spent in recovery after surgery is jumbled in my head. I remember sitting in a wheelchair, holding my stomach, calling the nurse, saying I didn't feel well. I was worried that I would throw up, that I would make a mess, that I would gross out the other people around me in their curtained areas. The nurse took her time, and I slowly realized that I was wearing a hospital gown; if I threw up, it wouldn't be my problem, my cleanup, or my clothes. It would be the nurse's fault for not getting me a bucket. I let myself relax.

Mom came in with her friend, who handed me a bottle of water and some saltines. She talked to me about her husband's ailing friend, who was raising ruckuses in his nursing home and almost got himself kicked out. She talked to me as I chewed on the crackers.

I found out later that for a surgery as serious as mine, they turn off your salivary glands so that you don't choke in the middle of it. The crackers just gummed up and wadded up in oatmeal-thick clumps. I used tiny bottles of cold water to break them up so they would go down my throat.

Mom was a couple of feet away, leaning on one of those over-the-bed tables that raise and lower and are used to hold the patient's food. She was on the phone, saying, "Wendy, she just got out of surgery. Wendy, she's not going to know who that is." Pause. "No. I'm not telling her." Another pause. "Wendy, she is barely awake. She's not feeling well. She's not feeling well … Fine. Fine."

She looked at me. "Kim, Wendy wants you to know that Maggie Honeychurch was just nominated as an aide to Obama."

"Holy shit. No way," I slurred.

Mom's eyes got wide. The phone dropped from her ear a little. "You know her?"

"Mom, remember when Wendy went to China on the Fulbright and came home dating that guy, Henry? Maggie Honeychurch is Henry's sister."

Mom put the phone back to her head and said, "Henry?"

I turned back to Mom's friend, who handed me more crackers and another bottle of water and said, "So, listen to this one …"

Meeting Dr. K One Last Time

After the surgery, Dr. K had to look at my sutures and the wound and make sure the space in my collarbone was healing as he expected. It was still a gash, red, puffy, and it didn't come back together completely. He said that it would come together and be barely a line.

My mom and I met with him in his office. His nurse practitioner told me that the amount of aching and pain I had in my collarbone was normal. She said Dr. K had big meaty hands and he'd been pushing his fingers around in there, moving things about, pulling skin away from where it lived. Those things caused my body trauma. Pain and aches were to be expected.

"I'm glad your mom made the decision to have the lymph node removed, rather than going through your rib cage," Dr. K said. "Many people, women especially, complain that the skin gets pulled into the space between the ribs. The cartilage normally keeps everything where it should be, but once the cartilage is gone, then things change. Some women really don't like how the skin occasionally feels pulled into the space between the ribs."

"You didn't tell me that," I said.

"Would knowing that have changed whether you had the surgery or not?" he asked.

"No," I responded. But I was thinking, *Knowing all of the side effects does make one feel more prepared when something wonky occurs. If it's expected, then it's not wonky.*

"That first time I met you …" he said.

"When I had everyone here?" I asked.

"And there was no place to sit," he added.

"Hey," I retorted, "we totally saved that rolling stool for you. No one took your chair."

"It was intimidating," he said, "coming in here with all of you. Waiting for me to state what was going to happen or not."

"It probably didn't help that I kept demanding that you take the lymph node out right there," I added.

He shook his head, "No, not really."

I asked, "Was that kid in the operating room bummed out that he didn't get to see the planned surgery?"

"What kid?" the doctor asked.

"The one who was there to observe," I said.

Dr. K rolled his eyes, "I have no idea."

I thought about that young guy, in all of his young blondness, having to go back to the other students and say, "No, the doctor didn't do the expected surgery. I got to see him pull out an enlarged lymph node. I was really looking forward to seeing some ribs and cartilage. It was a disappointing day."

But for Dr. K, the day was perfect and happy. He was pleased that he didn't have to open my chest, and he was pleased that he was able to diagnose Hodgkin's.

PRETREATMENT

Meeting Dr. N

Dr. K chose Dr. N because he thought my personality would resonate with hers. He said that doctors are doctors, and not all of them have the same bedside manner. He chose Dr. N because he thought we would get along well, which was important since she would be my doctor for years to come.

We—Dad, Mom, Jean, Giselle, and I—had our first meeting with Dr. N on May 18, 2010. I really thought that I would be able to meet with her and get my first chemotherapy dose right away, maybe that day or the next. But doctors don't work that way. They always have tests to complete.

It was an agonizingly long wait in the examination room of the cancer center on the third floor of the medical center. We waited and waited for a doctor to come and talk to us. The plan was that I would get chemo and then go back down to Jean and Aubrey's, so I could maybe work or be in a place filled with God's Spirit as I went through treatment. The women all took chairs. There wasn't one for Dad, so he leaned against the counter. I sat on the examination table, always my spot.

They talked; I might have too. But what was said didn't matter too much. It was the waiting. Always with the waiting.

Then there was a knock on the door, and a tall, thin, beautiful drink of water came in. He had short, curly hair that he tried to tame with gel. He reached out his hand and said that his name was Dr. A; he was Dr. N's fellow. Having had experience with fellows at this point, my mind didn't even access the definition of partner. Instead, my brain's first thought was, *Oh, he's almost an oncologist.*

Dr. A said Dr. N would be in soon, but that he would start without her, since we were going to be awhile. That was when the history lesson of Hodgkin's lymphoma began.

He said that if it were 1970, my diagnosis would have been a prognosis for a death sentence. Around the time of WWII, people who were diagnosed with Hodgkin's enlisted, because they knew they were going to die anyway; why not die for a cause? Then in battle, they were exposed to mustard gas. They survived the war, returned home, and saw the doctor, who discovered the Hodgkin's had been healed. They were healthy again and, ironically, mustard gas was the cure.[3]

In the 1960s, a sick man went to his doctor in France. (I could be wrong about the French thing, but I do remember the rest of what he said.) The doctor didn't know what to do. He knew his patient was dying, and there was little known about how to handle what was going on in the patient's body. In desperation, the doctor turned to the four most powerful drugs on his shelf, a concoction known as ABVD. The doctor pumped all four at once into the patient, and they worked. The patient was healed, cured even. The Hodgkin's never metastasized and never came back.

As a result, now ABVD is the treatment for Hodgkin's, with little deviation. ABVD. People don't want to find out if it's only three in the concoction or only two or one of the components that are responsible for the healing. They know ABVD works, and so ABVD is what people do, even if all four drugs aren't truly necessary. No one wants to risk not getting better to be a part of a trial for something less than what they know works.[4]

---

[3] For more information, go to: http://www.lymphomainfo.net/hodgkins/timeline.html.

[4] As it turns out, Dr. N is a part of a study that is changing the ABVD cocktail. They are taking out one of the drugs and putting in another one, which also starts with the letter A. This A is the drug they give the 15 percent of patients for whom ABVD doesn't work. Of the 15 percent of patients for whom ABVD doesn't work, 85 percent are cured using this second chemotherapy regime with this second A medication. I haven't been brave enough to ask about the 15 percent of the 15 percent for whom ABVD and then A doesn't work. I know the answer, but sometimes I don't like hearing the truth.

I joked that if you ever get handed cancer dice and are told to roll to find out what kind of cancer you are going to get, roll Hodgkin's. It's the only one that's truly curable.

Dr. A added, "But you don't get something for nothing." He said ABVD worked for 85 percent of the people who received it. He said if ABVD didn't work for me, we would talk about what the other 15 percent do. He hoped ABVD would work; however, there was a price to pay. Each drug had its own special side effect. Cancer cells grow fast, and one of the chemotherapy medications attacked fast-growing cells. However, the drug was not selective, and it attacked all fast-growing cells, including hair cells. Yes, I was going to lose my hair.

At that point, my hair was long and wavy. It was good Jewish hair. I must have looked horrified, because Dr. A pursed his lips together and nodded.

One of the drugs, he continued, causes heart damage. It was possible that the treatment could cause my heart to form a murmur. If it did so, I would have a murmur for the rest of my life.

He said one of the drugs causes pulmonary tissue to harden. It was possible treatment would cause my lungs to lose flexibility. He said, if that hardening happened, I would never be able to experience secondhand smoke again.

The third drug he talked about caused nerve damage. He explained during treatment, my hands and toes might get tingly. I was to call them immediately if that occurred. He repeated himself a couple of times: "Call immediately when you start tingling." He said the tingling could get really bad, which would set me up for potential severe nerve damage. He said keeping on top of the tingling could prevent that from happening.

He told us my blood count would go down, leaving me highly susceptible to infection. I was to avoid public places, germs, anyone under the age of fourteen, and caretakers of anyone under six years old. He said my colleagues from my high school could come visit, but they shouldn't touch me. He said if a colleague was living with a sick teenager, he or she should wait until the teenager was healthy before visiting. If anyone was living in a house with someone under the age of six, they could visit only if the child was healthy, but the child was not to be in my presence at all while I was sick. He said if I got sick with any kind of infection, the drugs they'd give me for it would cause back pain, and I would have to be hospitalized until the infection was cleared out.

I said, "Back pain?"

He responded, "Excruciating back pain, and you'll be trapped in a hospital bed." Then he repeated, "You don't get something for nothing."

He also said no one knows how you get Hodgkin's. They think it has something to do with mononucleosis. He said in families where one sibling gets mono and the other doesn't, the one that doesn't seems to be the one who gets Hodgkin's.

As a joke, I cheered and said I could blame one of my siblings. Later, my stepmom told me it made her sad that I was capable of blaming a family member for cancer, that the weight of that responsibility is unbearable. She said I was wrong to be excited and joke around.

I agreed; I was completely wrong. To this day, I have a hard time forgiving myself. I even apologized to the family member who had mono when I was growing up, although that person had not been present in the room. I told this person about my bad behavior and said, "It's not your fault. It's not."

Her response was, "Of course it's not. It can't be. It's not just siblings who don't get mono; it's best friends and partners and parents. All of those people aren't coming down with Hodgkin's."

When I cheered, Dr. A shook his head at me and said I wasn't exactly normal. I think I was still in denial at that point: this wasn't real, and it wasn't happening to me. I wasn't *really* in an oncologist's office, facing chemotherapy. To me, it seemed like a joke. However, it wasn't a joke to my family and Jean.

My dad asked, "Is it possible that my smoking when she was younger gave this to her?"

Dr. A said, "You mean, she was exposed to significant amounts of secondhand smoke in confined spaces?"

My dad said, "Yeah, like in my car and such."

Dr. A said, "I don't think we can rule it out as a possibility."

Dad turned a sickly olive pallor. I knew he felt guilty, but with the room full of people and the discussion revolving around my sickness, it wasn't the time to reassure him.

Somewhere in the middle of all of this, my stepmom caught my attention. She pointed to the crotch of her shorts and mouthed the words, "His fly is down."

I looked away from her quickly and looked at Dr. A. Yup. He was definitely flying low. I blushed and caught Jean's attention. She looked at me, confused, and when Dr. A's attention was focused on the computer in front of him, I mouthed, "His fly."

She saw and tried hard not to laugh.

Dr. A noticed something was going on in the room behind him. He turned to me, and I sat up straight, trying hard not to grin too widely. I know I was bright red. He looked around at the other people in the room and back at me. I was still sitting there, with a bright red face.

When he had finished giving me the information and checking some details on the computer, he got up and left the room. My father followed him out. They stood in the hallway for a couple of seconds, and then Dad came back in.

"Did you tell him his fly was down?" I asked.

"Of course," he said. "I would want someone to tell me."

I burst out laughing, "I agree. I would want someone to tell me too. But how is he going to walk in here after finding out he's been flying low?"

"Now who's making him feel bad?" Jean said. "How's he going to walk in here after hearing you laugh so loudly? He's going to know why you laughed."

A little while later, Dr. N came in; Dr. A was behind her. She was from India, tall, with long, black hair, a beautiful smile, and expressive eyes and face. She congratulated me on losing twenty-five pounds. I sensed something in the way she said it, though.

"You don't think it was just me?" I said.

She shook her head. "I think you had some help."

Dr. A took a seat at the computer, red faced and quiet. He barely spoke or interacted with us, but he did say a little, "We want to try to figure out when this started. Do you remember a night when you were really itchy?"

"Itchy?" I asked, "What kind of itchy?"

And then I remembered. It was a cold night in my apartment, which was above a not-so-well-insulated garage. It wasn't hard to have a cold winter's night. Sometimes, I'd get dry, itchy skin, but it was localized— my feet or my hands, sometimes my arms. On this one night, I had dry skin everywhere. I put body cream on my arms, hands, legs, feet— normal amounts, but it wasn't enough. I slathered myself with a thick layer of cream, all over. I flopped into bed wondering why the lotion wasn't working. The cream made my pajama bottoms stick to my legs, the sheet, and the comforter, and since I often sleep naked from the waist up, I wondered if I should put on a shirt.

I described this itchy night to the people in the room, and Dr. A said, "That was the night it started."

"I don't remember what night that was," I said.

"That's okay," he said. "We have a general idea."

Dr. N covered some of the material that Dr. A had already explained, reiterating the possible side effects:

- hardening of lung tissue
- heart murmurs or worse
- possible nerve damage, but probably tingling in my toes and hands
- hair loss
- low blood counts that could cause a serious infection

We all nodded to indicate we'd heard everything Dr. N said. Then she asked how I wanted to get my chemo.

"Pardon?" I asked, not realizing I had a choice.

"Well, this is the real question," she said. "How are your veins?"

"Okay, I think." I looked from Dr. N to Dr. A.

"Well, we recommend getting a port," Dr. N said.

A port. I had heard about this. One of my students had told me about his family's experiences during his late father's colon cancer. This student said that the port was the way to go; they just shoot the chemo into the spot in your chest, and boom, that's it. The student made a motion toward his own chest like he was injecting a shot and made a little farting sound.

I turned to Dr. A, and he nodded, "Get the port."

"Okay," I said. "A port is probably best."

Dr. N smiled. "Agreed."

She said that some people continue to work while on ABVD and others don't. She said that it just depended on how my body reacted. She said she suspected that it would take four months—a dose every other week, and eight doses in all. That is where it got a little confusing. Every person's situation is different, and what they call a "round" depends on the methods being used. In my case, a round consisted of two doses with a dose every other Tuesday. My first dose was scheduled for June 1, 2010, and my second was on June 15, 2010; those two doses combined would complete the first round. I had to have my doses exactly every other Tuesday, no matter what. It was important that I never missed a dose. Nothing was considered an acceptable excuse—not a hurricane, flood, earthquake, or alien invasion. I had to be at the cancer center for my doses as scheduled.

The conversation turned to wigs. Dr. N said if I were working and were bald, I might want a wig. She said insurance companies don't pay for wigs, but they will pay for a hair prosthesis. If I wanted a wig, down the road, she would write me a prescription for a hair prosthesis. To be honest, Dr. N couldn't keep a straight face as she was telling me this. She tried, but her mouth curved up at the sides.

"Really?" I asked.

"Seriously," she said.

My family made a couple of side comments about how my father didn't need a hair prosthesis, but what if he did? We also joked about how the phrase "hair prosthesis" didn't actually change the nature of a wig.

Dr. N wanted to run some baseline tests so she would be able to discern about halfway through if the chemo was affecting me adversely. She ordered a pulmonary test and an echocardiogram, saying I would have these tests again after dose 4, the end of the second round. If anything went awry, she might be able to lower the doses of some of the cocktail or maybe cut out one or two of the ingredients of ABVD. She also referred me to a fertility specialist. She said that ovaries usually go to sleep during chemotherapy, but she wanted me to know what options were available. She wanted me to have all of the information before I made any decisions.

One thing strikes me now: at every meeting along the way with Dr. K and Dr. N, the doctors asked me the same questions. They asked if I were having fevers or night sweats. They asked about chest pain, if I had trouble breathing, or if I were coughing a lot. They wanted to call my weight loss "unexplained." When I told doctors that I was eating everything in sight and still losing three pounds, they would say, "That sounds about right." The fact that I had lost fifteen to twenty pounds on my own, without Hodgkin's help, didn't seem to matter so much. It was because of Hodgkin's that I couldn't stop losing weight, even when I was eating cheesecake, cheese steaks, cookies, cupcakes, and pretzels with abandon. The amount of weight I had lost overwhelmed me when I was trying on shorts right before treatment. I had brought 8s into the dressing room, because that would have been my healthy size—not too big and not too small. Only it was the size 4s that fit.

As we were getting ready to leave the examination room where we had this meeting, Dr. N said, "There is an 85 percent chance you will survive, Kim; I want to dance at your wedding."

Staging

Dr. N sent me for a PET scan. She wanted to get the most recent baseline possible. It was now the end of May, almost two months since my first CT scan. I wasn't allowed to eat before the test, so by one or two o'clock in the afternoon, I was more than just Grumpy Pants. In addition, the tech was running more than an hour and half behind schedule.

I was hungry and miserable. Dad sat next to me, doing his Sudoku, one of those extreme puzzles for the X-Men of the Sudoku world. I tried to read and distract myself, but instead I was petrified a woman dressed as a clown was going to come up and talk to me. She had on a crazy outfit of mismatched stripes and plaids in bold reds and royal blues. She had bright red circles on her cheeks. She was going around talking to patients, saying she was a volunteer to cheer people up. What made me most uncomfortable was that she wore tea bags as earrings. I'm not sure how she slid the strings that hold the label through the holes in her ears, but she did. I leaned over and said, "Dad, does she have teabags in her ears?"

Dad looked over and made a duck face, saying, "One has to wonder why."[5]

---

[5]   Mom had to have a surgery at a hospital closer to home in the early months of 2013. The clown-woman showed up in the waiting room; one of her relatives was having an operation. I talked to her about her work at UBF. She said that by dressing as oddly as she did, she helped encourage patients who were insecure about their appearances to open up about their lives and bodies.

Just when I decided the tech was never going to come and was contemplating leaving to find food, he appeared. He took me to a room with a chair and a door; the door was attached to a waiting area with a couch, chair, and a table with accompanying mood lamp. The tech told me to take off my clothes and put on one of those gowns. Ugh, those gowns. I explained that I had on a tank top without a bra.

"No underwire?" he asked.

"Nope," I said.

"No wires of any kind?" he continued.

"Nope," I replied.

"My wife doesn't wear anything sexy like that," he said, indicating my lacy tank top, "so I guess that I don't understand how they work."

I didn't think my tank top was sexy in the least, which led me to wonder about this guy's private life, which made me a bit uncomfortable.

He left me in a side room, which had a reclining chair. He asked me to drink barium and let the radioactive material settle into my veins. I wasn't allowed to read or play on my phone. I wasn't to touch anything, to keep the radioactive material contained. He said if I felt ill, there was a garbage can. The tech wanted me to drink as much as possible of this thick, citrusy shake. He used a loud machine next to the chair to flood my IV with the radioactive material.

He put two of the hospital blankets over me to help keep me warm, an almost impossible feat as the hospital was always freezing. He turned off the light, but left the door open to the waiting room next door and its light came in around the partially shut door. I was left to drink the barium and wait.

As I was sitting there drinking and waiting, I heard two people, one male and one female, approach the door to the waiting room. They were talking, and I heard the male say, "Perhaps we could step in here and talk about this some more, in privacy."

I didn't even think to alert them to my presence. Once they sat down, the woman said how uncomfortable she was, that human resources wouldn't protect her, and she felt betrayed. The guy asked her to remind him of the backstory. I was excited by that, because I got to hear the whole story and it made my hour long wait fly by.

The tech came back and found them talking. I guess he pointed to the room I was in, because he said, "What are you doing in here? Do you know there's a patient in there?"

They made "oh my goodness" kinds of noises and left.

The tech didn't ask what they were talking about, but when I said it was one of the more interesting conversations I'd heard in a while, he asked, "They weren't making out or anything, were they?"

"No, no. Nothing like that," I said and gave him a brief summary of what I had heard.

***

He walked me down the hall to another room. The ceiling was really high, maybe two stories tall, and I remember it having metal-like walls, but that could be a mis-memory. The CT scanner took up much of the space. The tech asked me to take off my orange sherbet-colored fleece jacket and lie down on the CT scanner bed. He covered me with a couple more blankets and walked into a room with glass windows that looked out onto the scanner.

This is when I started to perfect the "moving/not moving" game. The CT scanner pulls the patient into and out of the doughnut holes; with PET scans there seem to be two doughnuts, upright and next to each other. The bed floats through the first and into the second; all the while the spinning thing inside the doughnuts makes this whirring noise that drowns out pretty much every other sound, even one's thoughts. Once in that mode, if you close your eyes, it feels like you are actually moving, even if you're not. You may convince yourself that your body is moving forward or backward on the bed; only opening your eyes allows you to determine if you are truly sliding. I was wrong more times than I was right that day. I would open my eyes and be moving, although I'd thought that I wasn't. Then I would close my eyes and think *I'm moving now*, and open them to find out that I was stationary.

Eventually, the tech pulled me all the way forward and told me to sit up.

"Can you see anything?" I asked him.

"Well," he said, "it's a rough picture."

"Right. I get that. But can you see anything below my diaphragm? The oncologist said that if there aren't any angry lymph nodes below my diaphragm, I won't have to have a bone marrow test, which I really don't want. I hear they hurt. I was wondering if you could tell."

"I'm not supposed to show you this, but come on," he said.

He led me into the back room with the windows, and we bent over the computer monitor. The image of my skeleton was on the screen, which didn't weird me out very much. I had been given the CD of my original scan to show the surgeon, and I'd pulled up those images on my computer. In fact, I even took the CD to the AP biology teacher at Boon Win High and showed him my skeleton, which he thought very cool.[6]

The tech explained that the images we were looking at were negatives, so what was "lit up" were the dark spots; when they processed the image, that would be reversed. He pointed out a number of dark spots in my chest cavity and under my arms. I merely glanced at them and asked him where my diaphragm was. He pointed to a faint line that ran horizontally above my pelvic bones. I looked for black spots below that line. I pointed out a couple, and he identified them. One was my bladder; one was "supposed to be like that." One of the spots was dark and was sitting at the base of my pelvic bone, sort of in the middle. It was small, though.

"What about this one?" I asked.

He said, "That's right at your urethra. It's probably a bit of urine that is holding the radioactive material but didn't come all the way out."

"So, you don't think I have any below my diaphragm?" I asked.

"I can't say no, but I will say that one round will probably take care of what's going on in there."

I replied, "My oncologist says I'm getting four rounds."

"They like to do that," he said.

***

When I talked to the oncologist after the scan, she said that I didn't have any cancerous lymph nodes below my diaphragm. That put me at stage 2A, since I didn't have shortness of breath, chest pain, coughing, or night sweats. If I were experiencing those things, I would be stage 2B. She also said that the mass behind my breastbone had grown.

---

[6]   When I went to see Dr. K the first time, Carla, his nurse practitioner, asked for the CD, and that's when she said that she definitely saw the mass. She took the CD in the back, away from me, to read it, and I had to wait for her to come back. She returned without the CD, and it was never seen again. I wish I had downloaded the information onto my computer. No one knows what happened to that CD, and the information is gone, as far as I know.

"Really?" I asked.

It had started out three by four by point four centimeters, but this newest scan revealed that it was six by eight by point eight centimeters. In just about two months, it had doubled in size.

"Do you feel any pain?" she asked.

"No. Not at all. I don't feel anything."

"You're lucky," she replied. "With all that is going on with each of your lymph nodes, you are losing space inside your chest cavity. There aren't a lot of nerves in there, so pain from one area may manifest someplace else altogether. But you aren't in pain anywhere?"

I shook my head no and was staged at 2A.[7]

Pre-Chemotherapy Testing

Though they ordered an echocardiogram, those who were in charge of schedules were unable to fit me into the calendar. As a result, I had what's called a MUGA scan; they never told me what the letters meant. I had no idea what one of those was, and I'm still not sure I completely understand.

The MUGA scan was scheduled to be administered in the Radiology Department in the Hospital of the University of Benjamin Franklin. This marked the first time I was on the third floor of the mothership. To get to the Radiology Department, one had to pass the Division of Infectious Disease. The first time we passed the olive-green sign, we all agreed that was a place I was to avoid, especially when my blood counts became low.

For the MUGA scan, the tech put an IV into my arm. He injected radioactive material into my arm and then waited for the material to

---

[7] Staging for Hodgkin's might be different than it is for other cancers, but they explained it like this: Because I had quite a number of lymph nodes in my upper chest full of Hodgkin's, I was stage 2. The letters A and B represented symptoms: shortness of breath, coughing, fevers, weight loss, night sweats, pain, etc. I wasn't having any of the symptoms except weight loss, so they said I was 2A. If I were having the symptoms, I would have been 2B. Stage 3 was given when a person had the lymph nodes below their diaphragm full of Hodgkin's, and the letters would be attached based on symptoms of side effects. Stage 4, the highest the numbers go, is when the Hodgkin's is in the bone marrow.

affect my heart, so he could count the different kinds of cells being pumped in and out with each pulsation.

The man was candid with me. He was wearing about three or four plastic rings on a couple of his brown fingers. Something happened; perhaps my vein blew? He had to pour the radioactive material from a vial into a syringe. If I recall, some fell onto the surface on which he was working. He said that the stuff in my veins wouldn't hurt me at all, but the liquid on the table could have a great impact on him. I asked about the rings, and he said, "They measure how much radioactivity I'm exposed to."

I watched the lit cells go out of my beating heart on the screen in front of me. He explained what we were looking at: cells rushing out, and others rushing in. It was cool to watch my heart beat. Instead of freaking me out, I found my breath deepening and my body relaxing as I watched my heart do what it was supposed to do. The tech said he couldn't tell based on the counts, because those weren't in yet, but based on activity and how things looked, my heart looked good.

***

I left the mothership and went over to the medical building for the additional tests that had been scheduled for that day. I used the elevator and got off on the ground floor, where people were lining up to pay for their parking. In front of me was a tall, elderly couple. They matched each other in frailty and hunched-over-ness. Their short, thinning, white hair matched. The male had his arm protectively around the female, and it was clear he was highly concerned about her. I turned to look at them as I walked by, to see if their faces matched as well.

Until this moment, I had been lamenting going bald. I couldn't get my head around it. I couldn't imagine what it would be like not to have hair. To be honest, it was a real struggle. In fact, at that very moment, my thoughts were on my head and my hair.

I turned to look at the elderly couple. The woman had a gauze pad over where her nose should have been. Instead of protruding out, as it would have if she had a nose, it sank in. It was concave against her face.

My stomach sank. It was revolting.

Two truths hit me in that instant. First, that is how to make a villain a true villain: remove his nose. Ralph Fiennes's portrayal of Voldemort is repulsive because he's lost his nose. Hannibal Lecter wears a face mask that obscures his nose. Most aliens are portrayed without noses. Second, I was being petty. I would only lose my hair. From then on, when I lamented my hair loss, I would say to myself, *It could be worse; I could have no nose.*

***

The pulmonary test, used to create a baseline on my lungs, was grueling. To be honest, I almost fainted. The person doing the test put me in a little round phone booth. It had a glass window and a little bench. When the circular door closed, I was squished in there, with just enough room to put my feet flat on the grey flooring. Inside the booth was a tube to breathe through and a speaker on the wall where I could hear the tech telling me what crazy breathing techniques she wanted.

One time she wanted me to breathe in and out quickly and repeatedly for ten seconds and then breathe out for as long as possible without losing steam. It turned out that she wanted me to exhale after hyperventilating for a total of thirty seconds. It was impossible, and I kept failing. Eventually she got the reading she wanted, but I had to hyperventilate on purpose to accomplish her test.

She wanted me to complete five different exercises to get a solid reading on my lungs; all of them were as challenging as the first.

One thing that struck me was how weak I was. Cancer takes all of your energy. This was an endurance test that my body was not equipped to complete. I would become exhausted after carrying a heavy schoolbag from my car to my classroom, and I needed a nap every day after teaching. The breathing exercises were more than my fragile form could accomplish. Before we were done, I was lightheaded. I told her I wasn't doing well, and she gave me crackers and water to get me through. After it was over, I slept on the way home.

The tech concluded with saying that my lungs looked healthy. She was compassionate about my weakness. She assured me that it was not due to a lung issue; it was a cancer issue.

Fertility Specialists

I was thirty-three and not dating anyone; I hadn't dated for about nine years. I had committed to God and was waiting for Him to come through with my husband. There was no need to date when God had brought Sarah together with Abraham, Hosea married Gomer (a prostitute), and Rahab married one of the spies who went into Jericho. I watched God introduce my friends to their future spouses. Of course, He would work miracles in my life as well.

When I met with Dr. G on the eighth floor of an office building on Market Street, at the University of Benjamin Franklin Fertility Care, I was not thinking about children or having children. Nor did I want children. I had always said I would make a rocking stepmom, but having children of my own was never a passion or a dream. Dr. G explained how chemotherapy affects ovaries and fertility in general. She said that people who had Hodgkin's and went on to have children afterward tended to have normal babies without birth defects. She stated that ovaries tend to go dormant and "hide" during chemotherapy. They don't take in the medication. They just hang out and wait for the battle to end; then they become productive again.

She asked if I were interested in harvesting my eggs to be replanted into my body.

I said, "I don't think so."

She said, "Let me give you all the information you might need to make an informed decision."

She discussed harvesting and how that was accomplished. It was doses of hormones and then when the eggs were ripe, she would collect them from my ovaries. She explained that fertilized eggs have higher chances of yielding a live birth than unfertilized eggs. If I harvested and fertilized ten eggs, three of them might yield a live baby. If unfertilized eggs were frozen, thawed, and fertilized later down the road, the chances of a live baby were lower than three out of ten.[8]

She asked if I were in a committed relationship, one where I might want to have a child with my partner.

I said, "No, I'm not with anyone."

"That's fine. We have a catalogue you can look through if you decide to harvest. There are plenty of options you can choose from."

The Dadalogue, as this catalogue is sometimes called, makes it sound so easy to find the father of your baby. But it takes the relationship

---

[8]   These statistics have changed. I don't know what they are now, but these were the statistics I was given in 2010.

out of it. To be honest, I had never thought of having kids, let alone artificial insemination with a sperm donor.

I said the first thing that came into my mind, "How did you get into this profession?" which I'm sure I said in a judgmental way.

Dr. G was gracious and walked me through her history and her educational experience. She explained that she'd become passionate about women who desperately wanted to have children but couldn't. Listening to her empathy toward would-be moms made me feel like an ass about my insensitive comment.

Dr. G offered me reading material and asked if I would participate in a study on how chemotherapy affects the fertility rate. She said that her nurse practitioner could give me details, but it basically included a pelvic exam, ultrasound, lengthy questionnaire, and blood test. I would go to the office for an examination in measured intervals during chemotherapy and afterward.[9] I agreed to participate. I would be reimbursed for parking and given either a $10 bill or a $10 Target gift card, depending on what they had on hand the day I was there.

Dr. G gave me a pelvic exam that day. First, she rolled a condom onto the ultrasound wand she would be inserting and lubed it up with ultrasound gel. She also moved the monitor on her computer, so I could see what the ultrasound was showing. When the wand was in place, she pointed out my uterus and my ovaries. She then measured the largest fertile spot and counted all the others on each ovary. I had twenty-four fertile spots on the first ovary and twenty-two on the second, which meant there were forty-six potential eggs to be released at my next ovulation or some ovulation upcoming, although, in theory, only one egg per ovulation is actually released.

To a person who didn't want children, this was a little overwhelming. Knowing that only one egg gets released per ovulation was comforting, but knowing there were so many eggs developing produced a little anxiety. Dr. G said my counts were normal and good. She wished me

---

[9]   During chemotherapy, Dr. N made it very clear that *nothing* was to be inserted vaginally, not a single thing. I also was not allowed to get a manicure, which might cut the cuticles and cause an infection that could be hard to heal when my blood counts were low. I was to avoid hot tubs and workout spaces for a whole host of reasons.

luck with treatment; her nurse practitioner and I set up time to do a phone interview and complete the big questionnaire.

Speed Bumps

I was at the prayer meeting at church on Monday night after the tests. When I walked in, Bruce said that the cancer was a speed bump. He pulled a chair into the center of the circle and had me sit in it to receive prayer. As everyone was praying, Bruce said, "If you take a speed bump really fast, it's a jolt. You definitely feel it. This is going to be a jolt to your body, but remember it's just a speed bump."

The First Haircut

My hair was long. It was dyed with red highlights and basically engulfed my face. I would pull it up in a ponytail or messy bun and teach with pens sticking out of it. When I lost pens, students would say, "Ms. Beam, did you check your hair?"

My appointment for the first dose was June 1, 2010.

On Memorial Day weekend, I drove to Nottingham, two driveways before the quarter-mile driveway where I used to live, and visited my former landlord's daughter. Laura has a beauty salon in her basement and gives a great haircut.

I guess I was beginning to admit the reality of my situation, because I asked Laura to give me a short haircut. I'd chopped all of my hair off before. I've had really short hair and really long hair and bobs in-between. Having the choice of my hair length taken from me was hard. Dr. N and her nurse practitioner didn't feel too bad for me. They had more sympathy for people who had never had short hair or had never even cut their hair who now had to cope with the reality of losing it all. I was mildly offended by their lack of compassion and sympathy, but now I get it. Now I understand I cut my hair short due to preference. Short hair might be against another person's religion, beliefs, or culture.

Laura gave me a cute haircut. It wasn't quite a pixie, but it wasn't floppy either. It was a good length, because it was short, but I didn't feel like a boy. She swept up my hair off her floor and put it in a disposable shower cap. I had visions of sending my hair down to New Orleans to help block the oil spills in the Gulf. Panty hose filled with hair were being used to trap the oil in the water. Laura said that she thought they would be happy to have my hair.

But when I was back at Aubrey and Jean's house, Jean said, "Oh my. Look at all this hair! I can spread it around my garden, and it will stop the deer from eating my hostas!"

"Really?" I asked.

"I read it in one of my gardening books. They said that it's natural and works well."

I never mailed my hair to New Orleans. When chemotherapy started, everything else just dropped away. Jean eventually used the hair around her hostas and hydrangeas. Those plants had one of their best years ever, because the deer barely touched them.

Treatment

Port Placement and First Dose

June 1, 2010

My port was placed the morning of my first dose. To be honest, I don't remember too much about it. I was in the Interventional Radiology Department, the same place I'd been for the ultrasound biopsy. It was a place that I was used to, although instead of taking me up the back ramp, they took me out the front and to the left. They put me on a gurney and again told me to gown up. I don't remember too much of what happened. They ensured that I hadn't had anything to eat, and then took me into yet another bright room. I woke with pain in the left side of my chest—an ache and a weight. That was the port sitting on top of my ribcage right above my left breast.

Once I was awake, they put me in a wheelchair and wheeled me over to the medical building for dose 1. Again, I remember very little of this. I know I was hungry; Mom went down to the restaurant in the lobby and got me a cheese pizza. I also got sympathetic looks from fellow waiting-room companions. Mom kept telling me I was pale and was worried I would throw up. I was weak and out of it from the sedatives used during the port placement.

Little did I know that when I got into the chemo room, I would get even more sedatives.

I think I saw Dr. N before I got dose 1, but again I have no recollection of it. I do remember a couple of moments during the dosing procedure itself, though.

I took the IV pole with me to the bathroom for pee number two. It was such a hassle to be attached to an IV pole, to have to walk around with a metal friend and lift it over the raised rubber threshold, especially when the arm moving the pole has the needle shoved in it and squeezing anything hurts.

"God," I said, as I tried to hover over the toilet and then just gave up and sat. "I don't know how much more of this I can take. I know it's only the first dose, but can it please be over?"

I heard God say, "It's going to get worse."

Okay. Get through this part then. I finished the stream, wiped, and headed back to my recliner.

Mom reports that the first dose was like truth serum. She asked me questions about all my major life events she wanted to know more about, and I answered her with the kind of detail she relishes. I told her more things than she'd ever known.

The whole day was fuzzy: the trip in the wheelchair down the elevator to the car; the trip home—I don't remember any of it. I got home and was hungry, really hungry. That I do remember.

"What do you want?" Mom asked, handing me a menu for a pub about two blocks from the house.

"Bacon cheeseburger," I said.

"Okay," Mom said.

Dr. N said I could eat whatever I wanted.

Mom got the food. I chowed down.

Then, I didn't feel so good. I crawled slowly up the stairs, on all fours like I was four. Only, four-year-olds charge up the stairs, racing to get up there first. I was an old woman, brittle and hunched, ridiculously slow. On the bed in the spare room, I opened my computer and started to watch the Joss Whedon's TV series *Firefly* on Netflix. Bombs were going off on the screen when the nausea became too much.

Pushing the computer to the other side of the double bed, I leaned forward over the metal bowl I used to bake with when I was little. Up came my dinner, looking like dog food.

Man. I had no idea my stomach could hold so much. I thought the bowl would overflow. I wanted to get away from the smell, but my stomach kept clenching, my mouth kept opening, and the burger kept coming.

I thought, *God, I don't know how much more of this I can take.*

He replied, "See? I told you it would get worse."

Believe it or not, in the middle of retching, I smiled. If God could tell me what would happen hours before it did, then this was not a surprise to Him. He was as present in this moment as He was in the bathroom and the chemo room and the drive home and during everything I didn't remember.

***

A day or two after chemo, Dad swung by Mom's and picked me up. He took me back to Aubrey and Jean's. Dad honored what I wanted; he said it was good for me to be with people who cared about me and that I should be where I was comfortable. He kept remarking on what amazing people Aubrey and Jean were.

Mom hated that I was leaving. She told me later that when I wasn't at her house, no matter where I was, if she couldn't check on me and see me for herself, she would worry. She worried until she made herself sick. She lost about twenty pounds during my treatment.

Dad drove up in his blue Ford Focus and told me to sit next to him in the front seat. He prepared for my nausea by putting a brown paper grocery bag inside a plastic grocery bag between my legs. I had my pink bucket from the hospital, but he liked his system better because it made clean up really easy.

I don't remember talking much on the trip. Aubrey and Jean live about an hour from my mom's, and Dad just zipped down I-95, to I-495, through the construction around the Christiana Mall, and then to their house off route 40 in Newark, Delaware.

***

Jean thought it was important for me to sleep in my own bed. While I had been away, they had their son, Mark, come and hang my giant, framed Matisse poster in the room where I would stay. One morning, I was in bed, reading *A Great and Terrible Beauty* by Libba Bray. I would go from dozing to reading. I remember lying on my belly and feeling the weight of the port pulling toward the bed. I felt the weight of the port all the time. It was heavy and present. It was foreign.

I talked to the port one morning. I said, "I accept you. I know you are doing me good, and I welcome you in my body." I used those words as a mantra for some time. It didn't make the port any more comfortable, but at least I was making room for it.

Jean told me later that she would wonder about me when she was doing tasks around the house. She would be ironing and realize that she hadn't heard from me for some time. She'd wonder if I were still alive and go in and look at me. Even then, there were times she wondered, "Is she dead?"

One night a couple of days after chemo, I ate my favorite lunch, a bagel. I adore bagels, but my body didn't keep it down. I threw it up. Eating also became painful. My jaw and my mouth became sore. Although I was hungry and really looked forward to a little snack, once in my mouth, the food became too painful to chew. I called Dr. N, who told me that the nerve pain might not just be in my fingers and toes; it could be in my mouth too. Salivation and digestion in my mouth were affected by chemotherapy. She prescribed Gabapentin to block some of the nerve pain, and Aubrey picked it up from the Walgreens around the corner.

That's when I started a list. I knew I'd have to talk to Dr. N about all the things my body was experiencing. I took the list with me when I went to see her again.

For the most part that week, I slept or read in my room. I sat on the swing on the back porch and stared at the deer. Jean put out birdseed every night for the deer. Around dusk, they would come down the path, eat, and occasionally stop to stare back at me. I drank tea and ate carbs. Once or twice, Jean ran a bath in the bathtub off the master bedroom and told me to lie in it. I wasn't allowed to get the sutures around my port too wet, so I would lie with the water just below the Steri-Strips, letting the warmth envelope me.

***

They did tell me that chemo would cause constipation. I didn't understand what constipation was until chemotherapy. To think that people live with that feeling on a regular basis makes me sad. It's so not comfortable. I didn't have strength. I was weak, and my body didn't have the ability to push, if you will.

I lived in constipation during most of my sickness. Doctors suggested I take a stool softener, but that would cause massive cramping that sent aches deep in my guts, deep into my back, and I hated the thought of being in that much pain. I was bloated the whole time I was in treatment. And I was a little uncomfortable.

One afternoon, I went to the bathroom. It was the first bowel movement since chemo had affected my lower intestines. After going, I was lighter. I felt like bouncing a little when I was walking down the hallway, which made me think of one of my father and stepmother's dogs, Dogi.

Dogi had been found at the Plymouth Meeting Mall one afternoon. The ASPCA set up a table and had a couple of furry friends ready to be adopted. Giselle and my stepsister stumbled upon Dogi there. He was part-corgi, part-beagle, maybe, and part neurotic. He had Yoda-like ears that flew out on both sides of his head. He hated being dressed in human clothes and wigs, which was tried when the family discovered William Wegman and his amazing Weimaraners. We joked that Dogi lived in his own little world.

Even though Dogi died years ago, Dogi stories tend to come up at every meal we have together. Even if we say, "No, we're not telling Dogi stories," he's still mentioned. Dogi had a disgusting pooping history. There is story after story of Dogi and his poop. But the more interesting point is this: after Dogi pooped, he would sort of dance. His feet would be lighter, and he would be a little happier. He would have more bounce in his step, and he would notice other people and dogs around him.

That morning I felt a little lighter and more interested in the people around me. I sent my Dad a text that said, "Now I understand why Dogi danced after he went to the bathroom."

Finances

I'm not really sure where to place this discussion, but it's one worth having, as my situation is definitely different than some. I've heard of people who were forced to go to work while on chemo, sit in their offices, and make it look like they were working just to keep their medical insurance. I've heard of people who lived off their spouses while they were sick. Me? I was lucky in ways I don't really understand.

Mr. Trebuchet told me as I was leaving one of those last days at work, "If you have any problems with HR and your benefits, let me know."

As it turned out, I didn't.

When I was first hired at Boon Win High School, I added a sick day or two to the sick leave bank and continued to add the requisite number of sick days to the sick bank each year I worked, so that I was eligible for the sick bank should I have ever needed it. This bank was for people who ran out of sick days and still needed coverage in order to keep their paychecks. As it was, my accumulated sick days covered me up until the last five days of school. Those five days were covered by the sick leave bank, which brought me to the end of the school year.

I was paid on a twelve-month pay schedule, even though I worked only ten months a year. This meant, no matter what was going on with me, I would be getting my school year's pay all year long—even during the summer.

I applied for Family Medical Leave (FMLA) once the summer came around and was informed that because I was in the middle of an approved life event that had been verified by my oncologist, I would be eligible to continue my medical coverage. Not only did I keep my health insurance, my paychecks continued to be direct deposited all the way up until I returned to work on the other end of treatment.

My treatment in total was a little less than a million dollars. My out-of-pocket expenses for co-pays and the little bit insurance didn't cover was about $4,000 total. Everything else was covered by medical insurance. I was actually able to put money away into savings while I was sick.

Like I said, this is not the normal experience for most Americans who are diagnosed with cancer. Many have to worry about keeping their medical insurance, since medical insurance is tied to employment. I happened to be a part of a fantastic insurance plan that didn't lapse while I was working. Everything was covered and I continued to be paid while I was out sick due to FMLA.

To: Important Contacts
From: Me
Subject: First dose
Date: June 8, 2010

I went in for treatment on Tuesday and promptly ceased to be myself. I sort of sank under the weight of the chemicals and still haven't resurfaced, to be honest. I've always been a side-effect queen when it comes to antibiotics, and it appears this is no exception. My neurons have been misfiring and I need a neuro inhibitor to stop throwing up. You know, when I was thirteen, I threw up. I didn't throw up again until I was twenty-six. And now, thirty-three.

I have this week off, and next week I go back for them to kill me again. Only next week, they will be better prepared for my nerves freaking out and my stomach tossing its contents.

But this is the major concern at the moment—besides serious constipation, not that you want to know that, but there it is: my body is currently sporting a fever of 99.7. It's been that high since last night. Granted, it's not going up at the moment, but I need prayer that it doesn't. If it gets to 100.5, which isn't very far away at all, I will have to be admitted to the hospital. This morning, I was up at 2:00, 3:00, 4:00, 5:00 and knew I had a fever, but I refused to take my temperature afraid of what the thermometer would say.

Besides asking God if I can die about once a day, at least, I think my faith is doing well. On Thursday, which was by far the worst, I had an image of me standing in front of a Mack truck, in much the same way that Rachel McAdams was hit by the bus in *Mean Girls*. Now, I'm beginning to fight a bit more, now that I can surface. Before I was just curled up in the front of the boat with Jesus, as the storms raged all around me. Now, I'm standing, like in 2 Chronicles 20:17—check that won't you?—and letting the Lord fight.

I guess that's it. Thank you for standing with me in this. I cannot, cannot do this without you.

Much love,
Kim

"Not all those who wander are lost." ~ J. R. R. Tolkien

Neutropenia

As it turns out, I did have to go to the medical building because of my possible fever, which indicated a possible infection.

I met with Dr. N and said, "Before we get started, can you cut this?"

I played a little with the wound in my collarbone. It wasn't healing well. One of the plastic "I promise it will dissolve" stitches was sticking out through the healing skin, making it impossible for the wound to close. The plastic stitch was no longer bound up inside the wound. It had come loose, and I could pull on the end. It would tighten up the skin and was clearly still attached in the back of the wound. It was sort of like when one pulls on a drawstring and the fabric bunches together.

Dr. N took one look at what I was asking her to do, and she said, "You know, you could get a family member to do this."

"But you're the doctor," I replied.

I came to recognize the look on her face as she came at me with the scissors. It was determined, with her eyebrows in a firm line and her mouth set into a tight-lipped pinch. This was her "I don't like this, but it is part of my job" look. Her scissors gave the plastic a tug, which definitely ached, and then I was left holding an inch or so of plastic. The rest slid back into the wound.[10]

She asked about my concerns, and I pulled out my index card of symptoms and read them off:

- nausea
- vomiting
- gum pain, especially when eating
- heaviness in my chest where my port sat
- achy legs, feet, arms, and hands
- problems keeping my breath
- extreme fatigue

---

[10] Even now, as I type this in 2013, I wonder what is up with the rest of that plastic string. Did it all dissolve, or are there still remnants of it in my collarbone region, just hanging out? One day, will I feel it there and pull out a few inches more? That happened to a distant relative of mine. He felt something pinching under the skin of his leg, and one day he pulled out ten inches of plastic thread.

- inability to concentrate or pay attention
- forgetting big chunks of conversations, etc.

She asked to see my index card and said, "I see you read the book."

"No," I said. "I was afraid that if I read any of the literature it would taint my experience and I would become a hypochondriac. I might think I had these symptoms because I'd read about them."

Mom seconded what I said. "We haven't read anything."

Dr. N smiled and said, "No, I mean this list is textbook. You are right in line with the side effects. You didn't miss one."

She upped my dosage of Gabapentin. As treatment went on, she said, I could increase the dosage as needed. I could take as many milligrams as I needed to keep the tingling in my legs, toes, hands, and mouth manageable.

She told me that they would admit me to the hospital, but there weren't any oncology rooms available at that moment. I would have to wait on the other side of the cancer center, where people get chemo. There the nurses could run tests and keep an eye on me. Mom had to scurry back to work, and Dad sat at the end of my bed for the day. He worked on Sudoku, and I played on my phone. I also watched the rain as it poured down.

A nurse came in and said she had to take blood to find out if I had an infection. She said that the results wouldn't be in for a couple of days because the blood had to interact with the material in two glass bottles she was holding. They looked exactly like hot sauce bottles, except they had medical stickers as labels, and one had a red top and the other had a purple top.

The nurse said, "Has your port been accessed since it was placed?"

"No," I said. I was lying on a bed instead of one of the chemo chairs, which reclined so far back one was practically lying down. In the bed, I wasn't reclined so far back.

The nurse said, "Okay, I'm going to access your port," and the next thing I knew, she stabbed me full in the chest. No warning, just stab! And then my port was ready to use. She filled her two bottles, lickety-split, but I was horrified. Horrified.

I looked at Dad, and he had turned his sick olive color again. After she left he made a "whoooew" noise and said, "That was rough."

The nurse left us alone as we waited for a room to become available at the hospital. A little while later, Aubrey called. He wanted to know how I was, what the doctors were saying and thinking. I told him that they were concerned I had an infection because of my blood counts.

That's when he said, "Jean and I have been talking. We live so far from the hospital, and if you were to get into trouble and needed to be there fast, we wouldn't be able to do that. In traffic, it's a two-hour drive. We want you to be close to where you need to be."

"But, I need to be with you guys," I said.

"And we want you with us," he said. "But we want you to be healthy and close to the hospital. We want you to be safe, and we want that more than being selfish and keeping you with us."

"I feel like you are abandoning me," I said.

"We aren't. We aren't. We are here for you, always. It's just that your mom lives twenty minutes from the hospital. That's a big difference from how far we are from there. We want you near where you have to be if there's an emergency."

Dad looked at me, concerned. I said to Aubrey, "I understand your point. It just hurts." The tears slid down my face.

After Aubrey and I hung up, Dad said, "They aren't going to have you down anymore?"

"No." I said. "They are concerned that they live too far from the hospital should I get into trouble."

"I understand their point, but I am disappointed for you."

Dad and I sat in silence for some time. He kept doing his puzzles. I just sat and allowed the tears to fall until they were done.

As I'd been sitting there for hours, I realized that my phone was dying. Dad looked up from his puzzle and said, "Do you have a charger?"

"No."

"Find out where I can get one," he said.

I looked it up, and he said, "I'll be back."

"But it's pouring," I replied.

He said, "I want to do this." He looked at me and said, "I love you. Call me if you need me," and he left with his umbrella to tread through the buckets of water pouring from the dark-gray sky.

Much later that afternoon, almost around 4:30, Whitherspoon from Boon Win High called. She had heard I was in the hospital, and she had just parked and wanted to know how to get to me. As she walked down Spruce Street, I was able to see her from my bed. She promised that since she was coming from school, she wouldn't hug me, but she wanted to be there for me. She found her way to the medical building and up to my room.

After some time, they moved me from the medical building over to the mothership's admission area. Zern and his wife joined us. Dad sat with his Sudoku as Whitherspoon, Zern, and I joked. I wanted to engage Zern's wife in conversation, but she is shy and only speaks a little English. Zern met her in Thailand. They married and then moved here to the States. Some weird twist of fate found us all together at Boon Win.

Eventually the hospital moved me down to a room off the emergency room. It was a section that was used for rollover for patients in the emergency room. The nurses who worked there were emergency-room nurses. The room was narrow and the bed faced the room's front windows, which looked out into the hallway. There was a curtain that could be pulled to give each room privacy, and that was when I started to hate the Hospital of Benjamin Franklin's curtains. They all have the same geometric designs, and one can only let one's eyes play with the designs so many ways before one gets annoyed.

This room was smaller than a regular hospital room and didn't have its own bathroom. Dad sat in a chair, watching the last game the Flyers were to play in the postseason that year. The Flyers were already losing, and when the nurse came in, she said, "Tell me this isn't an elimination night."

Dad told her it was.

She said, "Oh, man. No. I was hoping for an easy night tonight."

When we asked what she meant, she said, "When the Flyers lose and then are eliminated, people do stupid things like flip cars or riot. Then I get swamped. I don't want to be swamped."

She left, and Zern looked up at the screen. He said, "I do not understand hockey. How can you even tell where the puck is?"

I looked up at the screen and said, "It's in the corner over there. No, wait. That guy is charging down to the other end of the ice with it. You can tell who has the puck because they skate a little differently than the others and you can also tell where the puck is by who is going where."

Zern looked at me and then looked back up at the TV. "If you can tell that," he said, "you must be some sort of genius."

We also talked about my new short haircut. Whitherspoon, Zern, his wife, and my dad all agreed it was sharp. I said, "I think it looks a little like the bad guy's hair in *The Incredibles*. What's his name? Something like Symptom?"

We then talked about possible names for that guy, and they all said they didn't remember his hair well enough to say if mine looked like it. I eventually searched for the character on my iPhone, learned his name was Syndrome, and pulled up pictures. When I showed my friends Syndrome's head, they laughed and agreed my hair did resemble his, only I looked way better than he did.

They all stayed pretty late. Dad stayed until the end of the game. Whitherspoon and Zern both had to drive back down to Maryland and Delaware respectively and then be at Boon Win at 7:15 a.m. the next morning, ready to face the scholars who filled their classrooms.

After they left, the nurse came in and helped me get ready for bed. I didn't want to use a commode. I hated the idea of her having to empty it after I peed in it. She reluctantly allowed me to use the bathroom the nurses used. She was worried because I was neutropenic and was susceptible to some weird infection from using a bathroom the rest of the patients and staff were using. She also offered me food; there was a freezer filled with food for cancer patients in the ER. She said, "We always tell people we don't have food, but for cancer patients, especially those that are neutropenic, we have food on hand."

My regular blood test returned. (This was not the tests in the hot sauce bottles; those would take a couple of days.) The blood test said I was neutropenic, and it wasn't until we got back from the bathroom that the nurse explained what that really meant. She said that there are "good guys" in blood that go out and fight the bacteria and the bad things that try to enter the body. We should have six thousand of them in our blood samples. When my numbers dropped to below six hundred or so, I was considered neutropenic.

When a normal person eats raw fruits and veggies, the body fights off the bacteria on the produce, leaving the person able to take in all of the nutrition. When I was neutropenic, however, the bacteria on a raw red pepper, say, could keep me the hospital for a long time. After this moment, Dr. N said I had to be on a neutropenic diet for the rest of my time on chemo or until she said I was released from oncology. A neutropenic diet meant I wasn't allowed to eat raw fruit or raw vegetables. They all had to be cooked or frozen. I wasn't allowed to eat a salad, a celery stick, or even eat fresh baby carrots out of the bag. I could have melon, since it was under a thick rind, but that was the only fruit that wasn't frozen I was allowed. I could eat as many Cheez-Its, Twinkies, or potato chips as I wanted, but not a single blueberry or strawberry could pass my lips.

I got into bed and about three hours later, since I had a saline drip going into my port, I had to pee. When the nurse came in, she said, "I've been thinking. I don't want you using the bathroom anymore. It makes me too nervous."

"I don't want you to have to clean up after me," I said.

"That is much easier and my job," she replied. She helped me out of bed and had me sit on a commode. She left the room to give me some privacy.

It felt weird to be peeing in a spot that wasn't a toilet and was right next to my bed. It took me a little while to relax and let the pee come. After I was done, I wiped and climbed back into bed.

She came and grabbed the bucket in the chair saying, "Oh, this is much better."

I still felt a little weird about her cleaning up my pee.

***

The next day they released me from the hospital. Mom was working, and Dad wasn't available so Gail, my mom's childhood friend, said she would help out. She showed up around 2:00 p.m. She said she had to get on the road quickly, because she didn't want to get stuck in traffic heading back to her house in Bucks County. Eventually my discharge papers arrived, and the nurse wheeled me out to Gail's car.

Gail started to complain about how the traffic on 76 was going to be awful and how we were never going to get back to my house at that hour, which at that point was close to 3:30 p.m.

I said, "Why don't we just go the way Mom goes?"

"Where does your mom go?"

We were on Market or Chestnut at this point, and I said, "Make a left."

Gail argued with me about whether I knew the way and if I could get us there. She questioned my ability to navigate us home and didn't want to make the left I suggested.

"Fine," I said. "We will do it your way and sit in traffic."

Gail made the turn and continued to follow my directions until she knew where she was and was able to navigate herself through the back roads of Belmont Avenue and Wynnefield Avenue to the Main Line.

When we arrived home, my Aunt Maureen was at the house, which I didn't understand. Gail helped me into the house and asked Mom how she was doing and what was going on.

Mom said, "I'm having a heart attack, and Maureen is taking me to the hospital."

I looked at Mom and Aunt Maureen and watched as Mom took her purse and went out the door toward Maureen's bumper-sticker-covered minivan.

Gail said, "I have to go," and she turned right around, got in her car, and drove away.

I turned to Aunt Maureen, who could not believe that Gail had left just like that and asked me what I would do for dinner. I shrugged my shoulders and said, "The worst-case scenario is a bagel or a bowl of cereal." Then I said, "She's not having a heart attack. It's an anxiety attack."

Aunt Maureen nodded and winked at me. "I know," she whispered, "but let's just make sure."

I nodded and turned back into the house. The humor wasn't lost on me that I was coming home from the hospital just as my mother was leaving for one. I also wondered at Gail's ability to just leave when she heard that her oldest friend might be having a heart attack.

I plodded down the hall, collapsed on the pink sofa in the den, and proceeded to forget about most things for the next few hours.

Mom was admitted for observation overnight. Aunt Maureen came back to my house, made sure I had my evening medications, and spent the night in Mom's bed. She told me that Mom was doing just fine and was driving the nurses crazy. She was insisting that the nurses find the TV shows she wanted to watch and complaining about the food. The doctors gave her a stress test, which she did fine on, and most of her tests were completely negative. Mom said her primary-care physician visited and asked what in her life that might cause this kind of reaction.

Mom said, "My younger daughter was just released from the hospital today with complications around her Hodgkin's diagnosis."

"That would do it," the doctor said, and put my mom on an SSRI[11] to control her anxiety.

Aunt Maureen stayed the night and made sure I had my morning meds and breakfast before she headed back to the hospital to see my mom.

---

[11] SSRIs are medications used to treat certain mental health concerns, like anxiety and depression. The novel *It's Kind of a Funny Story* by Ned Vizzini has one of the best descriptions I have ever read on how SSRIs work.

To: Important Contacts
From: Me
Subject: Hospitalization and upcoming dose 2
Date: June 11, 2010

Just a quick note to let you all know I'm alive and actually back to my spunky self. I might be a little lethargic, but my wit is up and my snark is back. And today is not a day for dying, but living and breathing and pacing … we're not quite up to dancing yet.

I spent Wednesday hanging out in the cancer center of the medical building, and then Wednesday night, they eventually put me in a room in the Hospital of Benjamin Franklin. My dad stuck by me all day, which was just so sweet of him. He even went out in the rain to get me a charger for my phone, which in my haste (and not really believing I was going to be admitted) I didn't pack. My friends from work, Whitherspoon and Zern and his wife, came and hung out with me (and I have wanted to get to know Zern's wife, so I was really excited she came too). They stayed until really late, and then had to go to teach the next day after driving home.

Words fail me when I think of the love, prayer, and show of support I have had. You have been amazing. I was amazed when Whitherspoon and Zern both showed up. I have had constant texts, phone calls, Facebook messages, cards, presents and just such encouragement. Thank you so much.

Tuesday of next week they are going to load me up with antinausea medicine and steroids and a drug that replaces white blood cells (as the chemo destroys them). Hopefully it will go better this time than last. They also say, this being the second treatment, this will be the one that will make my hair fall out. I found out why: the chemo goes after fast-splitting cells because cancer cells are fast-splitting cells, but so are hair follicles … The chemicals aren't particular about which fast-splitting cells they are attacking; the chemicals are just doing their job. That's what makes your hair fall out; the chemo is working.

So, thank you, and I ask for prayer for next Tuesday and all of the rest of next week. I'm asking for grace and peace and mercy from God. I'm asking for a sense of His presence. Many of you have written to me about being in God's right hand and how His hand is the one that is steadying me. Many of you have written words of prayer and vision and scripture and those have been so comforting and grounding. You have helped me remember that this is but a light and momentary struggle creating eternal glory, even though at the moment it doesn't feel light or momentary at all.

Again, thank you.

I love you.
Kim

"Not all those who wander are lost." ~ J. R. R. Tolkien

Dose 2

It was close to dose 2, and I actually felt pretty good. One of Mom's friends, the one who helped me eat crackers and recover from surgery, asked me to take a quick walk to her house to see her dogs. As we were walking to her house, a couple of houses down from my mom's, my left arm got heavy and uncomfortable. It felt fat and weak.

I rubbed it and supported it with my right arm.

She turned to me and said, "What's wrong with your left arm?"

"I don't know; it just feels thick."

"Talk to the doctor when you see her this week."

"Oh, I will," I promised.

***

I was sitting in the medical building waiting for my appointment with Dr. N right before dose 2. Dad was sitting next to me, and I was still reading *A Great and Terrible Beauty*. I was about two-thirds of the way in, and the characters referenced a moment I didn't remember. I had no recollection at all what or whom they were talking about. I didn't recognize the new character that everyone in the book seemed to know. I looked back and back and back even more. More than halfway toward the front of the book, I found the last thing I remembered reading. I realized not only would reading be a problem, which was devastating enough, but I was losing my memory. I put the book down and decided I would only read books that I had read many times before; that way if I forgot parts, it wouldn't be a problem. I would know the story and fill in what I didn't remember reading.

The bigger implication: was I not remembering big sections of what was happening to me? That was something I wasn't willing to face. The problem of reading and not remembering I could fix by reading books I knew and loved. The problem about not remembering conversations or other large important things, I didn't have a solution for.

Dr. N and I met every time I went in for a dose. She talked to me about my blood levels, my side effects, what I was feeling and thinking. If she asked me how I was doing, the answer was usually, "I'm okay," but we both knew that wasn't exactly true.

"Okay" is a completely relative term. It's also a placeholder, a word you use when all of the other words are not enough, a word when other words are too much.

Before dose 1, they said they could give me something to manage the nausea if it got bad. But they also said that I could probably go about my life while being treated, that it wouldn't be that bad, that people continue to work while they were in treatment.

How was it possible to resume one's life as normal when one was glued to a couch, while her legs and bowling ball of a head were pulled down by gravity's force alone? How did one live normally when she had to eat gobs of crackers to keep from throwing up and when one, like a goldfish, forgot pretty much everything that happened about three seconds after it occurred?[12]

Dr. N had to put a whole bunch of orders into her computer, so she turned and did work she needed to do.

"I'm really worried about my left arm," I said.

She said, "I'll look at it," not turning from the screen.

I wasn't upset by this; she was doing what she needed to do to take good care of me and I still had hair.

She stood up; she was wearing her white lab coat, with her name embroidered in blue and hematology written underneath. "Anything else?"

"My left arm."

She came over, lifted it up, felt around on it, and then frowned at me. "As soon as you are done with chemo, I'm sending you for an ultrasound."

I don't remember chemo so much. I don't remember the trip down to get the ultrasound. I do remember lying on this gurney, and the guy with the ultrasound wand was moving it around my arm. I was

---

[12] Ani DiFranco has a song about goldfish with the line "the little plastic castle is a surprise every time." This is not so different from chemo brain. At one point I was hospitalized and, according to the nurse, I said a sentence. The nurse responded, and I said the exact same sentence a second time, not realizing I was repeating myself. When the nurse said, "You just told me that," I felt so small, humiliated, and ashamed. My gut sank deep inside. I got embarrassed every time I thought about this event until I recovered and realized I had no control over chemotherapy and its effect on my body and systems.

making all these jokes, which he didn't find funny. I thought they were hysterical. Maybe one is only funny to oneself when one is on steroids, Benadryl, Ativan, and ABVD.

The ultrasound guy took photos and rushed my stuff up to Dr. N.

Mom pushed my wheelchair, and I was cranky about her driving skills. Heck, my mom's driving skills always make me cranky. It was not really anything new that she was cutting people off, doing her own thing, and smacking my feet into walls as she steered me back to the Cancer Center.

We got back to the center, and Dr. N's nurse practitioner met us in a hallway. To be honest, I had no idea where I was. Now, by deduction, I can guess where that conversation took place. But in reality, at that moment, I had no idea where I was or what was going on. It was bright, and there was white linoleum on the floor.

Katrina, Dr. N's nurse practitioner, looked at me and said, "You need to stop being the queen of side effects."

And that was it. I was admitted to the hospital, because there were blood clots filling the major veins of my left arm and my neck on the left side of my body due to my port. And because it was immediately after dose 2 dripped into my body, I don't remember too much of what happened, neither getting to the room nor settling in. I do know that Mom schlepped a ridiculous amount of stuff into the room for me, the heaviest of which was *Jane Eyre*, which I had decided to read for the umpteenth time (seriously, I have no idea how many times I've read it). It was the only book I wanted to read. If I forgot big sections, it wouldn't matter; I would still want to marry Rochester.

I was given a hospital bed on the seventh floor of the mothership, and an IV in my arm that dripped Heparin into my system.

How Long Have You Had …

I was sitting on the hospital bed, with a hard-cover copy of *Jane Eyre* nearby. The pink bucket they give you to throw up in wasn't far from reach, and I was leaning on the raised back of the hospital bed. My IV pole was close, and my hand was aching from the IV needle. They would not use my port until the blood clots cleared up.

A herd of white-jacketed, doctor-type people walked in. They stood around my bed and stared. One older man, white, with a shock of receding curly hair, separated himself from the crowd of about ten to thirteen people and stood next to my bed. The rest of the crowd circled around the walls and faced me.

The first thing the curly haired man did was ask how I was feeling. I just looked at him. My stomach was foul and thinking about regurgitating itself. My brain was slow, and my thoughts weren't making their way to my tongue.

Seeing my look, he glanced down at my bed and said, "I see you have your pink-bucket friend with you."

I chuckled and nodded; during the first week after chemo the pink-bucket friend was never far. (In fact, we still call it that, and we have given pink-bucket friends to Wendy for her children and even have some left over. Pink-bucket friends are dead handy, not only when one is not feeling well, but when one has to mop a floor or wet-block some knitting.)

He went around and introduced everyone. Two were social workers. A number were interns and residents. One was in charge of what medication I was going to get.

I asked the medicine guy, "Are you going to give me anything good?"

His reply was, "That's the plan."

The man with crazy curly hair said to me, "How long have you had ..." He ended the sentence with a word that started with a "cl" but ended with something that sounded like "ap."

I asked him to repeat what he said, and he said the same thing, just as inarticulately.

"I'm sorry," I replied. "Did you just ask me how long I've had the clap?"[13]

The crowd chuckled.

"Yes," the doctor replied. "Yes, that's exactly what I asked. 'How long have you had the clap?' No. Not at all. How long have you had the *clot*?"

"I don't know. I noticed it about a week ago," I said. "It's made my arm very fat."

"It's not fat," he replied. "It's just filled with liquid."

"Fat and flabby," I replied, giving my left arm a disgusted look.

---

[13] One of the social workers later told me that she'd heard the same thing I had.

"That's what we're going to try to fix," he said.

As the conversation wrapped up, one of the gentlemen pointed at *Jane Eyre* sitting on the end of the bed. "Are you reading this?" he said. The book cover was now turned away from me and facing him. When he turned it to himself during this conversation, I couldn't say.

"Yup," I said. I thought about ten thousand more thoughts, but none of them came out. Apparently chemo makes you dull-witted and slow of tongue as well as forgetful.

"Really?" he asked.

I knew what he was saying. Most people read beach reads, light fluff in the hospital. Not many pick up classics.

"It's my favorite book," I replied.

"Really?" he repeated, clearly surprised.

"I've read it too many times to count," I said, as if that explained everything. And now I see, it explained nothing.

To: Important Contacts
From: Me
Subject: Blood clots?!
Date: June 15, 2012

Pardon all spelling and grammar errors, I'm typing this quickly on my iPhone. I had chemo today, and it went well. So far the hair is holding up; let's see what next week brings. Before chemo I met with the oncologist, Dr. N. I showed her my swollen left arm and underarm and she said, "Yeah. After chemo, you are going to ultrasound." And that's just what happened. The ultrasound tech was cute, and I gave him a hard time (so shocking), and he showed Mom my clots. I'm not sure if there are a number of them or if they are large in size. I don't know much about the blood clots in my left arm and up into my neck. As soon as the ultrasound tech was done printing the images of my arm and neck, he took off to find my doctor, saying the images looked serious. My mom and I gave chase. We met up with the nurse practitioner, Katrina, who is leaving today on maternity leave (Noooooooooo!). She looked at me and said, "Will you stop being the side-effect queen?" Then she said, "We're going to have to admit you."

Now I'm in a really nice room with a view in the hospital of the University of BF, in room 7014. They are using some sort of blood thinner called Heparin (that tastes wretched in the back of my throat, btw) to break up the clots.

I like my port. I like where it is. I like how easy it is to get the chemo into. There are options down the line that aren't so fantastic—like moving the port away from the clots and putting in a new one (I wonder if that will make new clots?). There is also talk of a something line, which stays outside my body and hooks into my heart as well …

I've had some great visitors, phone calls, deliveries, and chats. Mom sat with me through my babbling through chemo; goodness only knows what I said!! Mom and her friend/neighbor brought me my pajamas and some food. And now I'm going to wash up for bed before they come and check my vitals.

Much love (and hospital-bound for a number of days),

Kim

"Not all those who wander are lost." ~ J. R. R. Tolkien

Bad Boyfriend

I don't know why, perhaps to have a sense of being human or that nothing had changed, I put on makeup while I was in the hospital. I got up in the morning, took my IV pole to the bathroom, and put on foundation powder, sparkle powder, blush, and eye shadow. I put on mascara and returned to the hospital bed to sit, read, and stare.

One morning I was maneuvering back to the bed from the bathroom, carrying both the IV pole and the purple bag that held all of my makeup. One of the sweet CNAs came to check on me.

I was rolling the IV pole around. Picking it up over the bathroom's one-inch threshold was a pain in the ass—and hand—because grasping anything with an IV in one's hand hurts like hell. Makeup newly applied, I rolled past her as she pushed a blood-pressure and oxygen-level monitor in front of her.

"You got your boyfriend with you?" she asked, indicating the IV pole.

"This guy?" I said. "No way. I want a guy who will chase me down the street. This guy, I have to drag him everywhere I go. He's a bad boyfriend."

"What do you mean?" she asked with a laugh. "He sits by your bed all day, doesn't complain, doesn't talk back. He's loyal and undemanding."

I chuckled with her and said, "Nope. I want to be chased. This guy needs to be dragged everywhere. You can have him; he's a bad boyfriend."

***

At some point, they took the Heparin out of my IV drip. They said that they would change to a newer drug, one derived from Heparin, but better. They said I would be able to inject it myself and that I wouldn't need blood tests to check what the medication was doing to me, as I would with Heparin or Coumadin.

That evening a nurse came in and showed me what to do with the Fragmin. She showed me how to pinch a part of my poochy belly just under my belly button, and wipe it with an alcohol pad. She showed me how to press the syringe to my belly and press down on the stopper at the top with my thumb. It made a loud clicking noise and painfully pierced the soft flesh of my lower abdomen. She showed me how the contraption around the syringe made it a "safe sharp," in that it wouldn't stick anyone after I used it. She also explained I needed to inject myself every night before bed. After that first night, she had me do the injecting with her supervision. They continued to monitor me and my blood clots, but eventually discharged me with the instructions to shoot myself in the belly every night with the Fragmin, moving to new locations each night. I also had to keep an eye on my arm. If anything changed, I was to let the doctor know right away.

I realized much later how serious the blood clots had been. They went up the left side of my neck and down into my left arm. They made side veins in my neck bulge, because the blood clots in the main veins were taking up space, and the side veins had to be used. They also didn't say, and now I'm glad that they didn't remind me, blood clots cause strokes, which are very bad things. The clots in my neck and arm could have become free and done serious damage to my lungs, heart, or brain. I didn't register any of that until much, much later. I would say that's a good thing. In some ways, perhaps, chemo brain is a safety mechanism for cancer patients.

Visitors

I had dozed off in my hospital bed, too exhausted to read or to hold the heavy *Jane Eyre*. I was too tired to do much but sit and sleep.

It was late afternoon, the light dim, the hall relatively quiet. But I sensed I wasn't alone.

I looked over, and there was Aubrey, sitting in the chair next to my bed, a little out of my line of vision.

I mumbled, "What are you doing here?" Realizing that this sounded mean, I continued, "Did you have work at the Sunoco plant and just stopped by?"

"You're sick. In the hospital. I'm praying."

I nodded, tried to smile, and drifted back to sleep.

***

One night my hospital room was filled with visitors. Mom and her neighbor were there. Emma and Maeve from work were there too. They were all staring at me, watching my every move and talking about sickness. I felt on the hot seat. I turned to Emma and said, "So, what's up with your sickness?"

Emma got one of her favorite expressions on her face. It was a smile that didn't reach her eyes. It was a guilty dimple, and all of her teeth in the grin. It was a smile that I learned meant "I'm guilty, but I will cover it up with feigned ignorance."

She asked, "What sickness?"

I looked at Maeve, and Maeve turned to Emma with a serious look on her face.

"I don't know," I said. "Something about you coughing up blood."

My mom's neighbor almost fell out of her chair and yelled, "What?"

"I don't cough up blood," Emma said, turning red.

Maeve got all sarcastic and said, "Oh, yeah. Right. You never cough up blood or take steroids for it that make you crazy hungry. You've never forced me to stop for fast food because you were starving for food because of those steroids. In fact, we didn't even do that tonight."

"Seriously," I asked. "You stopped for fast food on the way here?"

"It's just the stupid steroids," Emma said. "I'll be fine when I'm off them."

My neighbor asked, "And you are on them why?"

Emma just grinned at my neighbor and refused to speak, so Maeve said, "For coughing up blood."

My neighbor said, "That's not normal."

"That's what we all say," I said. "But Emma here isn't too concerned about it."

I feel sort of bad for throwing Emma under the bus, so she could take some of the staring pressure off of me. I was the monkey in the zoo when I was lying in that hospital bed. It was nice to have someone else under scrutiny. But there are times when, even now, years later, I find myself worried about Emma and her health. Maeve and I hosted an intervention on her after I got better. We forced Emma to figure out her issues, and her doctors changed her diet completely and announced she was allergic to all sorts of food items. When Emma started the new diet, she claimed to be doing much better. But that was also around the time she moved away, and we stopped talking about her health issues so much—partly because she never brought them up and partly because we needed to see her face to determine if she was lying. Her voice alone didn't reveal what was happening.

***

Once I awoke and found three ladies from my church sitting in chairs around my bed, praying. One of them was the church bookkeeper. Another was a woman who had been to a leadership-training program with me—I'd harassed her by knocking into her with my knitting needles while she tried to type her notes. The third woman was a cancer survivor herself, whom I had come to adore. They said I didn't need to do anything, but sit there. I listened as they pleaded to God for my health, my restoration, and my body. Their presence was so uplifting and encouraging that I was reduced to tears.

***

One of my colleagues came to visit as well. He sat on the windowsill. He didn't say much, but he wasn't a big talker. His brown hair was pulled back in a ponytail, and we talked a little.

As he was visiting, my three cousins came into the room, bringing their crazy-fun energy. They brought Sour Patch Kids and Twizzlers. They sat on the windowsill next to my colleague and made all sorts of jokes and movie references. They asked questions about what was going on and how long I had to be there. They made it hard for my colleague and me to talk, not that we were saying too much to begin with. Eventually, my colleague thanked them for lightening the mood and said he had to get going.

Later, when I was a little better, I thanked him for coming and apologized for the chaos that was my family. He said that he appreciated their arrival. It made things fun and funny and that was just great in his eyes. Part of me wondered if there were something more he wanted to say that night but didn't get the chance.

***

I asked if the hospital chaplain could come and see me. One afternoon a very tall and thin black woman came and knocked on my door. "Hello, Kimberly? I'm the chaplain. You asked to talk to me?"

I sat up a little straighter and said, "You can call me Kim. When people call me Kimberly, I think I'm in trouble."

She came in and sat at the chair next to my bed. "Why don't you tell me a little about what's going on with you."

I told her that I had been diagnosed and was in treatment for Hodgkin's lymphoma. My body had rejected my port and was riddled with blood clots in my left arm and neck, which was why I was hospitalized. I told her that I was planning to go to Chicago for a master's in divinity, with a focus on being a hospital chaplain. I had some questions for her.

"How do you handle it when people of other faiths ask you to pray with them?"

She said, "I join in on their prayers. I don't pray aloud, for my faith is different from theirs, but I stand with them honoring their prayers."

"That makes sense," I said.

"Can I pray for you?" she asked.

"Absolutely," I replied.

I don't remember exactly what she said. Now, I wish that I had an audio recording of her on my smart phone. What I do recall is that she was leaning over, praying over me, and she was moved to tears. She said that my ministry would not have walls. She said that God's hand was on me.

Makeup

At some point, in the midst of this admittance to the hospital, being discharged and dealing with chemotherapy's effects, I decided wearing makeup was stupid. I was sick. I was tired. I was losing my eyelashes, which left nothing for the mascara to stick to. It was exhausting to stand in front of a mirror in the bathroom every morning to put on powders, blush, eye shadow, eyeliner, and mascara on what was left of my eyelashes so I could go downstairs, sit on the couch, stare at the television, fall asleep, and then wake up, only to crawl up the stairs to struggle to take it all off to get into bed. It seemed an awful waste of time; besides, was I hanging out with anyone who would care if I were wearing makeup or not? So, while I was sick-sick, I stopped wearing makeup most of the time. If I were taking photos of myself or hanging out with people other than my mom's friends, I would consider wearing makeup, but that was a rare thing.

Pre-cancer and post-cancer Kim believed in the power of well-placed sparkly eye shadow. We all need a little happiness, and sparkly eye shadow makes me smile.

During-cancer Kim realized there was too little energy in the day to be wasted on nonessentials. Besides, there wasn't much to smile about in those days.

***

Back at home from the hospital and feeling strong enough to get into the shower, I realized my hair was a problem. There was a massive amount of hair in the drain. I took a tissue, gingerly leaned over the tub, and swiped up as much hair as possible. I scooped up a whole handful. I grabbed another tissue and tried to get all of the rest. That too was a full scoop.

Trying hard not to think too much, I called my dad. It was a Saturday; both he and his wife were home.

"I left a small dog in the shower just now. I was wondering if you could come over and shave my head," I said.

Dad and his wife came over with his beard trimmer. He took me to the back part of my mother's driveway and had me sit on one of the lawn chairs. I was wearing the black tank top I always wore to doctor's appointments.

Using his beard trimmer, my dad slowly shaved my head. He was expecting something like we'd seen in *G. I. Jane*, where Demi Moore gets her head shaved by a number-1 razor, and it all just drops right off. My dad's beard trimmer made my head look like it had been shaved by a five-year-old. There was a spot in the back that was almost an inch long, and there were spots at the top where my hair was right to the scalp.

Erin told me later that the bad haircut and my bony frame made me look like a concentration-camp victim.

Giselle took my hand as Dad moved over my head. As she squeezed, my tears landed on our intertwined fingers. Before getting sick, that was one thing I could always say: I had big Jewish hair.

But now, there was no hair.

Giselle went upstairs with me. She sat in the tall, wingback chair in my room and waited for me to shower. I was weak after my first shower, and I was worried my body would give out during the second shower. She sat in the other room, just a yell away, ready to run to my aid, should I need it. Just knowing she was there was comforting.

I showered quickly and got out. When I looked at myself in the mirror, I didn't recognize myself. I no longer knew who I was.

What struck me most was something I had never thought about before. I had no idea that my hair was tied so closely to my identity. I think that's true for many women. And now, when I hear about people losing their hair—especially because of sickness and chemotherapy, but also alopecia, the condition that causes one's hair to fall out, and female baldness—my throat gets tight, and I cry. Baldness for men is somewhat expected, and men with full heads of hair shave their heads willingly. A family member had a girlfriend who shaved her head, and we were often asked if she was sick.

I had no idea how much being able to put a pen in my hair was a part of what made me Kim Beam. And with her hollowed out eyes, sharp cheekbones, and bald head, the woman looking back at me in the mirror was a complete stranger.

Erin's Visit

After dose 2, I called Erin. Erin and I taught together in my first teaching job on the North Shore of Boston, and that's where we met. Erin and I have remained close ever since, calling each other up about once a month and picking up right where the stories left off. Erin still lived north of Boston, in the space between 495 and 95 just below New Hampshire.

When I called her that day after dose 2, I was in what had turned from being the spare room in the upstairs of my mom's house to my room. Mom was in her office downstairs, working; I didn't want her to hear what I said to Erin. I didn't want to add to Mom's stress, and this would inevitably stress her out.

"Erin, I don't think I can do this," I said.

"It's hard," she replied.

"Not only that. I want to die. I don't want to do this. I don't think I have it in me."

"Physically, what's going on right now?" she asked.

"My stomach cries out all the time, hunger and nausea are combined, and if I don't eat crackers then it just gets worse. I don't have energy for showers, and you know how much I love showers."

"You do. Long ones," she replied.

"I can't even muster up a short one. The pounding water, the energy of standing. They exhaust me."

"What about a bath?" she asked.

"Too hot and then too cold," I replied. The truth is, I hadn't tried one. I was just projecting. "My legs are beyond hairy. They're gross."

"Can't you shave?"

"Nope. They're worried because I'm neutropenic. No shaving. The razor could nick me and that could cause infection."

The line went quiet for some time, and then I said, "I just want to die."

"That is not acceptable. You just started treatment."

That was true. I wasn't even one month into what would be four months of dosing and waiting to be dosed again.

"Can I just stop taking the chemo?" I asked her.

"No. Kim, there is more in you than you know. No. You don't just get to quit. I'm not giving up on you so easy."

"Okay," I said, tears rolling down my sharpened cheekbones.

Again, silence filled the line, and Erin, after taking a moment to inhale, said, "I'm coming down."

"What?" I asked, not understanding. I thought she meant she was going down her stairs to her kitchen, like she was talking to her husband, only she wasn't. She was talking to me. "I'm coming down to see you. I'm getting you out of the house, away from your mom for a couple of days. You don't need to take care of her; you need to take care of you. You need to get you well. What's a hotel near the hospital?"

"I don't know," I said, giving her a rough idea of where the medical building and hospital were.

"I will figure it all out. I'm coming down and getting you out of your house for a couple of days. We will stay near the hospital; that way if anything happens, you won't have too far to go."

"Okay," I said.

"I will get back to you on where and when," she said.

"Okay," I said. "You're really coming?"

"You bet your ass I am. I only have four friends whose friendships I work on long after we are near each other. You are one of them. Being my friend means I am there for you, no matter what, and when you start talking about wanting to die, I am not just going to sit up here."

Tears were streaming down my face, and all I could do was nod. I didn't know if she could hear my tears or my nodding or my appreciation.

She said, "I will call you with details."

"Okay," I croaked.

***

I found out much later that when I called, Erin was in a classroom that wasn't her own, sitting at some other teacher's desk. She heard about three minutes of this conversation and thought, *I don't want to have this conversation on the phone*, and started to search for plane flights on this colleague's computer. She said the big long gaps in the conversation were when she was browsing the Internet, looking for the cheapest flight.

She said, "I didn't know anything about Philadelphia, and I guessed that the closest airport was the Philadelphia airport. In that conversation, the most important thing for me to know was where I should be flying to."

***

Erin flew on Southwest, leaving her three- and five-year-old with her husband for three days. Mom and I went to the airport to pick her up. I was nervous and making jokes. Mom was irritated; she said that my leaving for the weekend and going to a big-named hotel near the hospital would be really hard on her. She worried about me more when she couldn't see me. She was also upset that I was going away for the weekend right after I had started to give myself Fragmin in my belly. If she wasn't there to see me do it, then she wouldn't be sure that I had.

I want to say, for the record, that Mom could not actually inject me with Fragmin, while Erin could if she had to. Mom had a hard time watching me inject myself, and she could not bring herself to inject me herself. If Mom was the only other person in the house and I couldn't inject myself, I probably would not get Fragmin that night.

Erin's flight landed, and we connected on the phone. She had never been in Philly before; she didn't know how the airport and its parking worked. I got out of the car when she said she was walking toward us.

"I'm wearing pink pajama pants," I told her. "Look for the concentration-camp victim wearing pink-striped pants."

When she saw me, she thought, *Oh God. She really does look like that.*

I had tufts of hair sticking up in the back, but I still had hair. Erin saw me and came running up. I saw her after she started running. She's white, tall, lithe, with brown hair and a smile that radiates out of her eyes. I braced myself and just stood there, waiting for impact. She slowed before we connected and gently, but firmly, as only Erin can, hugged the stuffing out of me.

After her suitcase was safely in the trunk and we were safely in the car, with Mom driving toward Chestnut Street, Erin said, "What the fuck is up with your pants?"

"What?" I asked.

"Seriously? What is up with your pants? Who let you out in public in those pants?"

"All my other pants hurt," I said. I went on to explain that jeans, corduroys, and other "normal" pants put too much pressure on my stabbed-up, injected belly. They put too much pressure on my innards too. They just hurt.

"But you would never be caught dead outside in pants like that," she said.

"I like them," I replied, thinking about how I usually dress with comfort in mind, and those pants were really comfortable. Maybe they did look like they were between clown pants and a print an ice-cream server would wear …

"Bullshit," she said. "You only like them because they are comfortable, and you don't feel well. If you were healthy, you would never have gone to the airport in such pants."

Her words hurt, and I wanted to get defensive, but she was right. I would never leave the house in those pants today, except to walk the dog or varnish some chairs in the driveway. I have done both in those pants since that day at the airport. But if I were healthy, I would never have left the house in those pants.

She got quiet. We all did. Erin broke the silence by saying, "Why didn't you get new ones?"

Since some time had passed. I didn't know if we were still talking about my pants, or if she had switched subjects. "Pants? Shopping isn't something I can do right now. It would take too much energy."

At that point, I felt hurt that she didn't understand how hard chemotherapy was and how much it was affecting every part of my life and being. I felt like she wanted *me* to go out and find clothes that worked with both my style and my current condition. I sat in hurt silence, unable to respond.

She knew all too well that I couldn't go shopping, I realize now; she wasn't talking to me. She was talking to my mom.

***

That night, we ordered up late room service from Flower Panda, the restaurant the family had eaten at the first time we had come to UBF's medical center to meet with Dr. K. The food arrived, and we ate sitting cross-legged, facing each other near the end of the king-sized bed in our room. We had Peking duck rolls and shrimp dumplings, which Erin couldn't get enough of. She kept eating and eating them.

I said to her, as I crawled up to the pillows, "If I keep eating all that food, I'm going to get fat again."

She gave me a horrified look and said, "I think your priorities are out of whack."

Shortly after that, I had to shoot myself in the belly with the Fragmin. I lowered the waist of my pants and rubbed a bit on the right side with an alcohol pad, since I had stuck myself on the left the day before. I pinched the flesh together. I stared down at the needle, as I held it with my fingers curved around the white cylinder and my thumb resting on the top. I waited as I mustered the strength to press the plunger down, to unleash the quick-releasing snap and experience the searing pain of a loaded needle into the tender flesh of my lower abdomen.

Erin was sitting next to me, resting against the headboard. She watched me staring at the poised needle, the trigger cocked and unable to do it. She said, "Many people look away. They can't stare at themselves do it, so they look away."

I turned my head slightly to the bed and stared at the dark colors of the bedspread weave into each other as I let my eyes go out of focus. As I relaxed and saw nothing, I allowed my thumb to do what it had to do. Click. The pain of a quick bee sting in my belly, and I rubbed the pain with the already open alcohol pad.

I threw the used needle away and curled up to fall asleep.

***

The next day was scheduled tightly. I had an ultrasound in radiology at the Hospital of the University of Benjamin Franklin.

Before I got up, Erin went for a swim. She said that it was early morning, and no one else was in the pool. She told me later that while she swam laps, she processed all that was bothering me. She thought about clothes that wouldn't put pressure on my belly—dresses. She thought about what would shave my legs but wouldn't be a razor—something like Nair. She thought about everything she was experiencing with me and allowed some of those feelings to release as she moved the water out of her way.

We went down to the restaurant and ate eggs, the same breakfast I ate every day of my sickness: two eggs over easy with buttered toast. Afterward, we walked to the hospital and waited in the Radiology Department. Once we were in the ultrasound room, Erin was fascinated by the internal workings of my body that appeared on the screen. She asked the tech all these questions, and the two had an anatomy lesson over veins and arteries in my neck and arm. It was actually interesting and made me less scared about what was going on inside my body.

Erin said, "When I retire from teaching in twelve years, I think I want to be an ultrasound tech."

"There's always work everywhere," the tech said. "I've lived in some amazing places all over because of it. In fact, some of the places I've lived have cut off my loans for me."

The tech couldn't say much about what she was looking at, but said that the radiologist would look at it and get back to my doctor by the afternoon.

My oncologist's nurse practitioner called me later and told me that everything looked better. She said to keep up with the Fragmin, and I should be set.

***

Erin planned a spa afternoon for us. We walked about four blocks total to get to the salon/spa. I thought I would never get there. It seemed to take hours to walk two-tenths of a mile. I walked in, exhausted and overwhelmed from the energy it took. Now, I look back and see why Erin didn't think it was a big effort. At the time, though, I wondered if Erin knew how weak I was.

Erin went off and had a massage. She and I both agreed that being touched, rubbed, and having my muscles pressed all over would probably be too much, particularly after that walk.

That left me with a mani-pedi. Pre-chemo, Dr. N had said no manicures or pedicures; the removal of the cuticle from around the nail would leave my hand or foot open to infection, and that would be more than my body could handle.

We walked up a set of stairs to a sky-lit room. Erin walked past me to go get her massage, leaving me with a large black woman to do my nails. She was quiet and clearly upset. I was bald and clearly sick. This was supposed to make me feel better, get out of my own head and body, be pampered. But in the middle of massaging my feet, the manicurist started to cry.

After I asked a couple of questions, she told me that since a new Adolf Biecker salon was opening in a few months just a few doors down, the managers at this salon were letting her go. She kept saying, "I don't know what I'm going to do. I don't know what I'm going to do."

So much for relaxing. And if I had been more myself, I would have had so much to give. But just a couple of days earlier, I had contemplated stopping chemo because I had nothing left to give. I felt bad for her, and my heart broke. I asked her if there were other salons she could apply to, and the answers were all no's with excuses.

She made a "tut" sound and asked, "Can't I cut your cuticles? Your nails would look so much better."

I wondered if she'd even seen me. Was she so wrapped up in her loss that she couldn't see my scrawny ankles, lanky frame, and badly shaved head? I couldn't say anything. I could barely talk. Just holding myself upright in the chair was hard enough. And there she was, across from me, tutting away, as if I meant to make her pedicure and manicure bad by not letting her touch my cuticles.

***

As we were leaving, there was a girl behind the checkout counter wearing a black wristband that said "Cancer Sucks" in white letters on her white wrist. I said I liked it very much. She said it was for a fund-raiser for a friend. Then she looked at me and said, "Do you want it?"

"Really?" I asked.

"Sure," she said. "Here, I can get more." She took it off and came around the counter to give it to me. I put it on immediately.

I know this sounds dumb, but I felt like that bracelet said what I couldn't say. A "Cancer Sucks" bracelet was the explanation I needed for my hunched shoulders, balding head, and greenish pallor. I thought people wouldn't get it—that they would think I was weird or malingering if they saw me and my slow, emaciated frame. I thought I had to explain to everyone that cancer and chemotherapy were making me this weak.

Silly me. I realize now, you don't have to explain it. But at that point, I wanted to.

***

After the spa, we went to a local restaurant that served organic, locally grown vegetables and locally and humanely raised meat for lunch. We sat near the front windows, and Erin was so excited about the locally grown organic produce in each of the dishes. I was secretly horrified. There was barely anything on the list that I could eat. I was on that damn neutropenic diet. No fresh vegetables for me. The only thing I could order and not have to change completely was the mushroom soup. I felt tears welling, but I shoved my nose deeper into my menu so Erin wouldn't see.

My body was achy from walking so far, from sitting so much, from not being in my own space.

The soup was amazing, and there was so much of it. I ate the whole bowl and was so completely full afterward.

Erin helped me back to the hotel. We rode the elevator, and she left me in the hotel room. I pulled the sheets down with effort and flopped, unable to do much more.

Erin went out. She tromped over to the Gap and took pictures of herself in different outfits and texted them to me. I commented on what I liked and what I didn't.

She was back in time to get ready for dinner. She was armed with Sally Hansen's hair remover in the blue aerosol can. "I talked to the pharmacist. He said that this should be fine." She had me get naked and stand in the shower. I followed her instructions. She sprayed my legs, followed the directions on the can and rinsed me off. Little brown hairs fell away from my legs, down the rivulets of water Erin was spraying on me and down the drain.

Afterward, she helped me get out of the tub, supporting me so I didn't fall. She helped me towel off. She then walked with me to the other room. As I tucked the towel tightly around myself, she showed me the purchases she'd made for me: two pairs of cotton pants, one periwinkle and the other sage. They had a wide cotton waistband and a drawstring and could be rolled up if I wanted to expose my ankles or calves. They were cut just like pajama pants, but weren't. They were exercise or lounge pants, and way better than the pink-striped pajama pants I had been wearing.

She also picked up two different dresses. One was a long, navy-blue dress with a T-back. The other was short, with white horizontal stripes of varying widths across a navy background. Both were cotton, and both were perfect.

I wore the long dress with a white sweater she'd bought. Erin put on a gray dress like the one I was wearing. My dad called to say he was in the lobby, and we went down to meet him.

When the elevator door opened, Dad looked at me and looked away, not realizing that it was me. Erin, whom Dad had never met, chuckled when I said, "I don't think Dad recognizes me."

We walked toward him, and as we got closer, Dad's eyes got a little wider and he smiled. "You look amazing," he said.

"Thank you," Erin replied, and I laughed.

Dad chose an Indian restaurant up the road. We walked the two or three blocks up and the restaurant was empty. Dad and Erin sat facing me, and I faced the empty restaurant. Dad and Erin did most of the talking. Erin told stories about our time together. Dad told Erin stories about me growing up.

On the walk back, I got weak. By the time we were on the block with the hotel, I was leaning heavily on Dad and apologizing that I was doing so.

His response to every apology was "My pleasure."

When we got to the hotel, Dad said, "I'm sorry. I think that walk was more than you could handle."

"I'm here now," I replied.

Dad and Erin bade each other good-bye and said how nice it was to meet each other. As we walked away from Dad, I teared up again.

***

Back in the hotel room, my left arm felt worse than before. It was heavy, yes, but painful now too. The only way to relieve the pain was to hold my arm up against the wall.

Erin looked at me as she rested against the bed frame. "What's the matter?"

"My arm really hurts."

She raised one eyebrow at me. The doctor had said that things in my arm and neck were getting better. It didn't feel that way.

Port Removal: Admittance

The next day marked the second time I was admitted to the hospital for an extended period. It was the day Erin was to head back to Massachusetts, and we were leaving the hotel. My oncologist's nurse practitioner called around 10:45 a.m., as we were packing up, and told me I needed to go to the hospital to have the port removed. We had to be out of the hotel room by 11:00 a.m.

When the nurse practitioner called back to discuss the plan for the day, I was walking down Spruce Street on my way to the medical building. She said something about going to the emergency room and being admitted there.

I had been to the emergency room once before. It was after dose 1, somewhere in the middle of all that chaos and not remembering things. I was achy all over and miserable. Mom called Dr. N's night service and was told to take me to the emergency room to see if I was neutropenic or had an infection. We walked through the sliding double doors of the Hospital of the University of Benjamin Franklin's emergency room. I felt the place was crawling with germs; I could practically see them on the chairs and the floors. I had been told to avoid people who had children younger than fourth- and fifth-graders, and here I was in a place that was dirtier than any daycare center I have ever been in. I refused to sit on anything. Even though I was exhausted, even though standing was painful and took strength, I refused to sit down. I'm sure that made Mom nuts, but I paced in the back corner, touched nothing, and stood while I waited to be seen.

Just the thought of that place sent shivers of infection down my spine, and I told the nurse practitioner, "No way. Find some other way to get me in. I'm headed to you now."

Erin and I walked down Chestnut. I rolled my suitcase, and Erin carried her bag, packed and ready to go to the airport.

"What?" the nurse practitioner said.

"I'm not going to the emergency room. Get me in some other way. I'll be up in the cancer center in about fifteen minutes," and I hung up.

Erin looked at me and said, "Way to go. Way to advocate for yourself." It may have been one of the first times in my life.

We turned onto Spruce and headed toward the hospital. My phone rang again. The nurse practitioner said, "Go to admissions, and they'll take you from there."

"Excellent," I said, as Erin and I turned into the hospital and went up the escalator to the plush admittance room.

Erin and I met my mom there, and we sat until it was time for Erin to catch a cab and go to the airport. It was a tearful good-bye. In front of me was surgery and six more doses. I didn't want her to leave.

Eventually I was wheeled to a room up on the sixth floor. It was a giant room with hardwood floors, a giant built-in wooden dresser with side bookshelves, and a huge-ass mirror. The bathroom had dark green and maroon marble tile and the bed next to mine was empty, at first.

As they settled me in, the rain that had threatened to pour down all day came. Water pounded the windows, and a flock of nurses came in to watch the sky, wind, and water. The lower, lighter-colored clouds zipped across the sky, leaving behind the dark, mean clouds, which never moved. The wind whipped the windows. The rain fell in a diagonal to the left; then it changed direction and slammed into the window with thunderous reverberations. With the rain whipping around, the Fisher Fine Arts Library, with tall Hogwarts-type towers, looked mysterious and looming. The nurses stared out at the weather in amazement, saying rain never fell like this and "this is so scary" and "I don't know if I feel safe up here," but they couldn't stop watching the wind and noise.

I found the weather display beautiful. If I felt any fear about it, it was probably wrapped up in all of the fear I was feeling at that moment. None of it registered. During all of this weather performance, my phone rang. Erin.

"I'm trapped on the tarmac, waiting for this weather to pass and I could be trapped on this plane for hours."

"Oh, hon, I am so sorry. That totally sucks. You came down here for me ..."

She cut me off. "To see you. To spend that time with you, I would sit here for hours. This has been one of the most important trips I've taken in years. I would do it all over and sit on this plane for twenty-four hours if it meant helping you feel better."

"Thank you," I whispered as tears streamed down my cheeks.

"I love you," she said.

"I love you too. Call me when you get in. Text me when you can take off."

"I promise I will," and she hung up.

The weather quieted a little, the nurses calmed down, and one started to do her admittance thing.

The nurses had a heck of time finding a vein. The doctor's call was to remove my port, and as a result they were going to use my veins for everything from here on out. All the chemo now would be intravenous instead of through the ease of the port. I had no idea what that meant, but *at first* I thought it was a good thing.

IVs no longer freaked me out as they had at that first surgery, when Fred told me I would just feel a pinch. I now understood that when blood poured from the vein, it meant that the needle was in and doing just what it should.

The nurse took my arm, put on the tourniquet, and started to slap my arm waiting for a vein to pop up. Nothing happened.

She smacked my arm a number of times and shook her head. "I'm not going to risk it. We have a genius at finding veins. I'm going to go get her."

She left my room and returned a little while later with another nurse, who walked in holding what she called "a baby needle." She said, "Let's hope that this works out easily."

She stabbed and scored a vein right away, with good blood return. I learned it works like this: the needle goes in, with a sheath over it. The needle pokes in and hopefully gets into the vein. If it is in the vein, when she pulls the needle out, leaving the sheath inside, blood oozes out. If the needle is just in no man's land, it won't ooze anything. I could also tell based on pain if they made it into the vein. If it was just uncomfortable, they weren't in the vein. They could jab around under my skin for minutes at a time, and for the most part it wasn't that bad. However, once they broke through the vein and actually made an emergency entrance ramp into my circulatory system, then the pain would register deep and force me to involuntarily cringe.

She hooked the IV up to its pole and its little monitor computer. We talked for a couple of seconds, and then she started to leave the room.

The IV pole started to beep.

She turned and looked at it, then at me, and then back at the pole. She walked over, pressed a button or two, and started to leave. It started to beep again.

"He's a bad boyfriend," I said. I was sure she had no idea what I was talking about, but I kept talking as if she knew exactly what I meant. "Whenever my boyfriends got grouchy, coffee normally made them feel better. Any way we can get this guy some coffee?"

She pushed a button or two, quieted "him" down, gave me a look that said "you are really strange," and said, "I don't think that's going to work." Then she looked at my arm and said, "I'm going to need you to not bend that way. It's cutting off the flow from the line."

I looked down at my hand. Bending my hand back so I could read my Kindle was not only mildly painful, but bad for the IV line. A bad boyfriend, indeed. Many of my boyfriends took umbrage to how much time I spent reading. Apparently, this IV pole was no exception.

***

A little while later, an intern came in and sat by my bedside. He was a really cute intern, I should add.

He looked at me and said, "I hear things have been rough for you. Can you tell me what's been going on?"

"You want to know what's been going on? You mean like the side effects and the symptoms?"

"Sure," he said. "Just tell me what's been happening these past two or three weeks."

"You want to hear all of it?" I asked.

"I really want to know. I want to learn what it's been like for you," he said.

And I started the list: the crazy nerve stuff in my gums, which surprised him. He wanted to know what it felt like, what it was like to chew.

When I was eating, my salivary glands made it even worse.

The memory loss.

The praying to die. Oh, wait. No, I didn't tell him that part.

In the midst of the litany, I stopped, looked at him and said, "Do you really want to hear this?" I thought about how people in books complain about their ailments and bore everyone around them. I have learned from reading Jane Austen and watching the BBC that no one likes a hypochondriac. Not that I was one, but still.

"Yes," he said. "This is really good to know."

I talked for some time about all of the symptoms I was experiencing. But in my head I was thinking, *Man, this guy is really cute. Too bad I'm bald.*

***

I made connections with a couple of my nurses during my hospital stays. One was when I was on the seventh floor and the nurse would come down to see me during her hectic day. That nurse stated that, with everything else going on during her shift, coming to talk to me was enough of a break to be able to go back and face all that she was responsible for. On my stay on the sixth floor, I would talk with a white nurse with freckles and red curly hair and she would smile. That's all I really needed, to be smiled at and reassured that maybe, one day, things would be okay again.

Before the curly-haired nurse's shift ended that first day, she came in with a yellow gown. I had watched people put on similar gowns to go into the room of MRSA patients.

She pulled out a chair and had me sit down. She wrapped the gown around me with the opening in the back, almost as if I were in a beautician's chair. She pulled out a buzzing hair clipper and put the setting down to number one to clean up the buzz cut my father had given me.

I put my head down and let her go to work. I didn't cry this time. It was just a trim.

Little hairs wound up all over the place, and I was itchy. It was an annoying itch around the back of my neck inside my gray hooded sweater. When I rubbed my head, it felt like my college boyfriend's head felt after his mom shaved his head too close by mistakenly putting the shaver on the wrong number. There aren't really words to describe the tickly, soft sensation of a newly shaved head, and it was weird that it was my own head that felt that way. I couldn't stop running my hand over it, just loving how it felt.

To: Important Contacts
From: Me
Subject: Port removal tomorrow
Date: June 25, 2010

Okay, I'm going to be quick about this.

For those who don't know, I was readmitted to the hospital yesterday afternoon. They are going to take out the port that has caused a whole mass of blood clots in my left underarm area. They are going to give me chemo through my veins from here on.

My oncologist was at the hospital as I was settling in my room. She said that I am her first Hodgkin's lymphoma patient to be admitted in seven years. Yeah, me! New award! Unfortunately, this is one honor I would rather forego.

Tomorrow morning, they are going to remove the port in what could be called surgery. Then they are going to continue blood thinners and watch me, for how long, I have no idea.

I have been giving myself shots in the belly since my last hospital stay, and I really don't like having to do it at all. Dr. N says I will have to keep that up for the next six months. (What???)

So I'm asking for prayer for the procedure tomorrow, this current hospital stay, wisdom for my doctors, my attitude toward the shots I have to give myself, and the aftereffects of the chemo treatment I will have this upcoming Tuesday, on the twenty-ninth. I don't want to drown again in the swamp and ooze that is my "treatment." If I were to be absolutely honest, I wonder if I leave me, God, and my faith behind whenever I have treatment; it takes over a week to even think about God again. And that is honestly the saddest thing. It actually makes me cry as I type this.

So good night. Thank you for standing with me through this, what has become a truly bizarre journey.

Much love,
Kim

"Not all those who wander are lost." ~ J. R. R. Tolkien

Port Removal: Surgery

I was wheeled down to interventional radiology and made to sit on a gurney. I didn't recognize where I was at first. As I got acclimated to this new area of IR, I realized I was on the other side of the hall from the time I had the needles shoved into my chest.

The interventional radiology nurses were all walking around and talking. I began to understand that the majority of them were pregnant. They were talking about morning sickness, saltines, and trimesters. One yelled out, "If you are ever infertile, just become a nurse for IR."

I so don't want kids, I thought to myself. All that Mom and Dad were going through with me being sick … all of the heartache and concern. A friend of mine says that having children is like having your heart outside of your body running around. All of these women were running around bringing life and possible major heartache into the world willy-nilly. But it's not like they didn't know what they were doing. They worked in a hospital. They saw sickness and heartache all of the time, and still they were diving in with their eyes wide open.

They had me take off my clothes from the waist up and put on the useless hospital gown, untied in the back. I sat on the gurney and waited a while. Then a small nurse, who called herself Jessa, came up and said, "Okay. We're going to go up there now." Jessa was white, with short, curly auburn hair; she was short and kind of petite.

She put her foot on the wheel lock of the gurney so it would roll and maneuvered me out of my spot, out into the hallway, and up a steep ramp.

"You okay?" I asked as I realized the gurney and I were not light.

She said, "It's just this hill. It gets me every time. I don't know why it's not flat around here. It doesn't make sense to have hills."

We entered a bright room, and she wheeled me to what felt to be the center of the room. She was walking around and talking to me as she prepped the room for the surgeon. There was a radio playing, and the announcer said, "Today makes the one-year anniversary of Michael Jackson's death." He lauded Jackson's greatness and then played, "Billie Jean."

I said, "I can't believe it's been a year since he died. You know, it's weird. Everyone forgot what a freak he was when he died."

The nurse paused, and I thought, *Oh crap! She's one of those people who adored him and I just insulted her!*

But then she said, "I think the same thing. I wonder where everyone's head went when he died. He held his baby over a balcony railing. He named his kids Prince and Blanket; these things are not normal."

That is what started our conversation. We moved on to Dansko shoes and how comfortable she found them, how after a day of teaching or nursing your feet didn't hurt at all. Only hers, like mine, squeaked. She said if I took them back to the outlet in Jennersville, where I bought my own, they might replace my squeaking pair for a silent pair. We then moved on to how she was feeling pressure to have a baby like the rest of interventional radiology.

"I really want one, but I'm not sure that my husband does."

"How are things with your husband now?" I asked.

"What?" she asked.

"How are you guys as a couple? How are you doing?"

She paused then said, "We fight a lot."

I thought for a second then said, "A baby isn't going to make that any better. In fact, it might just make things worse."

I am the child of divorce; my dad left when I was about two. Let me say for the record: divorce screws a kid up. My dad says that he didn't leave me, that he left Mom. He didn't walk out on his relationship with me; he fought for me. But explain that to my two-year-old abandoned heart.

She didn't like my response. She wanted to hear, "Yes! Go, get yourself pregnant!" Thankfully another CNA walked in. He was black, and from what I gathered from the discussion, he and his wife had a one-year-old son at home. Jessa started to ask him questions about how having a son changed their daily routines and how long it took them to get ready in the morning with a baby.

The doctor came in too. He was Jewish, with a tawny complexion and curly-curly hair. He introduced himself and said that he was going to put some Lidocaine in my chest so that I would be numb to everything that was going to happen. He explained that he would lift the port out and I would probably feel the rubber tube moving around deep in my chest as he did so. He said that I shouldn't have any pain. He would pause about halfway through pulling the tube out and put pressure on the major artery once the tube was out. His pressure would temporarily close off the hole in the artery when the tube was removed, allowing my body a chance to clot and close the hole itself. This would stop the major artery from bleeding into my body. Then, he would pull the tube out completely and stitch me up.

He was talking to me over the paper blue sheet-wall that Jessa had put between us. Jessa helped prep me for the surgery, but I distinctly remember her going into the hallway and talking for some time with the other nurse about his son and his routines, morning and night.

The doctor talked a little as he worked. He said he was in a band and that he thought about shaving his head for a cancer fundraiser where he'd performed, but then worried about what everyone at the hospital would think.

The doctor rooted around inside my chest, lifting out the port that had clogged the veins in my neck and arm. I felt the weight lift as he removed it, but there wasn't any pain. He started to pull on the port's tube. I could feel that. The sensation traveled way deep inside my chest cavity, up into a main line going into my heart; I could feel him pulling and pulling. I thought he was pulling and then cutting the tube and then pulling some more. But when it was over and the nurse handed me the port, I could see the whole line was intact. What was happening during the surgery was he was pinching the line to get a better hold on it; I couldn't see what he was doing, and I thought he was cutting the line. The rubber was probably wet and slick from being in my body, and with his gloves on, it was probably hard to get a good grip on the line and control the speed with which it came out.

As I felt the rubber tube sliding around deep inside my chest, my toes started to curl, a sure sign of an anxiety attack. To ward it off, I asked about the surgeries he liked to do. His response: the ones that have immediate impact, for example, he stopped the flow of blood spewing out of a major vein near a groin that was ripped open in an accident. The patient lived because he fixed it.

But then my heart started to pound really hard—deep chest pounding. Blood rushed into my head, making my ears throb. "My heart is starting to beat really hard," I said.

He glanced over the surgery blue wall at me and said, "All the girls say that to me."

Right about then I felt a warm and cold wash down the side of my chest, over the numb area and onto my side, where I still had feeling.

"Tell me that was not blood," I said.

"That was not blood," he replied. "I just washed you down with a spray bottle I have over here."

Way to give a warning, I thought.

My toes were going nuts, and my heart pounded. I eventually said, "Can you get that Jessa nurse in here to talk to me about shoes or something?"

He chuckled and said, "Jessa! She wants to talk about shoes!"

Jessa came in, flustered. "Just trying to figure out if I should have a baby," she sang in a light, lilting, joking manner. "What can I do?"

"Talk to her," the doctor said.

I could tell that he was beginning to stitch me up.

Jessa told a story about a guy hitting on her friend in traffic and how it didn't work out. The doctor was mad because the romantic story had a bad ending. I warned him I had a traffic story that also had a bad ending. My mom's niece, Wendy, had a guy come up and slip his business card through the crack in her window, years before she was married. He said his car was stopped in traffic right behind her, he saw her every day, she worked in the building next to his, and he didn't want to let this opportunity slip by. He wanted to introduce himself and just give it a shot. She put the business card in her ashtray. About a month later, she was in the car with her boyfriend and his brother. His brother was in the middle in the backseat and saw the business card still in the ashtray. He dove into the front seat and held it up saying, "What is this?" so Wendy told the story of the guy walking up to her car in bumper-to-bumper traffic. The twenty-something-year-old brother turned into a twelve-year-old. He turned to his brother, Wendy's boyfriend, and said, "She held onto the card. She still has it. Maybe she's planning on calling him. Maybe she has already called him. Maybe they've been seeing each other on the side for a month now and you don't even know it. Maybe she was going to pick up her phone after this weekend, on Monday, and ask him to lunch." Wendy's boyfriend snatched the business card out of his brother's hand and tossed it through the open sunroof.

"That's the worst ending I've ever heard! That's so disappointing!" my surgeon yelled.

"I told you it ended badly," I replied.

The doctor seemed to be done. He washed down my body and bandaged the port site.

He leaned over and looked at me, saying, "So, that liquid you felt? It was blood."

"What!" I yelled at him. "You lied! I can't believe you lied to me!"

He said, "I didn't want that kind of reaction when you were on the table."

Technically, I was still on the table. And the truth was, I could have dealt with the wash being blood. I would have asked, "Is this something that concerns you?" But what really got me riled was that he had *lied* to me. "Why was some of it warm and some of it cold?" I asked.

"Some of it was blood, but most of it was Lidocaine. It had just gone in and wasn't in there long enough to warm up."

When I was sitting up and they were getting ready to wrap things up, Jessa handed me the port. "You want to see it?"

"Yeah!" I replied.

The doctor said, "Don't show that to her!" but it was too late. The port was already in my hands.

It had a couple of parts. There was a metal base that had a couple of holes near the edges. Jessa pointed them out and said, "These holes are where the stitches go to hold it in place."

In the middle was a cylinder attached to the metal base at its bottom. There was a rubberized top on the cylinder, and Jessa said that was where the needles accessed the port.

"How come when it's stabbed the hole doesn't stay a hole?"

"It's specialized rubber. It goes back to its original form."

"Huh," I said, looking at the tube attached to the bottom area of the cylinder. It was almost a good foot long, if not longer. "This is longer than I thought it would be."

"It has a way to travel up into your neck and down the artery into the heart. It is a long tube."

Jessa returned the port back to the doctor and said, "I'll be right back." She came back a short time later and said, "Okay. I just called for transport. They are going to take you back up to your room."

"Every time someone says that," I said, "it makes me think I'm in some sci-fi movie."

My surgeon laughed and said, "I like her. She's funny. Can we keep her down here all day?"

I replied, "Nope, I'm going back up to the sixth floor." In my head, I thought, *You could stop by, though.* For the record, the cute doctor never showed.

Ordering Pancakes for Dinner

After my port was removed, I practically danced around my sixth floor, $19,000-a-night "hotel room." I don't know where the energy came from, but I had it. I moved about, pulling my IV pole/bad boyfriend around with me.

The nurse came in and said, "I can't believe how much you are moving about. Most people who come in here after surgery are dead on their feet, lying in bed, and not moving."

I was changing clothes, going to the bathroom. Now, I wonder if it was yet another side effect of the Lidocaine, that I just was energized from the whole thing.

The night before surgery, I talked to Wendy, who wished me luck for the surgery. She said I should ask for pancakes for dinner. Pancakes always made her feel better. Taking her suggestion, I wrote in pancakes for dinner, not knowing if the request would be honored.

By the time Dr. N arrived on her afternoon rounds, I was no longer dancing around my hotel room. I was back in the hospital bed, exhausted but still alert. She came up next to me and stood by my shoulder. "How was the removal?"

I grabbed her by the hand and said, "It was bad."

"What do you mean?"

I told her about being able to feel the tube moving around inside of me, about almost having a full-on anxiety attack. How the doctor made jokes with me to get my mind off the trauma, the wash of hot and cold liquid down my chest, and how the doctor lied to me. She gave me the "I'm being sympathetic but this *is* bad" look. Her lips were tight in a line, and her eyebrows crinkled together in empathy.

"I am so sorry that it was so bad," she said.

I shrugged. "Just another chapter for the Hodgkin's lymphoma book I'm going to write."

She smiled and said, "I'm going to write *The Indian Girl's Guide to Dating.*"

Gail, Mom's childhood friend, was there, and I think my mom was too. We were fascinated. "What do you mean?" I asked.

Dr. N then told a story, one to which I can't do justice, about coming home from Stanford after graduation. Her Indian mother and father had arranged a number of dates with their friends' children. One of them arrived at the house dressed in black biker leather, studded and tight. When her father asked if she was going to go out with this guy, Dr. N replied, "You set this one up," and out the door with the biker she went.

A nurse came in and insisted that I take Oxycodone. I really didn't want to. She said it would help with the pain. They didn't want to give me Tylenol or Advil or Aleve because those would mask a fever, which would herald an infection. It was only hard painkillers if I wanted one. I didn't really want a painkiller; I hated how loopy and out of control they made me. But she insisted I try one, and then I could decide if I wanted to have another one the next day.

Down the Oxycodone went.

Then two things happened. First, Jean and Aubrey came to visit. I was useless and couldn't talk. I don't remember a thing that was said, and I knew I was out of it. I hated how my brain wouldn't engage. People were there to see me, but I couldn't interact with them. It seemed like a waste of a visit.

Second, my dinner came. Two slices of tomato on about three leaves of Romaine lettuce. I have to admit that my stomach dropped a little in disappointment. I had been looking forward to pancakes for dinner. I don't really like pancakes that much; they sit in my stomach and make me feel sluggish. But on this day, high on painkillers and because of surgery, I'd had less food than normal; I was looking forward to pancakes.

My nurses looked at the tomato on Romaine and said, "You're neutropenic. You can't eat this."

If I was neutropenic, it meant I had to have less than six hundred army guys going out to fight bacteria. If my brain had been functioning and not high on Oxycodone, I would have asked what my actual numbers were. I would have asked the potential consequences of being neutropenic and having a gaping wound and stitches in my chest.

Instead, the nurses looked at me and said, "What about lasagna? We have some in the freezer down the hall just for cancer patients. It's yours if you want it."

I nodded and was soon delivered Stouffer's vegetable lasagna and, I have to say, it was better than pancakes.

My Hospital Roommate

I had a couple of hours alone in the giant room where the nurses watched the rain pour in. Late that night, a pale white woman was wheeled in. She had been brought to BFU from Delaware, where they were unable to control her pain.

Turns out she lived in Oxford, one town over from where I'd had the apartment down the quarter-mile driveway. My landlords' kids went to Oxford public schools, as did this woman's grandchild. My new roommate had been living with her daughter and granddaughter since her cancer diagnosis. She had it everywhere—lungs, heart, liver, and kidneys. I'm sure it was other places too, but I don't remember. It was all under control, except for the cancer in her liver. Doctors were trying to figure out how to control her pain while they tried a new treatment to stop the cancer's growth.

When she was wheeled into my room, she was pale. Sickly pale. She clutched her pink-bucket friend to her stomach. I took one look at her, and my anxiety kicked in. I pulled the bad-boyfriend behind me and approached one of my nurses outside the door and down the hall.

"If she throws up, I'm throwing up too," I hissed.

That's all I could think about: me and how someone else in the room would affect me. I didn't have any concern for her. It wasn't what had brought her in an ambulance from Delaware. It wasn't her condition. It was what another person in *my* hospital room meant for my comfort.

Thank goodness I didn't keep this attitude. I would have missed out.

The thing that struck me about my roommate was how positive she was. She was so kind and considerate, warm and excited to see anyone who came to visit. She had a makeover while she was there and tried on a number of wigs. She chose one that looked like a normal, well-styled hairdo. I felt some envy that she bought a wig, but even now I don't understand that emotion. I didn't really want one. I knew I could get one if I did, but I didn't. I was only going to be bald for four months;

buying a wig for a couple of hundred dollars for that short time didn't make sense.

What I saw in this woman was hope. She had hope for her future, despite her pain and despite her diagnosis. The doctors and interns who came to talk to her were gentle and quiet. They listened to her concerns. They took their time with her, and she appreciated everyone who helped her.

Her grace and kindness struck me because I knew she was dying. She knew she was dying. But beyond that, she was living. She was doing all she could to reach out and be present with everyone who came to visit her. Her granddaughter came and sat on her bed. Their conversation touched my heart. They talked about how lovely my roommate's new hair was, but more than that, they talked about what was going in her granddaughter's life, what was going on in school and classes and friendships.

After dinner and after my visitors left, the nurses came in and announced that since I was neutropenic, I would have to switch to a private room. I was moving two doors down the hall. We picked up my stuff and moved me to a room with less of a view, but my own bathroom. It was a room where I didn't have to worry about the possibility of hearing someone throw up.

I found out later that my roommate said to my mom, "I wish I could be the one to move so that she wouldn't have to relocate. But that wouldn't solve the problem. She's the one with the low blood counts. If I left, they would just move someone new in."

Mom kept me updated on my roommate's progress. She was discharged before I was.

I am so much richer for having lived with her for two days. I have never met a more beautiful person, one so engaged in others' well-being. She had grace and poise. She had true compassion, and I will never forget how she made her granddaughter her priority.

Yelling at Dr. N

The second day after the port removal I was grumpy. It was a Saturday morning. The light was blinding in the windows. Not even Dr. N doing rounds made me feel better. She had a number of interns and residents with her. They were all in white coats and following her about. When she came in and told me I should be happy to be in the hospital and not outside, that it was hot and gross outside, I grumped at her about the brightness of the room.

She just looked at me, smiled and said, "The vitamin D is good for you. Anything else I should know?"

I didn't think so.

"Are you in pain?" she asked.

I shook my head no. I was using an ice bag to keep my port site cold and that kept it from hurting.

"You don't want something stronger than ice?" she asked.

I think I snarked back that I preferred pain to loopiness.

She told me that she hoped I was feeling better soon and left the room. Out in the hallway, one of her white-coated entourage said, "You let your patients yell at you?"

"I have the best patients in the world," Dr. N replied before entering the next room.

Much later that morning, Dr. N came back. She was alone this time and pulled a chair up next to the left side of my bed. She took my hand and said, "Okay, now tell me what's going on."

My throat tightened, and my eyes started to burn a bit. I wanted to speak but my throat was too tight to talk.

"I'm so scared," I croaked. "I feel safer here. If something goes wrong, then I'm in a place where they can handle whatever weird thing my body is going to do."

"What are you scared of?" she asked.

I didn't really know, actually. I knew the blood clots were bad, but the doctors didn't seem to be doing anything beyond injecting the Fragmin in my belly every night.

"I just feel safer here," I said.

She thought for a moment and gave me solid look. "I'm sorry this has been so hard on you," she said. She thought some more, and we sat in silence for a few moments. Then she said, "I'm going to keep you here one more night. I was thinking of discharging you, but to help you through this, I'm going to keep you one more day. You'll be discharged tomorrow."

"Thank you," I whispered. My throat didn't allow for anything louder.

She gave my hand a squeeze and told me to have a good rest of the day, and she left. I don't remember much more—just that she was magically by my side holding my hand and then she was gone. I had one more day to be watched over by nurses and for some reason that gave me peace.

The Intern

Whitherspoon, my friend and colleague, visited me that Saturday night. She is fair–skinned, with blond hair. She sat at the end of my hospital bed on what turned out to be my last stay in the hospital during Hodgkin's lymphoma.

When Whitherspoon walked in, she asked, "How are you doing?"

I gave her my normal response to that specific question: I reached up, tugged on what was left of my hair, and painlessly pulled out a short clump. I wordlessly handed it to her, and she thanked me.

After talking for a while, she asked if she had to hold onto my hair any longer; it had been twenty minutes already, for goodness sake. My mom had gone to get us both chocolate peanut butter Häagen-Dazs ice cream.

Eventually, Whitherspoon said, "I am so uncomfortable on this bed."

It was one of those amazing beds that rotates within itself so that the bed-bound patient doesn't acquire bedsores. Even though it massaged her butt occasionally, Whitherspoon found it rather uncomfortable. She sank deep into her end of the bed; compared to me in the reclined and supporting spot, she was scrunched in a mass of cushy mattress.

I leaned over the side of the bed, making myself silly-dizzy in the process, and hit the buttons over and over until I figured out how to lift the end of the bed. It was some combination of the lock button and up, and the bed lifted, giving Whitherspoon much more support.

Mom came back with the ice cream, which started Whitherspoon's obsession with the chocolate peanut butter combination, an obsession so strong that she had it as one of the cake combinations at her wedding a year later.

We talked about things I don't even remember. Mom sat on the side and knitted; eventually, it got late, and Whitherspoon left. I found out later that she cried the whole two-hour drive home.

Mom left, and the nurses came in with my nightly Ativan. They took my blood pressure, pulse rate, and temperature and said, "We'll see you at 2:00 a.m."

"What?" I asked.

"See you around two in the morning."

"Is this new?" I asked.

The nurse and CNA looked at each other, and the CNA said, "No, every night you've been here, we've come around in the wee hours of the morning to check stats."

"I've never woken up for that," I replied.

"What?" the nurse said in disbelief, and in reply I shook my head no.

The CNA said, "Well, I'll see you at two o'clock."

I replied, "You might see me, but I won't see you."

They left the room, turning out all of the lights, as I requested so that I wouldn't have to bother them later. They also shut the drapes over the glass wall that separated my room from the hallway.

I took the Ativan and read a book on my Kindle for a while in the dark room by the light of a Petzl lamp on my bald head. Eventually, I got tired and put the Kindle on the rolling table to my right.

I used the controls to put the bed down flat. As I lowered the bed and started to get comfortable for sleep, I realized my feet were way up in the air. The end of the bed was much higher than the head of the bed.

Adjusting it for Whitherspoon had totally messed it up. I grabbed the Petzl, put it back on my head, and leaned over the side. Instead of silly-dizzy, I became sick-dizzy. I couldn't figure out which buttons to push, and if I didn't do so quickly, I was going to pass out or throw up, or both.

I soon figured the bed out well enough to be comfortable and pulled myself back up. I took off the Petzl, put on a black sleep mask, the kind I pictured Miss Piggy wearing (though hers were purple satin). I hoped wearing it would help me remain asleep through the brightness of the morning sun. That was one thing I learned: if I have to go to the hospital again, I will be sure that a sleep mask is one of the things that gets packed. The windows were always completely exposed to the sun, and very few had drawn curtains. The sun was blindingly bright and awakened the patient at some unnaturally early hour.

Once I was comfortable and wearing a sleep mask, I curled into a ball. I was just drifting off, when the man in the MRSA room next door yelled, "Can somebody help me?!?" I fell asleep with his words echoing in my ears.

***

It was dark, and I opened my eyes. Sitting on the side of my bed was one of the phlebotomists from the medical building, a really sweet African American woman who made my blood draws on chemo days fun.

"Girl, what are you doing here?" I mumbled.

"Making money. What are you doing here?" she asked.

"Blood clots," I slurred back.

"When I saw the list of who was admitted, I saw your name and said, 'I'm going to go see my girl.'"

"It's good to see you too," I said as I fell back to sleep.

***

The next morning I awoke to a white man in green (or were they blue?) scrubs in my room; he asked, "Why are your feet higher than your head?"

"What?" I mumbled. I pulled the sleep mask off and was immediately blinded by the sun burning through the window.

"Your head. It's lower than your feet," the intern said.

The answer zoomed through my head, but I knew it was never going to come out of my mouth in any coherent way. "I had a friend here. I went to bed, and I took Ativan and I couldn't …"

He cut me off. "You took Ativan. I get it." He acted as if Ativan were the only reason I would allow myself to sleep with my head lower than my feet.

"What time is it?" I asked.

"Eight a.m.," he replied.

And I was bummed. The longer I could sleep, the shorter my miserable day would be.

***

I was going to be discharged later that morning. I walked down to the nurse's station to find out when I might be bounced from the joint and to give away a box of chocolates that had been given to me during the stay. I didn't want to eat it (I was so scared of getting fat), and the caffeine, chemicals, and flavor were all just too much.

The nurses all dove at the chance of really good chocolate.

The white intern who confronted me earlier that morning turned to me with the same accusatory tone in his voice and asked, "Why are you getting two blood draws every morning?"

"Excuse me?" I asked.

"You're getting two blood draws—one at 5:00 a.m. and the other around 8:00 a.m."

"I didn't know I wasn't supposed to," I said. I also realized that I'd never felt the needle going in at 5:00 a.m. I would wake up from the needle, but once I was fully awake, the pain would be gone, and I wouldn't even realize it was the prick that woke me. I also wasn't the one who put in the orders. I just had to suffer with whatever was in the computer. If the computer said I was to get two blood draws, I got two blood draws.

"I just called Dr. N," he said.

I looked at him quizzically.

He said, "In your blood draw at 5:00 a.m., your neutropenes were at 570. And then at 8:00 a.m., they were at 530."

It slowly dawned on me what he was saying. Neutropene numbers were supposed to be 6,000. But mine were down to 530. Man, that was bad.

"Dr. N said we are going to call it a lab error."

I continued to just look at him, unclear about what any of this information meant.

"Otherwise," he continued, "we won't be able to discharge you."

"Yes," I said. "Let's say that. I want out of here."

I did too. I didn't know what happened to the fear I had the day before, but by this Sunday morning, I was ready to go home.

Below is a picture of me after surgery, when I returned home. I took the photo on my computer, and I posted it on Facebook, saying, "For those of you who don't believe I shaved my head." If you look closely at my lower chest, left of center, you can see the pretty bruise left by the port placement and removal. You see the line on the collarbone on the right side of the picture, the line that runs parallel with the pink shirt's collar? That's the diagnosis incision where they took out my lymph node. The two dots on the collarbone on the left? Those are from the port placement. When they put the port in, they had to guide the tube up and into the vein to the heart. To do that, they cut to find their way in.

Kimberly Joy Beam

To: Important Contacts
From: Me
Subject: After dose 3
Date: July 9, 2010

There have been a number of inquiries about how I'm doing. Yesterday and today seem to be good days. Today even more so than yesterday. So that's highly good news. I don't think I have to reiterate how much I can't stand chemo. I think that's understood, and we'll move on from there.

I've been asked for an address of where I've been staying, where I can receive mail.

I've been at my mom's for the past couple of weeks, and the next two weeks I will be with my dad. After that, I think for the remainder of this chemo crap, I will be at my mom's house.

I haven't been able to concentrate on anything heavy, so I've been reading sort of light and fluffy things—Meg Cabot, a murder mystery Erin recommended (btw, I finished it so we have to talk), *Jane Eyre* (okay, she's not so light and fluffy, but I think that was my fourth go-round, and I'm not so sure I want to marry Mr. Rochester anymore. Perhaps that's just the chemo brain talking, and he's still dashing and hot and romantic ...) So, if any of you out there have light and fluffy recommendations, I would be glad to take them. My brain wants to read serious things, but to tell the truth, it just can't right now.

Good news! I haven't been hospitalized with this third dose of chemo. Whee! Bad news? I think the blood clots are still lingering ...

1. Chemo this upcoming Tuesday, in my veins. Yuck and ugh all at once. It was fine until the last drip bag of what they call "D". It's got some big long name, and the regimen of chemo I'm taking is called ABVD, where each of the initials hides some really big long names. My veins were fine with all of the pre-chemo drip bags and push syringes and all the chemicals they shot in there, but D was ... uncomfortable. I need veins reinforced with titanium or stainless steel. Will you all pray that my veins will be mega veins and just take what they are shoving in there, without pain or blowing or collapsing or whatever it is veins like to do? I would really appreciate it.

2. This is huge too. The week after this upcoming dose is portentous. The big day is actually July 21; I'm being restaged. What that means is I

get to drink a ridiculous amount of sugared citrus shake, which I'm sure is made up of bad chemicals, and my veins are filled with radioactive material. Then, I am sent through the CT scan again, and they are going to see if any of my cells light up. This is so scary for me because I am so hopeful that I don't light up. My doctor thinks I won't, but I'm scared because how much longer I'm in chemo rests on this test. So, if I don't light up, I get four more doses, and if I do, I get eight more. Also, I don't want to throw up and I don't want to mess up this test by not being able to drink all of the sugar shake.

3. Along with the above test on the twenty-first, I am also going to have a pulmonary test and a heart test to make sure that the chemicals they are giving me aren't doing damage to my lungs and heart.

I am so thankful for all of you who have come and visited—Aubrey and Jean; my aunt; Gail; the women who filled my hospital room; Erin, who flew down from Boston and got a hotel room close to the hospital. (It was a good thing we were so close because I went straight from the hotel to the hospital. During her whole visit, we kept mixing up which building we were talking about—hotel, hospital, they're all the same, right? Beds, room service ...) I have loved the cards and the gifts—from Edible Arrangements (yeah!! thanks Peter; Erin and I loved it!) as well as hats and bagels and clothes. It's been overwhelmingly sweet and, yes, the cards and well-wishing e-mails and scripture verses have been buoying and help to remind me that this mire I am drowning in is temporary, and there will be joy and life on the other side. That's the point of it—living.

So, my plan is to be in church on Sunday. And things look good that I will be able to be there.

Much love,
Kim

"Not all those who wander are lost." ~ J. R. R. Tolkien

Nose Hair

The cough started a couple of days before dose 3. It was deep and rasping. It took my already sore body and stiffened it, pulling energy I didn't have, and left me aching after just one cough. Only, I coughed more than once in the series. The coughs made me scared that I would come down with a chest infection. Those kinds of coughs tend to become bronchitis with me. I was potentially sick, and that couldn't have been good.

Every time I got a reminder call of an upcoming appointment, the prerecorded voice would tell me that if I were sick, I should take necessary precautions to not share my germs. I had learned from all of my visits with Dr. N that necessary precautions were making sure I was using hand sanitizer frequently and to wear a face mask. The face masks were of a yellow cotton material and had a loop on each side that wrapped around your ears. As soon as I got into the Cancer Center at BFU's medical center, I sanitized my hands and put on a face mask.

By the time I got in to see Dr. N, I had been wearing the mask for something like two hours. Her first words to me were, "Why are you wearing that?"

"I have this really bad postnasal drip that has caused horrible coughing. I don't want to get anyone sick."

She said, "First, that mask is only good for about an hour. Once it gets wet, it no longer works."

My mask was wet. Something else I never really thought too much about before was the liquid in our breath. That is why we fog up when it's cold out—the liquid in our breath freezes. In this case, the liquid in my breath made the mask wet.

"Second," she continued, "you aren't sick."

"But my cough and postnasal drip?" I said.

"Nose hair," Dr. N replied.

"Nose hair?" I asked.

"Nose hair," she repeated. "You don't just lose the hair on your head and the hair on your legs. You lose all hair. You lost your nose hair."

I continued to stare at her, not getting it.

"Since you don't have nose hair, nothing is stopping your mucus from dripping down your throat."

At that moment, my body decided to start displaying the hacking cough that had been worrying me.

Dr. N looked at me, completely concerned, now understanding why I thought I was sick.

"Musinex," she said. "Take Musinex as directed by the instructions on the box every day until your hair starts to come back. Then you won't have this problem. Hopefully your lungs will clear up and we won't have to hospitalize you again."

Neuropathy

One night—it was a Monday, because it was a knitting night—my right leg started to itch. Not a small itch either, a deep itch, one that made me take a knitting needle and slide it up and down over my thigh muscle on the right side of my leg. It was the whole muscle. It wasn't going away either. I wished I could take the knitting needle, jab it deep into my thigh, and scratch the muscle from the inside out. I wanted to get down to the bone.

One of my mom's knitting friends, Brenda, said, "What is going on?"

"I don't know. But it's not good," I replied.

Her other friend, a cancer survivor herself, said, "No, that's really not. Call the doctor tomorrow."

The next day, I called and left a message. Dr. N eventually got back to me. I explained the itching, the deep intense itch that made me want to rip the muscle off my bone, like in the movie *Poltergeist* where that guy rips the skin off his face. Dr. N got quiet.

Eventually she said, "It's a side effect from the chemotherapy."

"How long does the itching last?"

"When did it start?" she asked.

"Last night."

"It should be over in two to three days," she replied.

Dr. N answered my question. The itching would end in two or three days. What she did not tell me was when the itching was over, my right leg would be weak, the muscle almost useless. What she didn't say was that the itching was actually the start of neuropathy and it wouldn't just affect my thigh, but it would numb the toes on my right foot too. She didn't explain that it would make me scared of stairs, because I knew my right leg could not support my body; that it would be hard to walk;

that it would make shoes feel weird; that it would take a long time to recover from it, if I recovered at all; nor that my right leg might never be 100 percent again.

She didn't say, "You may never run again."

She answered my question—how long would the itching last? I never thought to ask, "What will the end result be?" And since I didn't ask, Dr. N didn't volunteer that information.

Scarves, Hats, and Wigs

When I was about to have the surgery that would diagnose me—this was a little after Fred threatened to get my underwear—there were a number of other people in the presurgery room, all waiting for their own events to start. Dad and Mom were sitting next to my gurney, and we were people watching. It was easy to do, since only curtains separated us from each other.

Across the aisle was an elderly woman on her gurney. She was frail, yellowish, and had thinning hair. Her daughter was there, wanting to help her. Her daughter was wearing a black baseball cap with bright turquoise, hot pink, and vibrant yellow swaths. Dad pointed out that the daughter must have been in treatment, because she didn't have any hair. Her bald head was visible through the hole in the back of the hat.

That's when I first noticed that baseball caps do not hide the fact that a woman is bald. There are things we expect to see even when a woman is wearing a ball cap. Most women with short hair who wear caps have tufts of hair in front of their ears. Women with short hair often have hair below the end of the hat. Even if it's cut real short, their hairline is still visible below. Hair can be seen through the hole that is created by the adjustment strap.

Baseball caps do not hide baldness.

Neither do scarves.

When I found out that I was going to lose my hair, I went online and bought a bunch of scarves that came with a how-to booklet, which suggested different styles for tying the scarves to wrap one's head. I fiddled with them, putting them on, wrapping them, stepping back and looking in the mirror. My head is tiny as it is; I go to the junior department to buy my baseball caps. It is the one bonus to having a pinhead: ball caps are cheaper in junior sizing.

The scarves made my head look even smaller. They also didn't hide anything. Everyone looking at a white woman with a scarf on her head knows that she's bald underneath. Anyone looking at a white woman with my pallor and sunken eyes would know that I was in treatment. The scarf would only be another beacon that I was ill.

And wigs? One night I went to the emergency room; I was feeling achy all over. The doctors were concerned that my blood counts were low, i.e., neutropenic. They feared I had some sort of infection. This bout of neutropenia was actually my body reacting to my menstruation cycle, and I got my period about two hours after I got home. To avoid those 3:00 a.m. trips to the hospital, my oncologist prescribed a shot of Lupron in my bottom to put me into false menopause. What my oncologist didn't tell me was that I would get all of side effects of menopause, including hot flashes. There was no way I could put a wig (or hair prosthesis) on my head when I was living in a constant sauna brought on by Lupron-induced hormonal fluctuations.

I made the conscious decision to just be bald and not try to hide it.

***

After I was done with treatment and my hair started to grow back, people told me that I was brave for not hiding my baldness. They said that it showed a kind of strength that I (then and now) deny. It wasn't strength. It wasn't bravery. I just wasn't willing to hide the truth. That's how I saw a hat or scarf or wig: it is a mask, a façade that only hides the truth. And it is a shoddy mask at that. People see right through the hat and understand that the person doesn't have hair. The scarf screams, "I'm really bald under this thing!" And wigs? People have caught fire by standing too close to their ovens while wearing wigs.

Not that I was opening any ovens. It was the principle of the thing. I didn't want to spend to what I heard could be as much as $400 on a wig I would need for only four months. I didn't see the point in spending that much money on something I would detest when treatment was over. I also didn't see the point in spending $400 on a wig that would only make me sweat even more, given the damn hot flashes. It seemed a giant waste of money, so I walked around with my white shiny head with little hairs trying to grow.

And I was ugly, so ugly.

A thirty-four-year-old woman without hair is not attractive. Not when she is an emaciated concentration-camp victim who is being poisoned every other week. Not when her eyes are sunken in with dark bags under them. Not when she is so frail she can't get off the couch. Not when she lies in bed at night with silent tears streaming down her face.

***

Instead of being brave, I'd wrap my arms around my head, one in one direction, one in another, trying to hide as much of my head as possible. I would walk around the house, saying, "I'm so ugly."

Mom would yell back, "You are not!"

But she couldn't convince me, I knew the truth. Sick, bald, white women are not lookers.

Carolyn

Her first name is Carolyn; her last name is Sundheim. I called her Sunny all through high school; now that we are adults, what I call her is what pops out of my mouth: sometimes she's Sunny and sometimes she's Carolyn[14]. She is my oldest friend. She is petite, with dark, almost black, hair and a round milky white face. She has a sweet smile. She is also the only person I know with a size 5 foot, who can try on the sample shoes in department stores. We went to youth group together every Friday night. We stayed up late watching old movies like *Bringing Up Baby*, and *The Major and the Minor*. Other favorites included *The Philadelphia Story*, *A Room with a View*, and *Auntie Mame*. We drank ginger ale and ate pizza with black olives, because that was the only

---

[14] Poor Reader, you will have to forgive me, because I never keep it straight between Sunny and Carolyn and I hop around calling her both. Pretend this is a Russian novel. No, seriously. I thought about going back and changing her name to just one of them, and that wouldn't be authentic to the nature of our friendship. To me, Carolyn is Sunny and she's Carolyn; the name swapping is because I have known her since we were fourteen and on the same field hockey team. When I talk about other people interacting with her, she's Carolyn. When I talk to or about her, she's Sunny.

kind Sunny would eat. I hated black-olive pizza and would ask her if we could get half something else.

"No," she would say, "it will be all black olive, and you will learn to like it." Now, a pizza isn't complete without the black olives.

I called her parents Mom and Pop, just as she did. I became a part of their family and their dog, Skeeter, who was at least half-coyote (no joke), recognized me as one of the pack.

Sunny also saved me from my hard-working ways. One bright blue spring afternoon, she came to my house in the blue, diesel Ford Tempo nicknamed the Little Blue Wonder. She walked in the open front door and yelled, "Beam! What are you doing?"

"Writing our English paper!" I replied, barely looking up from the electric typewriter on which I was plunking away.

Only Sunny could fling open my front screen door and yell up at me without spooking me, which is a feat since I flinch and react to noises ridiculously easily.

"Come on! It's not due for two weeks!"

"Where are we going?" I asked looking down the stairs from my spot at the kitchen table.

She was standing on the landing at the bottom of the stairs; only the very top of her dark hair was visible. "The mall!" she would yell.

Off we would go.

***

After high school, we kept in touch a little. I bought her a picture frame, but I'm not sure I ever sent it to her. She went to Messiah College in Grantham, Pennsylvania. I went to Gordon, up on the north shore of Boston. By the time college graduation and life beyond happened, we barely saw each other.

In 2005, my mother, sister, and I took a three-week trip to Alaska. On the way home, we took a couple of days to visit Vancouver and then Seattle. When we were making plans, I got in touch with Sunny, who was working as a nurse in the emergency department of Seattle's children's hospital. She got the job after she graduated from Messiah. Her sister was out there, and all through high school it's where Sunny wanted to wind up.

We spent a delightful afternoon together, but afterward, again, we lost touch.

***

It was the last day of school in 2009. Technically, the last day with students was the day before. This was the last day for the teachers. We had cleaned out our classrooms, packed up our filing cabinets, and covered our bookcases with newspaper.

Zern convinced me to go out to the local bar with the teachers, and we agreed on Woody's on Main Street. The bar served peanuts, and you could throw the shells on the wooden floor. There was also a restaurant, which used white paper to cover the tables. It was my first time in there, as I wasn't really the "go out for happy hour" type.

We were sitting at the bar, and my back was directly to the door. An oval stained-glass window separated me from the foyer of the restaurant.

The door opened many times, as I sat there for hours. But at one point, it opened, and I can't explain why, but I turned and looked. Standing there was a man I knew that I knew. At first I thought it was Uncle Artie, my mom's cousin who had been my dentist when I was young. But it wasn't he. This man didn't look like Arty at all, but I knew him.

I stared and stared, until I realized I was being rude. I turned back to my friends and continued our conversation, yelling because it was so loud in there.

I was talking to the aide in charge of in-school suspension. Standing right behind her was the man I knew. She soon realized I wasn't paying attention to her, but to the tall, distinguished older gentleman behind her.

"Who are you staring at?" she asked me.

"Will you turn around and ask that man behind you if his name is Mr. Sundheim?"

"What?" she asked.

"Ask him if he's Mr. Sundheim," I repeated, wishing I could remember his first name.

"No!" she blurted, clearly embarrassed at the thought of doing something I wouldn't blink twice at doing.

I shouted really loud to be heard over the din in the room, "Mr. Sundheim!"

He turned, looked at me and with only a slight pause, he yelled, "Beamer!"

I screamed, leapt from my chair, and landed directly in his open arms. We had a long talk, and he called both Sunny in Seattle and his wife in New Jersey.

When he called Sunny, she answered with, "Hey, Pop!" and I responded with, "Do I look like your father?"

After only a second pause she said, "Beam?"

I laughed and told her how I wound up on her father's phone. We promised to keep in better touch.

***

In August, just two months after I bumped into her father, Sunny called.

I wasn't in Maryland, where I taught, but up in Massachusetts, house and dog sitting for Erin, who was visiting Japan with her family. I was on my way to Maine for a weeklong Great Books Discussion event at Colby College, where I would hang out with my dad and stepmom for the week.

Sunny called and said that she had a tough story to tell me. The details are hazy, but the facts linger. She was with her family at their camp in Speculator, New York. Her doctors in Seattle were processing a number of tests she'd had right before she left for vacation.

The long and the short of it was she had a tumor in her brain. When she took her pointer finger and pressed it in the center of her forehead, that's where all of the pain was centered. She would have surgery imminently (after two weeks of testing), after she returned to Seattle. The goal was to remove as much of the tumor as possible and to find out what was what up there.

I listened and heard her, but I don't think I believed any of it.

She told me stories of the entire family playing Uno; her brother and his wife were visiting from Alaska, where they lived. Her sister, who was from Tacoma, Washington, was there. Sunny's boyfriend was there too. They were playing cards and her brother, Eric, was shuffling; as he started to deal, Sunny blurted it out: "You're all here. I will only have to say this once. I have a brain tumor. I'll be having surgery when I get back to Seattle."

Eric stopped dealing midstream, and they all stared dumbly as Sunny outlined detail after detail of the conversations she'd been having with doctors in random spots away from the camp because of the spotty cell reception in the Adirondacks.

***

Sunny had surgery while I was in Maine. The tumor was somewhat bigger than a racquetball, but smaller than a tennis ball. It was bigger than the doctor had ever seen.

They had to wake her in the middle of surgery so the doctor would know what to cut and what to not cut, as the tumor was sitting near the communication section of her brain.

She came out of the surgery and the ordeal pretty well. They couldn't say anything definitive about the tumor in her head, and they had to wait to see if what remained turned wavy, meaning it was brain matter, or if stayed as it was, which meant it was tumor. Within a miraculous period of time, she was back to work in the children's hospital with a completely different perspective on sickness and suffering.

***

When I was in the midst of diagnosis, and in a pretty chipper spot, to be honest, I got a call from an unfamiliar phone number. It was the middle of the last period of the school day. Afterward, I was out by the softball field, because Whitherspoon's youngest sister was playing in a softball game against our high school. I checked my voicemail and discovered I had missed a call from Sunny's mom; she and Pop were at Woody's, and they were wondering if I could swing by and join them. By the time I listened to the message, they were long gone.

I called anyway. I got her voicemail and left a stupidly happy message:

> Hey, Mom! I'm so sad I missed you! Call me if you're still around and we'll get together. You know how Sunny has that tumor? Well, they think I have cancer too! Isn't that kind of funny? They don't know what it is or what is going on. They think lymphoma … But I would love to see you! Love you!

A colleague, Doug, was standing there as I left the message. He turned to me and said, "Kim?" his dark eyebrows furrowed and making a frown.

"What?" I asked, sincerely perplexed. I was grinning and happy and sure it was all one big joke. God would come through, and I would be healed. There was no way I was going to be sick-sick. The healing would be miraculous and would prove my faith in Christ was founded.

Doug shook his head and said nothing. Now I get that it was uncool to break my news to the Sundheims that way. Back then, I thought I was doing really well coping with diagnosis and the unknown, but looking back, I see now that I was just making it through.

***

Diagnosis came and went, and treatment started.

I was in the waiting room of BFU's Cancer Center. It was an early dose, maybe three. I was waiting to enter the door to hell, where they inject chemo into your body, when I realized I needed to talk to someone who got it, and so I called Sunny.

"Hey, you!" she yelled in my ear from across the country.

I laughed, and we chatted. A couple of seats down from me was a crotchety old man to whom I didn't pay any attention.

"How are you?" she asked in all sincerity.

I explained where I was sitting. "Sunny," I said, "if you ever need chemo, I'm coming out. I know your family is going to be there, but there is no way I'm going to let you do this alone. It's awful. You have no idea how awful."

I paused then said, "Yes, yes, you do. You work where you work."

She chuckled and asked me, "What's it like living at your mom's?"

I groaned. "She comes in the room and stares at me like I'm an animal in the zoo. She stands there and watches me lie there as if I'm dead, like I'm a koala or a naked mole rat."

She laughed really hard.

The crotchety old man turned to me and said, "You know what your problem is?"

"Hold on, Sunny," I said into the phone. Then I turned and looked into the sallow, yellow, wrinkled face of the man with piercing eyes and even less hair than I had.

"You have OCD," he said. "I know you do, because I do and you're just like me. You need to get yourself on medication. It will help. It's what will make it all better. You have OCD."

Mom showed up, and I looked at her. "What is he talking about?" I asked her.

Mom questioned the old man and his wife about what he said to me.

I had OCD, apparently. Mildly offended and pretty hurt, I picked myself up and walked out into the main entranceway of the third floor of the medical building, which the elevator describes as the second floor. "Sunny," I said, deeply wounded by this man's quick assessment of my personality, "I know I have anxiety. I could have told him that, but OCD?"

"Beam, relax. You don't have OCD."

Still shaken by his judgment and the reality of my being sick, I didn't follow when she said, "Why don't I?"

I said, "Why don't you, what?"

"Come out and see you. I could go see Mom and Pop from there."

"Really?" I asked. "You would fly in from Seattle?"

"Kim," she said, "I don't want you to have to do this alone either."

***

Chemo cycles consisted of pricking, dripping, dying, and waking up at the bottom of a cold, deep, muddy grave. I had to shove my fingers into the muck to climb out. During all this slop of unconsciousness and consciousness, all I could think about was that man saying my problem was OCD. It wasn't until the end of the week—after I came to and had many conversations with friends—that I could see that the man had no idea what he was talking about. My issue was not OCD; it was anxiety. I could not get certain thoughts out of my head, but that was mostly chemotherapy affecting my brain's normal patterns.

***

I was staying with Dad when Sunny flew in. He drove to the airport, and I weakly got out of the car. I was wearing the blue stretch pants Erin bought me, only the legs were way baggier and the tops were tight around my distended belly.

I eased myself out of the car and turned to the giant airport with tears in my eyes.

"Dad," I said weakly.

"What, Kim?" he asked, concern all over his face.

Tears started to pool in the corners of my eyes. "My head only makes sense at the medical building and cancer center," I replied.

The tense muscles in his shoulders relaxed. He came over to me as I walked slowly toward him. He stood tall next to me, supportive and strong. "It's okay. People like you walk around all the time."

I looked at him, "Where?"

He shook his head. "You aren't alone. Every one of these people in the airport knows someone who has gone through what you are going through. It will be fine." He walked slowly as I trudged next to him.

Sunny's plane was only mildly delayed.

Dad said he had to go to the bathroom and as much as I didn't want to, I had to too. Dad and I parted at the men's and women's rooms. I walked in and was instantly struck with an overwhelming fear of germs. I had no idea what my neutropene levels were, but I knew they were low. They were always low.

The white tile floors were gray. There were wet spots around the toilets and on the walkway between the stalls. There was water on the sink counters, and there were paper towels overflowing the metal waste bins attached to the wall under the holders. Scared of getting sick and winding up in the hospital again, I pushed the door of the first stall—which is reputed to be the statistically cleanest one—open with my elbow, careful not to touch any of the stall walls. I hovered over the toilet seat because there was no way I was going to sit down on it.

Here are two very embarrassing things that they don't tell you when you are diagnosed with cancer:

1. When your hair falls out, it's not just hair on your head; it's all hair. Which is nice because it means that you don't have to shave your armpits or your legs. But it also means pubic hair too. And what the oncologists don't tell you is that hair in that area is essential for aim. Seriously. It's not like girls are guys and can use their hands to direct their streams. Scout tells us in *To Kill a Mockingbird* that she cannot be a part of Jem and Dill's peeing contests because she does not have the proper apparatus. In college, my guy friends would go out in the snow, out to the main road that separated one half of campus from the other—Grapevine Road, or Route 127, depending on whom you talked to. As the road was free of traffic due to the weather,

they would stand at the crosswalk and write their names in the snow. Not owning a pen of my own, I was not allowed to join those shenanigans. Our trip to the airport was just after dose 4, and there was no hair to be found.

2. The weakness that overtakes your body makes simple things really difficult. I've always been a hoverer in public bathroom stalls. Lower your pants, separate your legs like you are going to squat some amount of weight, hold the pose, and let the stream go. Sorry to be so graphic but that's the honest truth. But when I was sick from chemo, my body couldn't do the weightlifting squat. It couldn't hold that position, so I had to put my hands out to either side, touching the nasty stall and the tile wall with each hand. I figured I could wash my hands as opposed to the part of my body that would make direct contact with the toilet seat.

Now I can hear you, dear reader, asking why I didn't put one of those toilet-seat covers down, you know, the ones that look like the outline of a human head when you pop out the middle. In my mind, I could imagine the nasty germs just waiting to put me in the hospital, lining up to work their way through that flimsy, translucent piece of tissue paper. I would rather take my chances with the walls than that "protective" layer of see-through paper.

I got myself into what was closest to a hover that I could muster, took aim and let go. Only it didn't land in the toilet, exactly. It was close, but it was landing on the toilet seat. In exhaustion, I sighed and continued the stream I now couldn't stop, figuring it would slide off the seat and land in the toilet. Some of it did, but not all of it. Instead of dripping down into the toilet, some of it dripped down and landed on my pants.

I peed on my pants.

In ultimate defeat, I wiped, pulled up my wet pants, washed my hands, and looked at my wet butt in the mirror. Fresh tears streamed out of my eyes. I unzipped the hoodie I was wearing, wrapped it around my waist to hide the wet spots, and made my way out of the bathroom. When I emerged, Dad was pacing right outside the door.

He took one look at my face, moved to me quickly, and said, "What's the matter?"

"I'm so embarrassed," I replied.

"What?" he sounded mad, but I knew it was just concern and frustration because he did not know what was wrong.

"I just peed on myself," I said, starting to cry harder.

"What?" he asked.

I explained how it happened, and he pulled me into a hug. "I'll do laundry when we get home," he said. "It will dry and no one will know."

As we walked toward the baggage claim to find Sunny—a very long walk indeed—he took my arm and guided me along, telling me his own embarrassing bathroom stories, which would have mortified me if they'd happened to me.

***

We eventually made our way to the baggage claim. I looked at everyone there and scanned all of the short people around the baggage conveyor belt. Most of them were clearly not her. There was a good candidate whose back was to me, but her dark brown hair had bright fire-red streaks. There was no way Sunny would dye her hair and not tell me. I stood by a brightly lit ad, waiting for her to show up.

I was standing really close to the girl with red streaks, when I heard Sunny yell, "Beam?!?"

I looked over, and streaky-red hair was looking right at me. The round face, warm brown eyes, and sweet smile were all Sunny's.

"No way!" I said. "I had said that that hair couldn't have been you. You would have told me to look for it!"

She laughed and said, "That's so funny, because I said to myself that there was no way that was you, but you're the only bald cancer patient around here."

We hugged around her suitcase, and Dad said, "I want to show you right where to stand, and I will come pick you two up. I don't want you walking any more than you have to." He greeted Carolyn warmly. We stood outside and talked nonstop until Dad came with the car.

***

Dad; Giselle, my stepmom; Juliette, my stepsister; and Sunny and I went out to a favorite local Chinese-Japanese-Thai restaurant down the road.

Giselle got a Bento box, which I had never experienced before. I craved all of those fresh vegetables that I wasn't allowed to eat on my neutropenic diet.

Dad made sure I got bottled water, and whenever my water was refilled he made sure it was filtered.

On our way to this restaurant I wanted Juliette to know that Sunny was not only sweet and amazing, but also a cancer survivor. I asked Sunny about her dye job and mentioned that the dye had also dyed the inch-wide scar on her head.

"Really?" Sunny asked, showing me the scar so I could get a better look.

"Juliette, you see that red?" I asked.

Juliette said, "How did you get that scar?"

Sunny smiled and said, "Brain tumor."

Juliette stopped, startled. Sunny kept smiling.

"Are you okay?" Juliette asked.

Sunny shrugged. "For now," which was not exactly a comforting response.

"How old are you?" Juliette asked.

"Thirty-four," Sunny said.

"Sunny and I graduated high school together," I chimed in.

Juliette thought for a second, and then she said, "That's sort of scary."

"Isn't it?" I replied. "I was thinking that we should pull an Erin Brockovich on the Byram/Stanhope area."

"What's that?" Juliette asked.

"You know, that movie with Julia Roberts where she worked for the lawyer who figured out the water in that one town was killing people."

Juliette shook her head, "I don't know it."

Dad, who was driving, said, "It's a lot like that *Civil Action* story that took place up by where you used to live, Kim."

"In Woburn," I said. "Bad water. Lots of cancer, I think. I was told by many people not to drink the water in Woburn."

Sunny said, "We should take a poll to see what weird diseases our graduating class got."

"I'm sure there were several. Dad, you remember David C, the actor who graduated ahead of me? At a recent reunion, he said that his dad died of Hodgkin's."

Hodgkin's was what the chemo in my body was fighting, and I'd just announced that David's dad didn't make it. The car got silent. Right. Good job, Kim. Way to keep the car ride to dinner nice and light. Trying to cover up my faux pas, I said, "He had diabetes too. It complicated things."

***

My father and Giselle adopted an insane Shiba Inu, whom they named Pico. This dog was over the top. I would have thought that being more than four years old would have settled this dog down, but not at all. He did backflips trying to catch butterflies. He pounced on mushrooms to eat them before my dad, who walks Pico regularly, even saw the poisonous plants. Pico destroyed stuffed toys and left their innards, what my stepmom called, "monkey brains," all over the carpet. He chased his own tail, over and over and over again. Daily.

Dad and Giselle had also adopted a sweet, sweet mutt of a girl named Sam, who didn't like to be petted rough, but gently and lightly. She often let her ears flop down, and she held her eyes, surrounded with white eyelashes, sad. She was dear and kind and a pack animal, following whoever was in the house. When I was sick, she often lay at the floor next to the couch and followed me wherever I went.

One morning, I got up, and Sam was lying on my bedroom floor. I went to the bathroom and then walked toward the stairs. As I was making my way, I heard Pico, the wonder dog, coming. I moved a little quicker and stood at the corner of the hallway, with Sam right at my heels. The two of us hid in the corner as we watched Pico fly past us to the hallway outside my bedroom. Then Pico ran into another bedroom, spun around a few times, and turned back into the hallway, charging back toward Dad and Giselle's room. Once there, he turned and charged back past us and past us again and past us again, with an occasional pause in a room to chase his tail.

I looked down at Sam and said, "Can you explain this to me?"

Sam looked up at me, her ears flat, her doe-eyes sad as if to say, "Why did they pick *him* to be my friend?"

"Right," I said to Sam as we waited for Pico to end his charge.

To say that Pico liked people is accurate. To say that Pico loved Sunny would be an understatement. Most important, the dog would sit, wait, stay, and was wicked obedient for her. But he loved to ignore the rest of us.

***

On the last day of Sunny's visit, I had to have a CT scan. She knew my test had been scheduled before she arrived and had no problem going with me. She and Dad got breakfast while I was having my test. When my test was finished, I went out into the lobby, but they weren't there. I curled up in a fluffy BFU blanket that I'd told the CT techs that I was taking with me. It was so fluffy compared to other BFU blankets and I was stinking freezing.

Sitting in the waiting room, I was phoneless. The techs wouldn't let my phone go where they were injecting radioactive material into my veins. Because I'd given my phone to Sunny, I just had to wait for their return when they were done with breakfast, since I couldn't alert them I was ready to leave.

In the waiting room near me, there was an equally cold man curled up on a woman next to him. Turned out the woman was there for tests, but the man was the one who made eye contact with me. "What are you being treated for?" he asked.

"Hodgkin's," I replied.

He asked questions about my treatment and dosages, how much time I had to spend in the hospital … Turned out he'd had Hodgkin's at a very young age and had to spend treatments in the hospital.

He said, "You're going to be fine. I'm fine and you will be too." He explained that he now had chronic fatigue syndrome. The doctors believed it came from the treatment for Hodgkin's.

I did the math—his age and the time it took for the chronic fatigue to develop. I figured I wouldn't have to worry about it until I was about sixty or so. And as Atticus Finch said, "It's not time to worry yet."

***

We talked about going to the Mutter Museum in Philadelphia before taking Sunny to the train. But instead, Sunny and I lay next to each other on my twin bed, staring at the ceiling and talking about our disappointment with God and our lives.

I stared at my white closet door a lot as we talked. "Sunny," I said, "when we were in high school, all you wanted to be was a nurse and a mom."

She talked about how hard it must be to be the parent of one of her patients. "It's made me rethink what being a parent means."

"I get that. I hate watching my mom and dad going through what they go through every treatment. I sometimes wonder if the needles hurt them more than they do me." My mom often said that she would take the treatment to save me from it, if she could. And I would say, "I would never want anyone to suffer like this for me."

"And those parents who are watching their children die at my hospital, they are suffering too," Sunny said. "How do I ask someone to join me in this life I'm living?"

I knew what she meant. People who had Sunny's kind of surgery are given a timeline of survival and it's a bell curve. When she first told me, Sunny said, "I have a bell curve left."

"What?" I asked.

Sunny explained, "After my kind of surgery, people die on a bell curve because of the surgery itself. Some, a small number, die right away. Then as the years go out, more and more die, until you reach the top of the bell curve. The top of the bell curve is the average length that most people live. Then the numbers of people who make it longer than that get fewer and fewer, making my surgery only a life prolonger."

"How long until you reach the top of the bell curve?" I had asked her.

"Ten years," Sunny replied.

She'd had surgery at thirty-three. That meant forty-three. Forty-three.

After a silence, Sunny said, "When I pictured my life, this is not what I expected."

I said, "Brain cancer was never on my list of expectations for your life. And it makes me mad. We, you and me, are God's children. We adore Jesus with everything we have, and yet, here you are with a brain tumor and I have Hodgkin's."

We lay there in silence, and then I said, "Chemo is hell."

She laughed, "I'll keep that in mind."

"Do. Do," I said. "It makes everything heavy—my head, my back, my shoulders. It all aches, but it's more like it's just so heavy, like my head is a bowling ball or my slippers have lead in them."

"Is that why you have that walk? I've seen it in other cancer patients."

"You mean the hunched, dog-headed look?" I asked. "Like Sammy when you go to put the leash on her, and she tries to push her head into the floor?"

She laughed, "Yeah, something like that."

"Everything aches. It's exhausting just standing up to go to the bathroom."

We were quiet, and then we both agreed: this had not been a part of our dreams.

I said, "And it makes me mad at God. He knew it. He could have stopped it before it even started. He could have stepped in at any point and said, 'No. No. This is not acceptable. She's my daughter.'" I paused. "Where the hell is He? Does He see this longing and aching and hurting we're in?"

Sunny added, "And how do we change our lives? I would love to pick up and go live near my brother in Alaska, but I can't change hospitals because I need to hold onto my medical insurance. I would have picked up a long time ago, but medical insurance won't let me."

I replied, "I've always wanted to be a full-time writer, to have a house filled with noise and a dog. This is not what I signed up for."

"Where is that clipboard that they pass around so you can volunteer to help with events?" she asked. "I'm going to scratch my name right off of it."

Exactly. And where was the clipboard that has my dreams listed and checked off as they come to pass?

"Sunny, you know I feel like God has left me, and He has no idea where I am. But there are moments when I think I'm hearing from Him, like when I'm in the bathroom. It's in those moments when I'm actually cognizant of washing my hands, when I hear, 'Don't worry about a thing, because every little thing is going to be all right.' Or I hear 'tenfold return.' But then I wonder, how the heck is that even possible? Isn't everything over?"

For her, ten years, now less and less every day, looms in front of her.

"I don't want it to be," she said softly.

"I don't want it to be either."

***

Catching up with Sunny was like sitting in the sun and being seventeen again. Only it was not at all the same.

Staying at Dad's

When I was at Dad's house for those two weeks, he and Giselle would go out at night, leaving me alone. He would say things like, "We are just going up the street," or "We are going to be fifteen minutes away. Call me if you need me."

I did need him, but I wouldn't call. I needed him present. Nighttime is the worst when you are sick, at least it was for me. That's when the symptoms worsened. I had strength in the morning to hold through. By the end of the day, those strength reserves were depleted, and everything seemed bleak. For me, night was when the sadness descended, and hope didn't exist. It was nice to know that you were not alone on the couch during those dark times, since time didn't seem to move forward.

***

Right before I left for Dad's, Mom's friend, Jane, told her, "Kim needs a knitting project."

I didn't understand and thought she was a little off her rocker for thinking I could knit while I was feeling that green. Jane gave me yarn and a pattern. She had to make two baby sweaters for a coworker who was having twins.

She said, "You are going to make the white sweater with green trim, and I'm going to make the green one with white trim."

"What if I throw up on it?" I asked. My pink-bucket friend was never far during a chemo week.

"You won't," was her response.

As I was sitting on Dad's leather sofa in the family room, I started to read the pattern and cast on my first knitting project in a couple of years. I had knit a baby blanket for a friend's daughter. I had knit a sweater for myself, but knitting wasn't necessarily something I was confident about.

I sat on the couch, knitting needles moving slowly, and I paid attention to my body. In my lower back, across my bum, and down my thigh muscles, the nerves were playing games. The sensation was one of worms under the skin, but since I've never actually felt that, it was how I thought worms would feel. They would go from my lower back, zoom down just under the skin across my bum, and then down into my thighs. They would dance. They would twirl and spin, lightly tickling. I would sit for hours and just feel the dance play out.

When I was tired of knitting, I closed my eyes and felt my nerves tintinnabulate around my body. Their playful antics could keep me entertained like little else did.

***

One night I was lying on the couch, half dead, and Dad was sitting next to me. He said that he wasn't going out that night; he was going to stay with me.

My stepsister walked in and said, "My mom and I are going out to dinner. Would you like to go with us?"

I was so touched by the invite. I had never been invited before to join the two of them going out to eat.

"Oh, Juliette, I wish I could," I said. "But I had treatment today. I'm not going to be eating anything, I don't think."

"Really?" she asked. "You had chemo today?"

"Yup. Chemo today. Feel like crap. But I so love the invite."

She soon left the room, and that remains one of the most touching conversations I have ever had with my stepsister.

***

Dad and I were watching *Firefly* together. This TV show was the one I watched on Netflix my first night of chemotherapy. I had Dad pop in the DVD, and we watched it together. He loved everything about the series, including Jayne, which is saying much since Jayne is the nasty thug who's always looking out for himself to the point of betraying those closest to him.

We watched as the horrible Reevers came onto the screen, with their pierced bodies and faces and forked tongues. They rape, skin, and kill their victims, and as one of the characters says, the killing comes before the raping and skinning if you're lucky. We watched the fear all of the characters had of Reevers. We watched as the authorities questioned Malcolm, the captain. During the time the captain was questioned, another person in custody sliced his own tongue in half.

I loved watching with Dad. I made Dad watch episodes with me while he was trying to work. I would yell, "You're going out tonight. Come watch *Firefly* with me."

One night when Dad was out, I walked upstairs when I couldn't endure being awake anymore. Sammy followed on my heels. I went into the bathroom; she lay down on the carpet outside the bathroom door. I got ready for bed and then sat in bed reading, staring, and paying attention to the weird sensations of the nerves dancing in my back, legs, and bum. Eventually I nodded off.

And I fell into a Reever dream.

I was on a dark ship, deep in space. I was alone, but not completely. Reevers were working their way in. The last thing I saw was their faces, with metal piercings shooting out of their cheeks and foreheads and necks. They had deep holes in their cheeks. Just as they approached to skin me and rape me, Sammy barked.

I awoke with a start.

Sammy, standing near the end of my bed was facing in the direction of the driveway, and she was barking her head off. But there was nothing to bark at. Dad and Giselle weren't home yet. I was still alone, but I was no longer in a petrifying Reever dream.

I wonder if Sammy knew I was in trouble and needed her help.

***

One afternoon I walked out onto the porch where Dad was setting out lunch. I was sort of shuffling my feet and worried that I would stub my soles on the slate flooring.

I carried my heavy head and body out onto the porch and said, "Dad, I have a question."

"Yeah?" he replied as he was putting silverware out around the plates.

"Is it 2010?" I asked as I sat in one of the heavy wooden white chairs with blue cushions.

"Yes, it's 2010," he replied.

Later Dad brought this moment up with me, and said, "It was at that moment I realized how truly sick you were. You couldn't even remember what year it was. Don't we ask that question to find out senility?"

Yes. Yes. Clinicians do. As well as asking a person to spell the word "world" backward and remember three named objects and repeat them back five minutes later.

***

One day while I was at Dad's, my cell phone rang, and the caller ID showed Boon Win High School. I picked up the phone, and on the other end was Joe, one of the assistant principals, the AP to whom I was closest.

"How are you doing?" he asked.

"This is awful. Never get cancer, Joe. Never do it. Chemotherapy is just awful."

We talked a little, and then he wanted to know when I would be coming back.

I said, "November."

"Good," the AP said. "Things are just not the same without you here."

"What are you talking about?" I asked him. "I am not that important."

"You might not think so," Joe said, "but we all have noticed a difference. Your classroom isn't the same. The whole tenor of the building is different without you here. The kids are just different, even down in Lower C."

"What?" I said. "My room isn't anywhere near Lower C."

I could hear Joe smiling and nodding on the other end. "Doesn't matter. Your presence makes a difference. We're all looking forward to having you back. I'm looking forward to having you back."

"November," I replied.

***

One night Aunt Maureen stayed with me while Dad was out. She brought her harp in from the rain. We sat and talked for hours. It was delightful. She talked about plans for her daughter's wedding. She talked about other things related to her children. We talked about me, treatment, side effects, and family members who were behaving badly.

I knew Mom had sent her. I knew that Mom was worried about how much time I spent alone at night, and Aunt Maureen sat with me until it was late.

We both agreed that it was a special time and one we should repeat.

***

Gail took me to the tests. It was sweet of her to do so. She sat and waited for me. She read magazines and discussed the articles with me when I came out of testing. She was very kind to run me into the city, but I'm not sure she understood how hard the tests were and how much they took out of me. I had to breathe in the phone booth again, only I had no energy. I had to have an ultrasound of my heart, so they took the wand and shoved it high and deep into my belly under my rib cage.

When I told the tech the wand hurt, he responded, "If we want to see your heart, this is what we have to do. Roll over more onto your side; I need to press this higher up."

I didn't have the patience or endurance for the challenges of the day. I could barely walk at the end of it.

During those two weeks with my Dad, my tests results came in. I called Dr. N on the day they were to be ready, and she called me back in the afternoon.

"Things are looking good," Dr. N said. "They are looking very good, which is why I want to offer you an option."

"Okay," I said.

"I know the chemo has been rough on you," she said. "I'm going to give you the choice of chemotherapy or radiation."

I thought for a couple of seconds and asked about timelines. She said I'd have to wait a month before radiation could start. I would have to be at the medical building at the same time every day for a month for treatment. She said that the timelines were the same: I'd finish chemotherapy or radiation at the same time.

I asked, "At our first meeting, didn't you say that radiation could give me heart, liver, lung, pancreatic cancer … basically cancer of any of the organs in my chest?"

"Yes," she said. "It would be down the road, but I would watch you closely if you decide to have radiation."

I thought about how hard it was for my parents to take off from their responsibilities every other Tuesday for chemotherapy. How much harder would things be if I had to go into the city each day for a half-hour appointment?

"Dr. N," I said, "if you were me, and you were offered this choice, what would you do?"

"I would stick with the chemo," she said.

"Okay," I said. "I will see you Tuesday for chemotherapy."

"You are an intelligent woman, and I knew you would make the right choice," she said. "That's why I gave you the option. I don't do that for all of my patients."

I walked into the kitchen after this conversation ended, and both my stepmom and my dad were there.

"I'm glad you're both here," I said. "I don't want to have to say this more than I need to. I will have to call Mom, but I wanted to tell you about my conversation with Dr. N."

That got their attention.

"I'm good. I look good. My scans look clean, or better. She said that she likes what she's seeing, and she's giving me the option of radiation."

Giselle, who had been at my first doctor's appointment, said, "Didn't they say that radiation could bring in cancer down the line?"

"Yeah," I said, "cancer of the liver, heart, lungs, kidneys …"

Dad cut me off saying, "Basically cancer of anything in your chest."

"Yeah," I repeated. "Basically cancer of anything inside my chest."

"What did you tell her?" Giselle asked.

I repeated my Dr. N conversation and added, "But she said that we would talk about it again, to see if I change my mind before chemo on Tuesday."

When Dr. N and I talked again, we decided I would continue with four more doses, or two more rounds, of chemotherapy. The side effect of this decision was surprising to me. It was insidious, and I didn't realize it was going on until much later, after I was done with treatment and was back to work.

I walked around after my conversation with Dr. N feeling like poop because of treatment. I was weak and miserable. I had been thrown down into the giant grave surrounded by the darkness of treatment, and had only my skeleton fingers to slowly climb back out again. It took a whole week to get out of it, and as treatment progressed, it took longer and longer to struggle out of the chemo grave. As I was working on emerging, I was barely cognizant of life—I would walk to or fro from the bathroom, or eat, or sleep, or breathe. I would have the condemning thought, *You chose this,* which to my addled brain meant *this suffering is your fault; you chose this pain.*

I'd chosen this method of healing that was destroying my ability to think, feel, and exist. I'd chosen this grave. I'd chosen all that I was going through. The crunchy veins under my skin where the D shredded its way up, I'd chosen that. I'd chosen the back pain that wrenched my muscles and made me unable to move.

I'd chosen the vein pain that seared days and days after treatment. My mom would wrap this canvas pad filled with sand that she put in boiling water for twenty minutes and then place in a towel and wrap it around my arms in the hopes of getting the veins to return to normal and the pain to stop. Or she would make me lie on the boiled sand bag in the hopes that it would relieve my back muscles. I chose that.

For the last four doses, I chose all of the side effects. I chose the nausea, the inability to eat a raw red pepper, which I craved, and the deadness that was my right leg. I chose all of it.

To: Important Contacts
From: Me
Subject: After dose 4
Date: July 26, 2010

This is the first time I've cracked open my computer since the last update I sent.

For those who haven't heard, on the twenty-first I went to the hospital with my dad and my best friend from high school, Carolyn, and went up to the nuclear medicine area (right past the center for rare diseases; Dad keeps telling me to not go into that office). I drank a sugar shake and was filled intravenously with radioactive sugar. I shivered on the bed of the CT scanner, and they covered me with three blankets, one of which I walked out with. I asked the tech if he saw anything on my scans, and his response was "just a bunch of dots" but my doctor should have answers by the end of the day.

I called the next day, Thursday, three times. I finally got her secretary on the phone who said Dr. N was in clinical all day. On Friday, Dr. N called, and we had a long talk. First she started in on the nerves on the outside of my legs, what was going on with them. Turns out she thinks that my bones are trying to make new blood cells, and that's why it hurts/aches. I wanted to hear about my scan, and she's talking about nerve/bone pain? Well, I asked about my scan and she said it looked amazing. In fact, she even sang the word—"amazing!"—that's how amazing it looked. I moved into my right arm being achy and miserable, and all my veins hurting, and how my right arm was warmer than my left—not hot, not swollen or red, just achy beyond belief and physically warmer. That's when she said, "Your scan was so good, I want to offer you another option." We talked about the other "option," which became clear wasn't an option at all. I asked her, "If you were me in this situation, which would you choose?" and she said, "chemotherapy." I asked her many other questions, and the key one was, "Can we start using my left arm for chemo this week?" She thought about it and agreed that would be okay, that the blood clots should be down enough to be able to handle chemo.

So, the short of it is this: I have four more doses to go, and then I'm done. Four more doses administered every other week. The last one is September 7. The second to last one is August 24, my birthday. No drug in my ABVD cocktail will be decreased. I'm going to be slammed for the next eight weeks, and then I'll recover. My hair will grow back. I will have strength and spunk, and I will be able to sit down with God for long, long conversations about all of this.

Here are some of my concerns:

- I really want my left arm to be the trooper my right arm has been. I hope that my left arm will be able to handle two chemos in a row. (Since the right arm has been slammed not only with two chemos so far, but every blood test, every hospital stay, even the radioactive IV I had on Wednesday. I want my left arm to take the next two doses of chemo, giving my right arm a break, and then go back to my right for one and my left for one, and then we're done.)
- I want there to be no more side effects and hope that I will just power through these next eight weeks.
- I hope to gain about five pounds. Everyone who has seen me this week has been saying that I weigh too little and that I should put weight on. If you saw what I eat, I should be a bit pudgier than I am, but apparently with my body trying to survive the poison, taking in nutrition to maintain weight isn't a priority.

So, that's my story. Thanks for being a part of this journey. I'm not really sure where I am in it, emotionally I mean, what I think of all of this. Everyone is just so excited to hear that the cancer is dead, and that is really, really, really good news. But I still have four more doses to survive. I told someone today that I think of it like the way I would imagine a marathon runner would feel: yeah, I just completed 13.1 miles and that's an accomplishment, but there are still 13.1 miles to go. And that is daunting and scary, and I wonder if I will be able to get through it. So I'm daunted and sad and wish there were some other way to live the next two months, but this is what I have to do in order to have the future that some of my friends have told me is still to come.

All my heart.

Kim

"Not all those who wander are lost." ~ J. R. R. Tolkien

Waiting Room People

When I was waiting in line for triage to receive my chemo dose, a little white woman with dyed auburn hair was behind me. We were talking about our diagnoses and the effects chemo had on our bodies. We were joking about some things, like how chemo is like being thrown into the back of a dark walk-in closet, and you slowly wake up and come to yourself. One thing we did not joke about—her diagnosis of multiple myeloma. I told her my grandmother had it; I didn't tell her that she died in one year. Well, we did celebrate that her prognosis was for ten years. She even said, "They've made great gains since you were little."

Later, as I sat in the waiting room, waiting for my opportunity to be treated, she came out of the treatment door. I didn't see her at first. However, when she got close and reached out her hand to touch my arm, I was all attention.

"Thank you," she said, "I just hate coming here. I hate everything about it, even if it is just for a little shot like I had today." I nodded in understanding.

"But I have to thank you. You made it fun. You made me laugh and joke about these things. Some people are just so serious, and it's depressing. Thank you, and keep that spirit about you."

I smiled at her. "Thank you," I replied. "That is really sweet. I'll try to. It's hard though."

She nodded, "I know that too. But you, you helped me today, and for that I thank you." Her husband took her other arm as she turned to him, and he helped her walk out of the cancer center and onto the elevator to go home.

***

When I was waiting to see Dr. N for the first dose, there was a man in the waiting room, about my age, maybe a bit older. He was usually treated on Mondays, but the day before had been a holiday, and no one was being treated. He had to wait until Tuesday—my dose day—for his dose. The waiting room could get overloaded as they doubled up Monday and Tuesday regulars, trying to get everyone in.

There was something striking about him, something that pulled my attention, but at first I couldn't place it. His head was shaved, and he was wearing a T-shirt. He looked like everyone else, but he said he had been in treatment for years, and he was getting tired of it.

That's when I realized the striking thing about him: he didn't have eyebrows.

He was also holding a gallon-size Ziploc bag. Inside were orange pill bottles with white lids. There were tons in there. The bag was bulging, even though it was closed. As he moved it around, it rattled.

I'm sure my eyebrows went up as I looked at it. "Ridiculous, right?" he asked.

I nodded, "But surely you don't need all of them. Some are like leftovers?"

"Nope. I need them all."

I saw him later in my treatment. He was across the waiting room from me. I was bald, and I don't think he recognized me at that point. I wanted to ask him how he was doing. I was feeling shy and tired that day. He also didn't look like he was in the mood for talking. That was the last time I saw him, but now, whenever I go to the medical building, I keep my eye open for him. I would like to check in, if he is willing to talk with me again.

***

Around dose 2, I was in the waiting room, already impatient about what being there meant. I was done with treatment. I was done with feeling like shit. I was without hope. I was praying to die.

There was a young white woman with a brown pixie cut on the other side of the waiting room. She was smiling and joking. She was sharing her story to a rapt audience of other waiting people. She talked about how this time was easier and she was out running in the mornings. She talked about her happiness and joy during this treatment go-round. I wanted to ask how she could be so happy, since her cancer had been in remission and was now back. She said that they were using the port in her head. (They put a port in her head?) She said that the tube went down to a vein that pumped into her heart.

She said her boyfriend was with her in this, that he was so supportive. This woman said that she was still exercising frequently and that very little had changed in her life with her chemotherapy.

I picked up some of her hopeful energy. I also felt jealous of how great things were going in her life. She had a boyfriend. She had energy to run, which was shocking. She just seemed to have it all. I didn't see her again, but as my treatment went on, I found out something that made me worry about this woman's prognosis.

I discovered from the oncology nurses and some of the oncology residents, interns and doctors I met, the rougher chemotherapy was for an individual, the more good it was doing in the patient's body. I told them that I was miserable and nothing seemed to be working right—my fingers and toes were tingling, my right leg was dead and not worthy of trust, my mouth occasionally hurt, even water tasted funky all the time. I wasn't allowed to drink caffeine, and green tea was out, no matter if I drank it decaffeinated. In my normal life, I lived on green tea. I was bald. I had no energy. I felt like shit, and at times my mother found me crying on my bed. These things gave the nurses, oncology residents, interns and doctors hope. These bad things going on in my body meant the chemotherapy was working.

Choosing to Live

I was on my bed in my room. I was wearing a short, pink satin nightgown with thin spaghetti straps. It hung loosely all over, resting on my sharp shoulder blades, exposing my pale, pale flesh and the pink, pink scar where the port used to be.

I had already shot myself in the belly with the blood thinner, Fragmin. The light was off, but the light from the hall was shining bright into the room.

Mom was moving around, making going-to-bed noises: helping the weakened and aged dog, Emily, onto the bed. Mom washed her face and walked between her bedroom and the bathroom, stopping to tuck me in and kiss me goodnight.

My stick legs stuck out from below the flowing satin. My bony, cracking feet were useless for support. My bald bowling ball of a head forced my frame to the mattress.

Mom studied me and said, "Are you crying?"

"Let me go," I replied. "Please. Can't I just die? Please? Can't you just let me die?"

She came in and sat on the bed and rubbed my back. "Nope. We've come too far to stop now. We've done too much. I have too much invested in you to give you up."

"Please. Just let me die."

Her response was to rub my back and kiss my face. She said, "I love you."

And I realized that it was easy to die, really, really simple. It's choosing to live that's hard.

Family Behaving Badly

This was a hard section to write. Some might even question why I did. But if I'm going to be honest about my experience, I have to admit that family doesn't always react gracefully to sickness, and family dynamics change after a diagnosis. In fact, some family members who are incredibly helpful at one moment might be incredibly hurtful at another.

In this book, as I say in the note to readers, I have changed names and relationships to protect the innocent and the guilty; and all are innocent in some way. People do things, myself included, without realizing the ramifications of their actions. Please know, the events I'm recording here involve family members who were close to me and whose actions hurt me deeply. It's possible the things that happened occurred unintentionally or because, like I said earlier, not everyone handles sickness well, the doctors, family members, caretakers, and sick person included.

I'm recording this for people who are going through treatment; if your family also behaves badly, then you'll know you are not alone.

***

I used to make a joke about families. They are further evidence of God's sense of humor. He puts us in families with people we would never be friends with under "normal" circumstances. Because we are all related, we have to figure out life together.

But now, I don't see it as funny at all. The pain families put each other through is cruel. I would rather choose people to be in my family than have to celebrate holidays with people who are insulting and mean.

***

Wendy had two little children in daycare, and those children were often sick. Wendy would call the house and say, "I'm calling to give the nurse's update," and relate the sickness that was in her home at that moment: fevers, ear infections, and stomach bugs were the most common illnesses in her household. Someone was always sick during the four months I was in treatment. The one time that everyone was fine, Wendy showed up to make breakfast for my mom and me. Wendy received a phone call about ten minutes after her arrival saying that her child was sick in daycare, and Wendy had to go to pick her up. Mom, who had been looking forward to a morning off, then stepped in and made Wendy breakfast before she left.

My numbers were low; we know that. I was living on the neutropenic diet because there was no knowing when my numbers would be down, and a raw red pepper would put me in the hospital. My oncologist told me to avoid children in contact with germs (which would include young children in daycare). The only time Wendy should be welcome was when her family was healthy, but I shouldn't have contact with Wendy's children even if they were healthy. There was even concern about my contact with Wendy during this time, since she often picked up the daycare germs.

Wendy was upset that Whitherspoon had visited me in the hospital. She was offended that Whitherspoon, who worked in a germ-ridden high school, was allowed to go to the hospital right from work. I pointed out that Whitherspoon didn't touch me, and she wasn't living with sick children, but Wendy didn't recognize the difference.

My mom has been really helpful to those who need her. Before I was sick, Wendy would take her children over for Mom to babysit. Mom was happy to spend time with Wendy's two kids. But when Wendy picked up her kids, she wouldn't clean up after them. The Fisher-Price people and their cars, planes, and houses would be on my mom's den floor. The kids' board books would be all over the two couches. The chairs her husband brought up from the basement for the children's high chairs would be in the eating area, with the high chairs still attached to them. Often there was Cheerio goo and juice on the trays and seats.

When Mom became my full-time caretaker—she was also working full-time—she didn't have the time or energy to help Wendy as she once had. Wendy didn't understand this. On more than one occasion, Wendy confronted my mom about not being there for her. Wendy kept telling my mom that she wanted things to go back to the way they were before I got sick. My mom was always hurt by these conversations. She would turn to me, weak on the couch, and explain that she couldn't do it all; it was too much. I would apologize because she had to choose between Wendy and me. It wasn't fair to Mom that I got sick. Not that I asked for it, but it was hard to watch Mom be torn between one of her best friends and her sick daughter.

***

Gail, one of my mom's childhood friends and therefore a family member as those things go, made chicken noodle soup every week I had a treatment. She used another family member's recipe and made such a good batch of sick soup. She would deliver the soup and sometimes stay to visit with me as I lay on the couch.

People visiting could be very hard on me. I would have to sit up, pay attention, and be alert and personable; after a short period of time that became exhausting. After someone visited, I would need to sleep for a bit. Please don't think I wasn't happy to see visitors; they were my lifeline. They made me tired, but they also made me know that I wasn't alone in my battle.

One time, Gail came to see how I was doing. She took one of the eating-area chairs and pulled it around to face me on the couch, her back to the television. It was a bad day. I could barely lift my head off the couch. My face was just sort of smeared there. My legs were stretched out in front of me. I was covered with the white-with-blue-stripes BFU blanket we took home from treatment.

Gail, who has a background in psychiatry, looked at my body, all sticks of bone and my bowling ball head, and said, seriously, "You know not showering is a sign of insanity?"

I flopped my head in her direction. I was truly concerned when I said, "Really?"—the way I was concerned about that guy in the waiting room who accused me of being OCD. My heart raced, and I thought about my not showering. I loved showers. Before I was sick, I took really long, really hot showers. It was something of an issue with some family members who felt I took too long in the shower. Now Gail was telling me that my sanity was in question because I was too exhausted during the first week of treatment to move my body into the pelting water and overwhelming thundering rain of the showerhead. I would shower every day of the second week and then when treatment came around again, I wouldn't be able to muster the strength for a shower until that first week had passed and my body had recovered a little. Gail had clout; with her terminal degree in the mind and the way it works, I really believed that it was possible chemotherapy was making me clinically insane. For example, I couldn't remember squat.

She paused and then said, "No, not really. I just wanted to see if it would get you off the couch and into the shower."

Later, when I was better and able to process this moment a little, I was stymied. If she felt really strongly about my showering, why didn't she offer to help me upstairs and run me a bath? After Dad and Giselle shaved my head, since I had just had a shower and was weak, Giselle followed me upstairs and sat in the armchair in the bedroom. She sat there for the entire shower, as I rinsed off all of the little hairs that were itching my entire body, in case I lost my ability to stand and needed help. If Gail felt so strongly about my need to shower, she could have figured out an alternative: run a bath, helped me up the stairs, helped me undress, helped me into the bath, and, if necessary, helped me wash. Instead, she made me feel like crap for not having the ability to pull my head and body off the couch.

***

Gail did other hurtful things too. She wondered to other family members (and it got back to me) why my mom was so upset about my being sick. According to the statistics, I had an 85 percent chance of the chemotherapy working. She said, "Kim's going to be fine. I don't know why her mom is so worried."

She also called a couple of times and said, "I'm coming over to visit."

Mom would say, "Please don't. Kim doesn't feel well at all. It's a bad day. She wants to be left alone on the couch."

Gail would come over anyway. Mom had to run interference and sit with Gail to keep her from bothering me in the den. I would hear them in the living room as I lay on the pink couch under the BFU blanket. Gail's visits really upset me, but I couldn't even muster the strength to talk; how could I possibly confront her? Mom would sit with her until Gail felt better about my being sick, then Mom would get back to work (since she worked at home), staying at her desk a couple of hours longer than usual to make up for the time she'd missed.

***

But that wasn't the worst of it, not by a long shot.

I received an e-mail from a family member. I won't say who this person is, but please know that this is someone I really care about. This person hadn't called or been by since I was diagnosed. Friends and other family members crawled out of the woodwork when I was diagnosed and treated. This guy? Nowhere to be found.

I sent him an e-mail that said, "Where are you? Do you know that I've been hospitalized in your city? Where have you been? If you don't show up soon, you're not going to be my relative anymore but just some guy I know."

His response? "Your cancer comes at a bad time for me."

That's right, because I love that I have cancer. I love that my plans for going to Chicago and studying for a master's in divinity have been uprooted. I love that people have to rearrange their schedules for me—take me to the hospital, make me soup, and stay with me because it's not good for me to be alone for too long. This is exactly what I planned for the end of my thirty-third and the beginning of my thirty-fourth year.

He did show up, under threat. While he visited, he drank an entire sixty-four-ounce bottle of cranberry-raspberry juice, and he had to visit the bathroom many times.

After lunch, we sat on one of the leather couches, and I talked about shooting myself in the belly every night with blood thinner, about surgery, about being bald, about how nothing seemed to be working right in my body as a result of the chemotherapy. He listened, sat with me, and asked a couple of questions, but that was the only contact we had throughout my entire sickness.

After I was better, I was at a family gathering, and one of our family members confessed that she was having a hard time forgiving the way he'd treated me when I was sick. I told her that I might not have completely gotten over it, but that I was choosing to forgive him. I might not feel forgiving yet, but I would come around to it. She said that I was better than she was, for she feared she wouldn't be able to forgive him; that's how strong her feelings were. I assured her it was work on my end, but that I was willing to do the work necessary. I also said I knew she would too.

***

There were other family behaving badly stories, but I stopped here. As I thought about it, I wondered if the ones here are too much. Would they be hurtful to my family members to read? Would they feel exposed because I wrote about them? The point was not to hurt them, but to say, we were all a little human and don't do the best possible job at being gracious to each other. Does that mean by writing these I'm not being gracious? When does being vulnerable about my own story and my authentic reactions to those who interact with me encroach on other people's privacy? And so the self-doubt continues.

Marinol

Around dose 6 I turned to Dr. N as I was heading to the chemo room. I said, "Can't you just give me pot?" My voice was dripping with frustration and anger.

She looked at me and said, "It's not legal in Pennsylvania."

"What about the pill form?" I asked.

"Oh, Marinol? We can do that. What? Forty pills?"

Mom reacted, "Oh, she doesn't need that many."

Dr. N thought for a second and said, "We can always refill it if we need to," and wrote a prescription for twenty pills.

When Mom went to fill the prescription, she took my credit card and told me she was really curious about how much legal pot would cost. Turned out, with my amazing medical coverage through the school system and because the Marinol was generic, it cost nothing. Mom was amazed and told me how lucky a girl I was. My pot didn't cost a thing.

***

It took me a couple of weeks to get the chutzpah to actually take it. When I did muster up the courage (for I had never used pot before), I called up an old teaching colleague and told him that he had to stay on the phone with me while I went through the pot thing. He agreed and warned me that the first time he did pot he didn't feel anything. We were on the phone for an hour and a half before I finally said, "I don't think I'm high."

"I don't think you are either," he said.

I took it a couple of days later and, yes, I did get high off it. I also got the munchies. Each time I took the Marinol, I asked Mom to make me popcorn. She only had kettle corn in the house, the sweet and mildly salty popcorn. I would ask her to bring me the salt shaker and, since all of the salt would fall to the bottom of the bowl, I would keep shaking it onto the popcorn.

I watched a couple of movies on Marinol; one of them was *500 Days of Summer*. Later, when I watched *Whip It*, a movie about roller derby, I thought, *This movie would be way better on Marinol.*

***

I only took the Marinol on especially bad days, like a chemo day or during that first week after a dose when I didn't know if I was alive or dead.

One day after one of my last four doses, my aunt and cousin came over. My cousin's wedding was at the end of October. My aunt was not only the mother of the bride but would play the harp for her daughter to walk down the aisle. Finding a dress was a concern for her, so she wanted to model the dress she had found for the event. It was a lovely purple satin affair. However, I don't remember too much from those moments we spent together on my pink sofa.

I had taken Marinol. I would be in the middle of a sentence and pause, staring off into space. I would be thinking and then wave my hand over my face in a circular motion, drawing my fingers together at the end of the circle. I would repeat "Marinol," as if that explained why my brain had suddenly shut off.

Aunt Maureen and my cousin thought it amusing. They both had experienced being high and recognized all of the symptoms. They were so patient as I couldn't articulate myself in any coherent way. Apparently I thought what I was saying was deep and important, but they saw right through all of that to my inebriated state.

Joan of Arc

Months before I even knew I was sick, I went with our church to Hagerstown, Maryland, to participate in a prophetic conference held at the Vineyard. My pastor was doing a workshop on the prophetic, and I was there to minister to people who wanted to hear from God.

The first night was a Friday night. As the night was drawing to a close, this younger guy who was a pastor near the Washington, DC, area turned to me and said, "I see you as a warrior. I see you as Joan of Arc leading men into battle, but it's not battle against flesh and blood. You are going to lead men into spiritual warfare. You are going to train them on how to stand, put on the armor of God, and wield the sword of the Spirit."

I held onto his words. Even after I was diagnosed, it seemed impossible that I would get terribly sick. I was to be Joan of Arc; that meant that there had to be a future for me. Unfortunately, I did get really sick, and the chemo every two weeks after two weeks after two weeks destroyed me.

One Tuesday morning, this might have been dose 5 or so, I was going to treatment with my father, who drove into the city past the art museum.

Outside the museum and around the surrounding property were a number of statues. The most famous was the one of Sylvester Stallone in *Rocky*. Right after the filming of the movie, they moved Rocky's statue to the Spectrum, but a little while ago, the city moved it back to the base of the art museum's hill, around the corner from the famous museum steps that Rocky ran up. Whenever you drove past, there was a line of people waiting to take their picture with the Rocky statue.

On the opposite side of the street, in the median between east and west, down the road from the museum's Perelman Annex, was another statue. It was a tarnished, garish, mustardy yellow statue of Joan of Arc. I had often overlooked her statue, never being a fan of gold jewelry or gold in general.

She sat atop a horse in her armor. In her right hand, she raised a flapping flag, and the cape on her back fluttered as if she were moving. She held her left hand down low, near the saddle, which came up high in front of her. Her horse had extended eyelids because of his armor. She wore laurel leaves in her hair and a firm determined look on her face.

After I received the "Joan of Arc" word, I made a new claim to her statue every time we passed it going into the city.

On this particular Tuesday, I turned all of my attention to Joan, because I needed her presence, her strength, her boldness, her armor. I needed all of them. I needed so much more than just glancing at her could give me.

As we drove, I kept my eyes focused, and she came into view. There she was, but she wasn't a mustard gold or burnt yellow. The art museum had polished her up. She was soft golden. She was sunshine and light. She glowed with fire.

My mouth wanted to bite down on her. Her beauty was so deep, so palpable, gleaming and unreal, I wanted her beauty inside of me.

As Dad drove past, my attention was pulled away to the roads leading to chemotherapy, and before I realized it, tears were streaming down my cheeks. I thought about hiding them from Dad; I couldn't even utter what that freshly buffed statue meant to me.

I knew Dad would think the tears were because we were headed to chemo. I'm sure he thought they represented fear mixed with anticipation. I'm sure they were, partly.

But I saw this, at that point, as a brand-new promise. It was a certainty that one day I would gleam and be brilliant in ways I had never been before.

Adventures with Jane

After I finished the baby sweater for Jane's friend, she decided I needed other projects to keep me busy. She also decided that I needed to get out of the house.

She took me to Slip Knot on Route 3, also known as West Chester Pike, where they were having a Blue Heron trunk show. Until that point, I had no idea what a trunk show was. I found out.

Blue Heron representatives were in the store, and they brought a boatload of yarn with them. There was chenille and rayon and rayon with sparkly bits. There was yarn that I couldn't put down. But worse, there were people everywhere. The store was mobbed and crowded, and I became quickly overwhelmed and exhausted.

I bought yarn. I learned about the knitting designer Stephen West and his shawls that play with color. On the way home, I crashed and slept the entire way.

***

The Blue Heron day was when the adventures started. They continued with trips to the Tangled Web in Chestnut Hill, where I bought yarn to make a pair of purple fingerless gloves and a Debbie Bliss book to follow the recipe.

Again, at the Tangled Web, I found myself getting grumpy and wanting to rest. But yarn and the pull of yarn and the recipes of delightful confections swept me up.

Again, I slept on the way home.

***

Then Jane showed up one afternoon and said, "You need to get out of the house, and I need to go to Neiman Marcus."

I knew my blood counts were down so I said something about people and getting sick.

Jane said, "This is Neiman Marcus. You'll be fine. I have to find a present for a friend's daughter's wedding, and then we will have lunch. Besides, you won't walk very much. We'll valet park."

We spent most of that visit to Neiman Marcus in the dishware and fancy gift section, right near the Neiman Marcus restaurant.

Jane and I wandered around and looked at the dishes. I felt most of them were old-ladyish or too busy to put food on. Down in the back, there were some very simple, substantially heavy dishes in solid white for the dinner and butter plates, and mocha for the salad plates. What sold me were the solid white mugs. They were also simple, but they held the only design on the whole set. The mugs had monkeys on the side, with long tails and round heads. Jane and I fell in love with them.

While Jane was checking out, I overheard her conversation with the cashier, an older gentleman wearing a suit that was a little baggy on him. He asked, "Is she doing okay? I lost someone very close to me from cancer."

Jane smiled. "She's doing great. She's just been in the house too long, and I can see her becoming depressed. I drag her around to safe spots, like here and yarn stores, to get her spirits up and change her view a bit."

The man smiled. "I'm glad to hear that she's doing well."

"She'll be fine," Jane said. "She just needed a little adventure today."

Just when I thought I wouldn't make it any longer, Jane steered me into the restaurant for lunch. Little mugs of chicken stock started the meal with little bits of toasted bread. There was a bridal party going on and even a fashion show of the latest designs. Tall women in different fancy dresses walked around and showed off what a person could buy around the store.

I had never been in a department store with Neiman Marcus's prices or had food like that in a department store.

By the end of the shopping excursion, I was done. I crawled into Jane's car and sat in silence on the way home. I may have even gone to sleep.

One of the things that struck me was, yes, I was bald. Yes, I was emaciated and sickly. Yes, I looked wretched, but when I was with Jane—someone who had fought breast cancer and won, someone who had an elective double-mastectomy at a rather young age—I felt understood and supported. It was okay I was bald. She would know what to say if someone said anything rude. She knew that I needed to get out of the house. She knew I was depressed and exhausted, but she also knew an adventure would do me good.

Dose 6

Dad drove me to dose 6. That was the last day I lived in his house during treatment. As we got into the car to go, the rain was pouring down. As we got closer and closer to Roxborough and Manayunk, the rain was in sheets, and trees had come down all over the roads. Roads were flooded out, and traffic was everywhere. Dad would use route A to get to the medical center, only to find a tree across the road and detour to route B. By the time we were on route G or route H, I was about two hours late for my appointment and was fretting. To get me to forget my worries a little, Dad told me this joke:

> A man and his wife were in the middle of Death Valley. They had driven exactly halfway when the man stopped the car, leaned over his wife, and opened the passenger door, telling his wife to get out. She said she didn't want to. But because he insisted, she did.
>
> He slammed the door behind her, locked it and said, "Consider this a divorce," and drove away. Her purse was still in the car. She had no water, no money, no cell phone, and was in the exact center of Death Valley.
>
> She started to walk, but she had no idea where she was going or in what direction she was headed.

Up ahead, she saw something shiny in the sand. Thinking it was a mirage, the woman didn't pay any attention until she was right on top of it. It was a bit of brass. Leaning down and brushing a bit of the sand away, she found that the object was bigger than a coin. As she dug it out, and rubbed it clean, she realized it was an old-fashioned oil lamp. She rubbed the engraving on the side, trying to make it clearer to find it out if it was tiny lettering or scrollwork, and out popped a genie, who, of course, gave her three wishes. But he said, "Be careful, because whatever you wish for, the person you hate most in the world gets double."

"Okay," she said. "For my first wish, I want a top-of-the-line, fancy car, like a Tesla, and I want it to never run out of gas, and I want it to never break down."

"Okay," the genie replied. "Just remember that the person you hate the most gets two cars."

"That's fine," she said.

And poof there was a silver Tesla with a full tank of gas. "Hop in," she said to the genie, as she maneuvered the car back to the road and picked a direction out of the desert.

"For my next wish," she said.

"Be careful, the person you hate the most in the world gets two," the genie replied.

"For my next wish," she continued, "I want a suitcase that is full of money and no matter how much I take out of it, whenever it's closed, it will be restocked with money. That way, I will always have enough for everything."

"Okay," the genie said, "but the person you hate the most will get two of them."

"That's fine," she said. "My husband can have two cars and two magic suitcases. That's fine."

Once outside Death Valley, she started to program a hospital into the Tesla's GPS. If the genie thought this odd, he didn't say anything.

When they got to the hospital, she parked the car and checked the trunk for her money suitcase. It was there. She pulled a whole wad out and put it in her front pocket. Again, if the genie thought this weird, he didn't say anything. Then, she had the genie come with her to the sliding doors in front of the entrance of the emergency room.

"If I wish for anything, the person I hate most will get double?" she asked the genie.

He nodded. "Double."

"For my third wish," she said to the genie, "I want you to beat me half to death."

When Dad was done with the joke, he said, "I guess that it's not so funny when chemo beats you half to death."

"I wouldn't wish this, not even halved, on the person I hate most in the world."

"Yeah," Dad said, "who do you hate most in the world?"

I paused and said, "Probably some stupid politician. But even if I am beaten half to death …" I said.

"Yeah?" Dad asked.

"I don't have a miracle Tesla or a suitcase that is going to pay for all of this and my medical insurance in the future. It also will not pay for me to change my life, however I choose, after all of this is over."

Dad was quiet after this, and we sat in silence as he drove. Then he broke the quiet by saying, "But there will be life after this, and that's worth all of it."

"If you say so," I replied.

He said, "I know so," and rubbed my left knee with his hand.

***

Dose 6 went into my left arm, but they couldn't find a vein. This became a theme for chemotherapy. Once a vein was used, the D drug of ABVD would destroy it and keep it from being used again. One of the nurses said that D was like an ice pick gouging the vein and ripping up the inside as it traveled to my heart and the rest of my body. Once one of my veins took the chemo, that vein turned hard and crunchy-bumpy beneath my skin. I would have visitors like Whitherspoon and Aubrey and Jean roll their fingers over my skin and feel the enlarged, hardened, and bumpy line under my skin. They would cringe. Other people would say, "No, thank you. I trust you. It's gross."

Why do we do that? Look at people and say, "Oh my gosh! This smells so disgusting! Smell it." Or "This tastes nasty. You try it." Or, "This feels gross. Here, touch my arm right here."

The problem with enlarged, hardened, and bumpy veins, besides the obvious—veins aren't supposed to be enlarged, hardened, or bumpy—they also hurt. All the time. There were weird aches, centralized in a thin line from wherever the insertion was all the way into deep sections of my armpit that I didn't even know existed.

One only has so many accessible veins in one's arms. With dose 6, they got creative. They entered my vascular system in the left bicep using a ridiculously tiny needle with two blue wings on the side, called a butterfly needle. It was used on children since it is so tiny. This particular needle was jammed into a vein under my arm, just down the line from my armpit.

When I saw Dr. N after this dose, I lifted up my arm and showed her the aftereffects. A spider-web-like kind of grid had formed under my left arm; it consisted of dark brown lines and white spaces between the lines. I asked Dr. N, "Is this a problem?"

She looked at it and didn't mask her horror. "Why didn't they use a bigger vein?"

"They couldn't find one."

The not-so-fun effect of the spider web? Each brown line ached the way the veins did. Vein pain was something we measured in my house when I was in chemo. Ten meant unbearable, and I would be crying. One meant "What's vein pain? That just sounds weird." I lived at seven and eight most of the time, waiting for a ten, which I imagined would take a blown vein and the chemo just spilling out into no man's land. I'm sure that had to hurt like hell. But since that never happened, I never reached a ten. There were times when I cried silent tears from vein pain. That's when Mom would boil that white canvas pillow filled with sand, pull it out of the boiling water with tongs, and wrap it around my arms with just a towel to protect me from the intense heat. When I was focused on the heat, the vein pain wasn't so bad.

***

During chemotherapy, the nurses used an ice pack to fool my body into thinking that the burning in my vein from the chemo was actually the burning from the ice pack. The moment they started the D, they'd place an ice pack on the burning vein, and my body would be able to tolerate all that was going on. The burning cold masked the burning heat of the D. I would even look at the ice pack and think, "The cold burn makes the chemo burn not as noticeable." Even with my eyes seeing the reality of the situation, my body was still fooled.

***

While I was in the waiting room, waiting to be called through the door of hell to get my dose 6, there was a white young man with short, blond hair in one of the chairs against the opposing wall. He looked to be in his mid-twenties. Someone around his age was with him. She had long, blond, curly hair, and she looked pissed off. I caught a few of her words, and they were harsh and blaming. I picked up she was hateful because she had to be there with him as he got his chemotherapy. My heart went out to him, but I didn't know what to say.

I eventually got called through the door to hell and put in a chemo chair. That was when they stabbed the vein in my bicep. While they were pouring my pre-chemo cocktail into my IV, there was the clear sound of retching from the other room.

The nurse with me sighed and said, "No matter what we do, every time, the poor guy gets sick. That's his sister in there with him. It would be better for him to be alone than be with her. She blames him for all of this. He's just so miserable."

Mom looked at me and said, "Can I go visit with him?"

"Absolutely," I replied. "Do what you can for him. I'm just going to be knocked out from these drugs."

I sat and stared and stopped trying to stay awake. Mom walked next door and talked to the guy. She told him about Marinol and that he had to ask for it. She told him how rough I was having it and that it was normal. She talked to him about all she had learned from walking through Hodgkin's with me, and all that we found helpful along the way. She wrote down notes for him because she knew he would probably forget, like I did. She sat with him and supported him in ways his sister couldn't.

Long after that meeting, Mom continued to talk about that guy. She talked about how worried she was for him and how good it felt to support him.

I suggested she volunteer with the University of Benjamin Franklin when I recovered. I said she could support other people going through what I had gone through. She was now, practically, an expert in

Hodgkin's lymphoma. She said she wasn't credentialed, and she didn't believe she would be wanted. She never pursued it for whatever reason—maybe it would be too hard to go back into the chemo rooms or maybe she really believed she wouldn't be helpful. When I asked her about it, she wasn't comfortable with the conversation.

I too wonder about that guy. I wonder if he was ever able to salvage his relationship with his sister. I wonder if he wanted to. I wonder how he changed as a result of his walk through Hodgkin's.

Occasionally, I wonder about how our lives intersected because we were in adjacent chemotherapy rooms, and my mom was able to share the compassion she always had for me with him as well.

***

That night after they used my bicep, I went home, feeling wretched. That was usual. Around bedtime, I was sitting on my bed, trying to prepare my belly for the Fragmin. But I had the shakes.

I'm somewhat used to them. When I was little, before I threw up, or if I was peeing, or sitting on the toilet waiting to be sick, my legs would start to shake and then bounce. The balls of my feet would be firmly planted to the ground, but my legs would do this uncontrollable, jerky, bouncing movement.

That night, as I was sitting on my bed, trying to wipe my belly with the alcohol swab, my arms and legs started to shake violently. I couldn't hold onto the alcohol pad, and it dropped to the bed.

I looked at Mom, who was watching me from the doorway. She watched me shoot myself in the belly every night. I said, "I don't know if I will be able to do this tonight."

Mom walked in. She took a new alcohol pad and wiped a spot on my belly. Then she said, "I don't think I can do this either." She picked up the needle that I had already prepared. She started to aim the needle at my belly, but then said, "I can't. I can't do it."

"Neither can I," I replied, as my arms and legs continued to shake, shiver, and mildly bounce around on the bed. I was not able to control my movements.

Mom climbed on the bed and said, "You are going to have to."

"How?" I asked.

She wrapped her arms around my chest and arms and put her legs around my spastic bouncing ones. "Okay, I'm going to hold you tight, and let's see if it's enough for you to inject yourself."

Mom squeezed. I put the needle to my belly in the area she had swabbed, took a deep breath, looked away, and pushed the plunger down. All this took less than ten seconds to accomplish, which was good, because Mom wasn't able to stop my bouncing for much longer than that.

Birthday Dose: Dose 7

Because I place significance on numbers, when my age became those numbers, I believed things were supposed to be better during that year. Take twenty-four. I turned twenty-four on the twenty-fourth. I thought that was my worst year. I lost my apartment to a fire, my heart was stomped on by a not-so-wonderful guy, and I stopped trying to hear from God for most of that year and into the next.[15]

There are two other numbers on which I place significance: thirty-four and forty-two. John Vanbiesbrouck's number was thirty-four; he was the goalie of the New York Rangers, but at that point in their history, their nickname was the "Strangers" because Phil Esposito kept trading guys off the team. During games, they would put a mic on Beezer, and you could hear what the guys were saying to each other down on the ice. They could do it because Beezer didn't swear, but then other guys would skate near him, and they would have to turn it off when those other players pulled out potty words. Ever since my middle school and college obsession over John Vanbiesbrouck, later the goalie for the Philadelphia Flyers, I'd had high expectations for the number thirty-four.[16]

The day I turned thirty-four, I received dose 7.

---

[15] My thinking there was I would rather not hear from God at all than to think I was hearing from God and be wrong.

[16] The next portentous age is forty-two. I've believed that ever since I read Douglas Adams's *The Hitchhiker's Guide to the Galaxy* in my early twenties and learned that forty-two is the answer to life, the universe, and everything. I do find myself a little troubled as forty-two approaches. Twenty-four sucked. Thirty-four was not so great; it was better, yes, but it wasn't fantastic. I think my expectations for forty-two might set it up for failure; or perhaps, because I expect one crappy year, it will be one of the best.

Thirty-three was diagnosis and chemo. Thirty-four was chemotherapy and recovery. It was the year I didn't die. It was the year I lived.

The day I turned thirty-four, I had chemo in a bed, rather than one of those chemo chairs that lies almost flat. Mom said that I did worse in a bed than a chemo chair. I don't know why she thought that, but she did.

What was different about the birthday dose was I watched it go in. I usually watched them root around looking for a spot to jab the vein. Once the needle was in, I rarely looked down to see what the nurses were doing. I would talk to others and sit while the steroids, Ativan, Zofran, and other pre-chemo cocktail dripped into my arm. On my birthday, when the nurse said it was time for the chemo, I roused myself from the stupor pre-chemo cocktails elicited. This time, I stared at my arm. The nurse undid the IV drip and attached the first plunger, which was bright red, a thick cherry red, the kind of red Swedish Fish would be if you melted them down. Then there were two other plungers of clear liquid, and the last was the drip. It was the D of ABVD. It burned as it went in; it burned and ripped up the veins. The D is what left my veins hard and crunchy, able to be felt with little effort weeks after chemo was over. The D left my arms aching in a way that's hard to describe. It was a sharp ache, one that made me want to rub the vein to soothe it, but it was thin, thinner than a pencil width. It was more like a number-three knitting needle. The pain runs up the length of your arm—sharp, stabbing, and inconsolable.

It had been my modus operandi to eat a popsicle while getting chemo, because we had been informed that something cold in my mouth would close the nerve endings and stop some of the chemo from getting into my mouth, thereby reducing some of the pain in the days afterward when my salivary glands kicked into gear. Mom would go up to the breast-cancer floor and find popsicles. Rarely did she come back with cherry, the only kind of popsicle flavor I really liked. I can't stand fake grape flavor. Once when I was little, I threw up orange soda, so orange flavor is not my favorite either. However, eating cold was necessary, so Mom approached me.

Something happened in my belly as I watched the chemo go in. I don't know if it was horror, just a psychobiological reaction, or if it was all in my head, but I didn't feel so good after watching. I was queasy and lightheaded. Mom came at me, popsicle outstretched.

"No, I don't want it," I said.

"You have to eat it," she insisted. "It's better for you to have it to cut down on the chemo's side effects."

"No," I shook my head.

But Mom was insistent and standing over me. She shoved the popsicle in my mouth, and I was forced to taste all of its fake orangeness. Not even five minutes later, I said, "I'm going to be sick." One of those kidney-shaped bowls was put in front of my mouth and without realizing what was going on—thanks to the mind-altering effects of the Benadryl, Ativan, and steroids—I chucked up all of the popsicle.

Dad made that face he makes when he's a little grossed out; his eyebrows scrunched, and a "whoosh," sound came out of his mouth.

The nurse said to my mom, "Well, she did say she didn't want it."

The rest of that dose was a blur. I didn't remember it. When this picture arrived in my inbox a couple of days later, I looked at mom and said, "I ate after I threw up?"

"You don't remember?" she replied. Then she told me that I'd wanted pizza, of all things, and Dad went down and got it for me. She said I ate two slices of pizza, and for a birthday dessert, the nurses brought me this little Danish thing. Apparently, I gobbled it all right up.

"Even after being sick?" I asked.

"Being sick didn't even faze you. You got hungry and wanted food."

"How many times did I get up to go to the bathroom?" I asked.

"Oh, around three or four," Mom said.

I had no recollection of that either.

***

I chose not to celebrate my birthday that year. I put it off until I was feeling better, and then it wasn't a celebration of the day of my birth, but a celebration that I was alive.

***

Before I received the birthday dose, I met with Dr. N. It was a little weird because it was my last pre-chemo meeting. The next time I had chemo, dose 8, Dr. N and her family would be in Italy for a one-month vacation. The nurses would run the blood tests, check everything, and administer dose 8 without her. Then, as would have happened had she been around, I wouldn't see her again until after my body was rescanned one month after chemo ended.

However, Dr. N asked me to come back the day after my birthday dose, as she sometimes did, so I could get a shot of Neulasta. At the hospital, they discovered how dangerously low my blood count had dropped. They gave me a shot of Neupogin, which apparently made my white blood count soar to crazy heights, but the second week, it plummeted scary low. Dr. N didn't want me to have too many white blood cells, because that would cause other problems. Instead, she chose Neulasta; it was like Neupogin, only slow releasing. My blood count dropped the second week after my dose. Neulasta the day after treatment would allow my body to have support for the two weeks when the chemo was destroying my blood cells; Neulasta would go into action, helping me create blood cells as chemo destroyed them. That way, my white blood cell count would never get completely out of control.

Dose 7 didn't go well, as I stated above. I threw up. Mom didn't think I'd received all of the medication I needed to help my body fight the chemo's effects. The nurse was uncommunicative and unreceptive to Mom's concerns. Mom called Dr. N the night after the dose and told her how badly things had gone.

When I showed up for the Neulasta the next day, one of the nurses told me not to leave immediately afterward. Dr. N wanted to talk to me. I waited with my father. I was wearing the outfit I usually wore when I was at home: tank top, navy blue cotton hoodie, and my favorite pajama bottoms—a pair of light blue, almost green, Life is Good cotton pants that had tea cups all over them in jaunty angles. Each cup had a tea bag, indicated by a black string, and a white tag flopping off the side.

When Dr. N came out, she took one look at me and yelled, "You're in your pajamas!"

Without even thinking, I replied in a similar tone. "I feel like shit!"

She asked what had happened the day before and what was going on now. But we were standing right in front of the nurse with whom Mom had the grievance. I didn't feel like I could tell Dr. N the truth. I repeated that I had thrown up and that I felt like crap. She nodded and hugged me, wishing me luck for dose 8.

Later, when Dr. N got back from her vacation, I told her we had been standing right in front of the offending nurse, and I didn't feel right talking about her.

Dr. N chewed on the side of her mouth and nodded her head. "So it was bad?" she asked.

"It wasn't the worst one. That was dose 8."

Speed Bump

"It's a speed bump," my pastor, Bruce, had said before my treatment started.

I looked at him. The diagnosis was almost in, and I "knew," at least I was barely admitting to myself, that I had cancer.

Bruce said, "Speed bumps are jarring, and you think you'll lose the bottom of your car and you wonder if all is all right, but this is just a speed bump."

Just a speed bump.

It was just a speed bump when my hair fell out. My lack of strength, my inability to think or make my own decisions or make any type of decision at all were all speed bumps.

If it was a speed bump, I wondered if the bottom had dropped out, my exhaust had been ripped off, and if my muffler was dragging behind.

There were a set of rubber speed bumps in the middle of the road on the way to the medical building, near the Starbucks and the University of Benjamin Franklin bookstore. As I was going to the medical building to meet with Dr. K and Dr. N, I would stare out the window at the black-and-yellow rubber speed bumps, which broke up the walkway where the UBF students had the right of way.

Speed bump, I would think as we went over it. *This is just a speed bump.*

We drove over those rubber speed bumps with every dose. We drove over them the day after the dose, when I sometimes had to get a shot of Neulasta. When I went to the emergency room or when Erin was visiting, there were more trips over the rubber speed bumps in the road.

As we drove into the city for dose 7, Dad crossed over Market and Chestnut to Spruce. We passed the place where students cross, and the rubber speed bumps we had been going over every week were gone. Nothing. Not there.

I looked down at the road where they used to be.

"No speed bumps," I said to my dad.

"One has to wonder why not," he replied.

Dread had been filling me. It was my birthday, yes, but it was also dose 7. Dose 7. It would kill me, and I would be miserable.

The speed bump had not returned by the time we traveled down the road to the hospital, and the medical building loomed large and smelly in front of us for dose 8. It wasn't until later that they built official asphalt speed bumps that would never go away.

Only that day, when the speed bumps were gone, even in all of my dread, I looked at the road and smiled. I found a moment of hope, the kind of hope I feel when I first smell spring after a particularly harsh winter.

Dose 8

It was the last dose. Tuesday, September 7. I sat outside the door of hell, anticipating the call into room 10. A white family (a mom and dad and son) sat under the picture on the wall. The son, probably a freshman in college, was the patient; I could tell by his bracelet—plastic, white, and marked with his birthday and a special patient number given to him by the hospital. Of course, I couldn't see all of that on his bracelet. All

I had to do was look down at my own to know what was on his. He still had his blond hair.

I was against the other wall, the one with the windows that overlooked the drop down to the second floor. My dad was next to me. Both families were eavesdropping on each other.

I complained to my father that I had to buy size 10 pants, because I had chemo bloat. Although my legs were sticks, nothing but 10s would close around my belly, though my legs swam in the stretchy legs of jeans, which were supposed to hug. Dad looked down at me and said, "Where do you buy Barbie pants? At a Barbie store in the mall?"

I shook my head, looking not at Dad but straight ahead, and said, "No, Dad. I buy my Barbie pants on consignment."

The mother of the boy paused and said, "Did you talk to your economics professor? I want to make sure you have everything you need to get everything done."

"Mom," the boy said, "I'll go to class Thursday. I will get the work done."

No, you won't, I wanted to say. You won't. The drugs will kill you. They will throw you down a hole; you won't be able to breathe, you won't know who you are, what you are saying. You won't be able to think. In about a week, you will be walking out of the bathroom and down the hall, back to the pink couch you have lived on all summer, and you will think,

> *I am standing up. One foot is stepping. Oh, and look there is the other foot. It too is walking. How did I get here? Did I just pee? I must have. I must have just gone to the bathroom. Oh, the couch. The couch. How far you are from the bathroom.*

And that will be the only cognizant thought for the day.

The next day, you will be at the bottom of a massive hole, a grave, and there will be no ladder, no way out. But somehow, you dig your boney fingers into the dirt walls. You clutch at rocks and muck to crawl, slowly, to the top, to see the sun and the trees out the window. *It's summer, right? Still?* Yes, it's still summer.

The very next week, right after you have surfaced, you will get back in the car, and they will kill you again. And the week after that, you'll walk from the bathroom and have your first cognizant thought about … walking.

How could I tell this kid all of that? How could I tell these parents what they were about to go through?

I didn't say anything as I walked through the door to hell. Perhaps he would be able to study economics.

***

I was in the room, in the armchair that lies almost flat when fully reclined.

The nurse was going for a vein. Good luck to her. All of my veins were crunchy and hard below my skin. One in my bicep had been mad since dose 6; it was bloated, black, and blue, with spider veins all around it and a weird dark web pattern under my armpit.

For dose 8, the first stab was a jab all around the area, which yielded nothing. Like kids playing in a pool where swimming underwater meant you couldn't be tagged "it," my veins saw the needle coming. They would duck and hide. No amount of rooting around would yield "blood return."

I didn't mind the needle fishing around. Go ahead, shove it in there. Nope, no vein yet. Doesn't hurt. Go ahead, poke around in there.

Needle two. Nothing but some deep prods.

Needle number three. Still nothing. Now Mom and Dad were in pain. Dad's face had turned a sick olive, and he paced the hallway. Mom was freaking out. Seriously. She went to find a doctor. What could the doctors do? They hadn't touched a needle in years. She went out to the receptionist, tears streaming down her face, speaking so the whole waiting room could hear, yelling at the check-in guy:

"They're hurting her. Hurting her, and they can't find a vein. Get a doctor. I know Dr. N is in Italy. Get someone! Someone! They're hurting her!" Then she came back and found me waiting for attempt number four.

I was still sitting in the chair. I looked at the nurse who was like a mom to everyone, one of those moms who tells you the truth when you don't want to hear it. She said, "If we don't get it on this try, we're sending you home."

Yes! I would get out of dose 8 and I wouldn't have to do any more.

But a different nurse came in, and she found a vein I never knew I had on the under part of my left wrist. She felt along the bone in the turkey leg of my forearm and shoved her needle in, getting good blood return.

"Shit," I said as the pain of creating an emergency entrance ramp onto the superhighway of my circulatory system registered.

The nurse looked at me, upset, "What?"

"I was hoping you weren't going to find one."

Dad spoke for me. "Someone made the mistake of saying that if you didn't get in, we would be going home without the chemo."

The nurse turned back to me and shook her head. "You are funny."

They hooked me up to the pre-chemo cocktail, the drugs that trick your body into thinking chemo isn't all bad.

The mom of the nurses, wearing the navy blue scrubs all the chemo nurses wore, turned to me and said, "It would be much easier if you had a port."

Seriously? thought my Ativan and Benadryl groggy head.

I grabbed my shirt and pulled down the collar. "I did," I said, exposing the scar above my left breast, maybe even exposing a bit of my boob—I was high; who knew what I was doing? "My body rejected it. Blood clots. Hospitalized for nine days."

She said nothing. Maybe my words were slurred. Maybe I only said it in my head.

Duct Tape

Around dose 7 or 8, I informed my family about my intentions. I wanted them to be completely clear about my decision, if it came down to it.

There was not going to be another dose after dose 8. Dose 8 would be it. I'd signed up for four rounds, eight doses; anything beyond that wasn't going to happen.

I told my mom and then I told my dad. My mom's reaction was silence. My dad's was, "Don't tell your mom that; it will just stress her out."

A little later he said, "So, you're not going beyond dose eight?"

"Nope," I replied definitively.

"That's what they make duct tape for," he replied.

"What?" I asked.

"Duct tape," he said. "I will strap your hands and feet together and throw you in the backseat of my car. You won't have any choice."

When Dr. N found out I had decided that I wasn't doing any more rounds, she said, "That's okay. I would have admitted you to the hospital and told them you were a flight risk. That would have taken care of the issue as well."

***

Thankfully it didn't come to that. Eight doses were all that my body had to endure.

I gave myself from September 7, the day of the last dose, to November 1 to recover, and then I went back to work.

RECOVERY

Roller Coasters

You know how I said I don't wait very well?

When I was little, my dad, his second wife, and her family used to go to amusement parks. My father was a big fan of roller coasters. He still is. I, however, find the wait overwhelming. When I was little, waiting in the maze that corrals riders closer and closer to the death cars, my stomach would flip over and over. My teeth would sometimes chatter. I would be in a constant debate with myself: *should I or shouldn't I?* If I didn't and just stepped right through the cars to the safety of solid ground, I would feel a coward, a wimp, someone scared of what is supposed to be a totally exciting and thrilling experience. Once on the ride, strapped in and clicking up the first hill, I would look at the stairs that led back down off the ride and think, *It's not too late. I can still take those down and get off this thing.*

I have experienced harrowing roller-coaster rides in my life. Some were not personal, like the guy who pulled a Superman off the Superman ride in Massachusetts and died. There were problems with the G-forces, and they had closed the ride to figure them out. They decided to speed the ride up to get past some of the glitches. It was one of those hanging feet rides and on a curve, with the increased speed, the guy was pulled right out of his seat.

Other roller-coaster moments were my own harrowing experiences, like the time I was on Dorney Park's wooden roller coaster, named Hercules. According to DorneyPark.com, Hercules was ninety-five feet tall and had a 151-foot drop. If I remember correctly, at the time, it was the highest drop of any wooden roller coaster. I was with my dad, and he was much bigger than I was. I was a scrawny thirteen or so at the time. The attendants pulled the lap bar down, and it was snug on my dad, but not so much on me. When we went down the drop, I wound up standing with the bar resting on my thighs.

The summer of chemotherapy was the summer Universal opened Hogwarts and Harry Potter land in Orlando. *AAA World* magazine had a whole write-up about it. Of course I read it, being a Harry Potter fan and belonging to Ravenclaw myself. As the article talked about the thrills of playing Quidditch and riding a broomstick, I put it together. As each dose day came close, I found myself reacting to the anticipation of the chemo cocktail in much the same way as I had to roller coasters. There is nothing fun about torturing oneself. There is nothing fun in feeling the expectation to be someone you aren't. That was the moment I said, "I am done with roller coasters."

Of course that thought played with my head in another way. I began to fret about having children; what if my children love roller coasters and want to go on them? After all, they will have some of my father's genes. I decided roller coasters would be my husband's area. Not only was I dreaming of a man with dark hair, blue eyes, and a fondness for drinking tea, but I now wanted a willing roller coaster participant who did not expect me to participate with him. But that was only if kids were involved.

Now, let me put a caveat on all of this, lest you think me a total wimp.

I have jumped off rocks into the ocean from great heights. I have put my foot over the edge of the Cliffs of Moher in Ireland (and have the photos to prove it). I have swum in the Atlantic Ocean off the North Shore of Boston in February, when there was still snow on the ground.

If there is no wait time and we do it *now* without giving my brain a chance to think or rationalize, then I am willing to try anything. But if you put me in a car and drive me to an airport (always a place of high stress for me), put me into a jumpsuit, strap me into the plane, and explain I will have to jump out in thirty minutes, I will be okay for about five of those thirty minutes. If you teleport me to the jump site and give me no time think about it, great—I'll do it. If you leave room for think time, then no, it's not happening. That's why I run and jump directly into ocean the second I get there, why I dive into pools instead of getting in slowly. It's why I rarely tell guys how I feel about them; I'm too concerned about the consequences to be bold enough to say what I feel.

That day, I made the decision to not ride roller coasters, unless … unless there is no line of torture to wait on. Then I reserve the right to change my mind.

Yom Kippur

It was September 17, not yet the twenty-first; I was not yet allowed to get off the Neutropene diet, not yet allowed to eat uncooked or fresh fruit and vegetables. But I was close, so close. Just four days away.

Mom and I drove Aunt Grace, the nonagenarian who wasn't really an aunt but had been in the family so long she was of course an aunt, to my real aunt's house for Yom Kippur.

I sat in the front. Going to visit my family always makes me a bit uncomfortable. And I love my family, I do. They drive me insane at times, and there are a few I naturally gravitate toward, like in all families.

I got out of the car and instead of braving the grass, I walked a little down the street to the driveway. I moved slowly, cautiously. Each step was uncertain. Damn neuropathy. Damn useless right leg.

My head was gleaming, an ever humbling beacon—an ever-present reminder of how weak and sick the chemo had made me and of how ugly I was.

Mom came around the other side of the car and helped Aunt Grace get out. Holding her arm out, Aunt Grace leaned against her as they crossed the front yard.

As I bumbled along, barely faster than the ninety-year-old, I found that I was jealous of Aunt Grace because Mom was holding her up. I wanted Mom's protection too.

As I got about halfway down the drive, Wendy stuck her head out the front door, watching my turtle-like progress.

I looked at her. Perhaps I smiled, but only for a second, because instead of coming out and giving me her arm to help me along, or instead of going to help Mom with Aunt Grace, she looked at my sick frame and ugly head and yelled, "Hey, Baldy!"

I said nothing. I'm sure my face registered hurt and anger because I am unable of hiding my feelings.

When I got to the door, I looked Wendy in the face and for the first time in my life, I stood up to her force.

"I need you to know I'm really self-conscious about my head."

She looked at me in shock for about two seconds and then said, "No, you're not. You're not. If you were, you would be wearing a scarf, a wig, or something."

I nodded at her cluelessness and walked into the house. I decided it wasn't worth fighting insensitivity.

Kim's Well Party

When I was released from oncology and told I could start eating fresh fruit and vegetables again, Mom threw me a party. She catered it from a restaurant down the road, which put together meat and vegetable trays. We also had at least two platters of my favorite cookies, the butter-sugar kind that are half dipped in chocolate and then dunked in sprinkles or nonpareils.

More than one hundred people were invited, and about seventy-five wandered in and out throughout the day.

I was blown over when my friend Jessica walked in the door. She lived in Buffalo and had come down that morning, picking up her mother in Cortland (just outside of Ithaca) along the way. Jess said it had been an eight-hour trip.

Her mother said, "We would have been here sooner. I'm working on a project for you. I wanted to finish it to bring it to you, but I'm going to have to mail it."[17]

"Thank you, but your being here means everything," I said. "You don't have to send me anything."

"Whatever," Jess replied, laughing.

Jess and I spent some time together on the couch in my living room. We talked about my illness and how I was doing. We got caught up on what was going on in her life and what her current struggles were. Jess's and her mom's presence at the party touched me deeply.

---

[17] Jess's mother sent me a package a little later. It was an amazing handmade quilt. She said in the note when she heard I was sick, she and her whole family were devastated. By working on the quilt, she was able to keep me at the forefront of her mind, heart, and prayers.

There were family members in the back den. There were Boon Win colleagues in the living room. There were church friends in the kitchen, and Lancaster friends in the study. My house was overflowing with people.

At one point, one of mom's knitting friends came in. She was a lovely black woman with a soft voice and a silent strength. She liked to get her head shaved about once every two weeks, leaving her silver hair laying flat along her well-shaped head. She and I had a bet about whose hair would be longer at this party. Months before I was done with treatment, we each put a ten-dollar bill in a brass container in the den. I said there was no way my hair would be longer than hers and she said hers would be way shorter than mine. Brenda went to the barber the morning of the party and had him cut her hair really short just to be sure that she would win the bet.

At different times, my father and Aubrey called me over and said, "Where did all these people come from?"

"They're friends," I said. "They helped carry me through."

Later I told Dad I had been a little overwhelmed by the number of people in my house. Dad laughed and said, "I was too. It's amazing the amount of people you know and keep in touch with."

At the end of the night, my legs were aching, and I could barely stand. I wanted to get up and help my mom clean up, but she made me stay on the couch.

"I've thrown parties before and cleaned them up on my own," she said. "I don't want to worry about you overdoing yourself to help me."

The neighbor down the street helped her clean up.

I didn't celebrate my birthday that year, although my Aunt Maureen had insisted I open a birthday gift from her and my cousins. This party was a celebration of my life. It was a way of acknowledging all I had gone through to keep air going in and out of my body, to keep my heart beating, and to keep my lymph nodes from killing me.

I was alive, and I wanted to have as many people around me as possible to celebrate that fact.

Post-Cancer Fertility Study

As soon as I was released from oncology, I went back to the fertility specialists. I was still getting hot flashes from the medication they'd given me to stop my period, and I was still very weak. However, I was able to eat a raw red pepper, and I was allowed to use a tampon when my period showed up again. That meant I could have an internal exam.

Again, the doctor had me disrobe. She rolled a condom onto the ultrasound wand and then put ultrasound gel on the wand. They turned down the lights and had me slide down on the examination table.

My uterus looked unchanged, she said. But where I'd had forty-six fertile spots in the first exam, I now had six on one ovary and five on the other—a total of eleven. And as time has passed since the chemotherapy, those low numbers remain consistent. I have between ten and thirteen spots whenever I am examined.

The doctor's response? "As soon as you are cleared to have children, you'd better get on that."

"Excuse me?" I said.

"You're thirty-four. You're fertile at present, but your count is low. The longer you wait, the harder it will be to get pregnant. As soon as you can, you better get on that. You are running out of time, and it's only going to get harder to get pregnant as you get older."

Anxiety and Other Side Effects

I went back to school on November 1. I entered the hallways, and they smelled exactly the same. Nothing had changed, and everything had changed.

I'd discovered another side effect from chemotherapy only a couple of days before I went back to work. I had been with Wendy and her family, eating outside at a metal table in the cold of October during a Halloween parade in her town. We were enjoying our dinner, and I was resting my tired arms on the table. The cold started to bother my fingers a little, and before I knew it, the middle finger on my right hand had turned a sick yellow color. Even the fingernail turned a wonky yellow-white color. The other fingers were flesh peach—not white, not yellow, a little pink, a healthy tone. But not my middle finger, and it hurt. It hurt in a weird, "I'm angry" way. When I touched it with the fingers on my left hand, my right middle finger was cold to the touch.

Feeling myself panic, I went in to the restroom. After I peed, I washed my hands in hot water and the effect quickly faded. As my finger stopped aching and returned to my normal coloring, I also started to calm down and the anxiety dissipated.

I called Dr. N the next day and talked to her nurse practitioner about what had happened. I explained the discoloration and the painful ache that filled the finger. I explained how I'd had my hands on a cold wrought-iron table that we were eating on outside.

She said, "It sounds like Raynaud's."

"What's that?" I asked.

"Another side effect of chemotherapy" was the reply.

I paused then said, "I really thought it could be leprosy. Is my finger going to fall off?"

The nurse practitioner chuckled and said, "No, no. Nothing like that. It's just that your blood vessels are messed up from the chemo."

"So, you're saying that this happens to some people after chemotherapy?"

"Yes," she said. "Yes it does."

"And my fingers aren't going to fall off?" I asked.

Again, she gave a small chuckle and then said, "No, not at all."

"How long will this last?" I asked.

She said, "It could be a couple of months. It could be the rest of your life."

Right. I had heard that before about my right leg: a couple of months or the rest of your life.

A few weeks later, at school, I walked up to Whitherspoon and showed her my hand. The middle finger again was flaming yellow; the color was unnatural.

"Check out this side effect," I said.

She turned to me hesitantly. After being grossed out by the crunchy vein under my skin, she wasn't looking forward to this one. I held out my hand, and her eyes widened. "What is wrong with you?"

I shrugged. "Apparently this happens. I've learned hot water helps it go away faster. I'm going to the faculty room, which has the only hot water in the building, if anyone is looking for me."

I walked down the hall a little to the Upper B planning room. I unlocked the door and didn't bother to turn on the light. I went over to the sink, turned the hot water tap, and waited about twenty seconds for the water gushing out to get warm. When it was, I shoved my right hand under the only warmth to be found in the building.

Not even a minute later, as I was massaging the finger and rubbing it with my left hand, the door opened. Doug, the science teacher, walked in saying, "Whitherspoon told me to come in here and look at your hand. She said that you have something abnormal going on."

I stepped back a little to give him a view of my hand. All of my fingers and the palm of my hand were a sharp pink from the water, except my middle finger. My middle finger was still a nasty dead-yellow, though pink was starting to show at the base and near the major knuckle in the middle.

Doug leaned over the sink, took a look, horror coming up on his white face with brown goatee, and shouted, "What the fuck is wrong with you?"

I laughed and said, "Side effect from chemotherapy. Hot water makes it go away faster."

"Did they tell you this might happen?" he asked, still appalled.

"Nope," I replied. "They did tell me you don't get something for nothing. I'm alive. My fingers are fucked up though."

As we were talking, I continued to rub my hands together, and the rest of the finger stopped being yellow as the pink spread from the bottom up to the fingernail.

"You are gross," Doug said as he left the room. "You better get someone to look at that."

"I have," I called after his turned back. "They say this is normal."

"Nothing about that is normal," he yelled, as the door slammed closed behind him.

***

I went to lunch, and Rob was sitting in a red recliner. It was on wheels and rolled smoothly. Rob, one of my English colleagues, was demonstrating the wonder of the recliner, as the chair rested back so far he was practically lying flat. I looked at him, and my lunch stuck in my throat. Then I said, "Way to play with the chemo chair."

Everyone stopped chewing.

"What?" Rob said.

"That thing you're sitting on. It's a chemo chair."

I looked around the lunchroom and asked, "How the hell did a chemo chair get up here?"

Awkward silence was my only response.

***

As I got further and further away from chemotherapy and gained a little more strength as time went on, Jean would ask me to do the dishes after dinner. I had more energy to deal with the students. But something else happened, something I was not expecting. I started to have panic attacks in school. When I was sitting on the back porch at Jean and Aubrey's or driving around, I was fine. But at school, with the activity and closed-in walls and halls, when I was surrounded by noise and some form of chaos, my body started to react.

One day I was standing in front of the blue lockers outside my classroom, and the world tilted a little to the right. It was like everyone was sliding down toward the bathrooms and the Bat Cave.

In panic, I reached up with both arms and grabbed the counter, which was a little lower than shoulder height.

Berry and Rob were out in the hallway with me. Berry said, "All right, Beam?"

"What is wrong with me?" I asked.

"You're better now. Your body is beginning to realize it's okay, and it now has energy to react to all that has happened to you."

I made an appointment with a nurse practitioner in Syndersville, who had been recommended by my landlord's daughter. When I went to see her the first time, I told her all that I had been through. I told her I was having anxiety, which she said was perfectly understandable. I told her my body was really sensitive to drugs and, since I'd been on SSRIs before, I didn't want one that made me sleepy. I told her Lexapro and Effexor conked me right out.

She said that Prozac wouldn't make me tired. "If anything," she said, "it will make you wired."

She put me on an adolescent dose since my body was so sensitive.

Taking the ten milligrams of Prozac, I would be okay most of the time, and then, out of nowhere, I would be slammed with anxiety, a full-on panic attack that I wasn't able to control.

I made another appointment with my nurse practitioner and said, "I think the ten milligrams is strong enough to take care of the beginning symptoms, but it's not strong enough to take care of the whole attack. I can get slammed with a major attack without any warning that it's coming. My arms get tingly, which is new for me, and I think about wanting to kill myself to end it quickly."

"Do you have a plan?" she asked. "Are you safe?"

"I just think in the moment, 'I could grab that whole bottle and take it all and be done with these things.' But then, I leave the room and breathe it out. When it passes I'm ashamed and stunned the idea was even as strong as it was."

The nurse practitioner said, "I want to hug you. You know what's going on. You are right. The Prozac is taking care of the little anxiety symptoms, but it's not strong enough to handle a big panic attack. I'm going to increase you to twenty milligrams, which is a low adult dose."

She said, "I'm going to be checking on you for the next couple of weeks, frequently. I want to talk about suicidality. As we increase medication, I want to know if it's still giving you these panic attacks that make you want to kill yourself. I'm hoping that as your body adjusts to twenty milligrams, all those thoughts will just go away."

All I wanted to do was sit out on the back porch with a book and never move.

I'd called Wendy a week earlier, to ask about the plans for a family event. She said she hadn't even thought about it. I said, "When you do, let me know what you need me to do."

The night before the said event, Wendy called. She gave me a list of what she wanted me to do. It had been a bad anxiety day. I was shaking, exhausted, and—let me be completely honest—a little scared to leave the house. It was hard enough to go to work and back home every day. Adding a grocery run or plans on top of that did me in. In addition, the next day was already pretty full. In the morning, I was meeting my father at the Christiana Mall; he was going to buy me a MacBook Pro, because I was applying to graduate schools so I could change my life. After that, I planned to go to Wendy's house.

I confronted Wendy for maybe the second time in my life. I said, "Are you really calling me one night before the event when I called you a week ago to ask what you needed?"

She lost it. I rarely tell Wendy what I think, and this is why. "Fine!" she said. "If you can't help me out and you are too busy to be useful, then I will just do it myself."

"Wendy, I'm just trying to figure out why you are calling me now, at seven o'clock on Saturday night, to tell me to figure out dessert and decorations." I added, "I have a lot going on right now," referring to the anxiety I was going through and my plans for the next day.

Her response was, "What can you possibly have going on?" and she went off on a long tirade listing all that she was responsible for.

I wanted to cut her off and say:

> Yeah, my grades might be in, and I don't have a husband and kids. However, the hallways are tilting down ahead of me and I feel like we're all going to slide down a steep slope. I've started to take anti-anxiety medicine that has changed my anxiety attacks. My upper arms tingle, my mind whirrs, and my arms and legs want to bounce off my body. My insides sink and I think, "I'm better off dead than living like this." I'm mad at God; in fact, I don't trust God, and I'm not even sure I want to talk to Him ever again. I want to change my life, stop teaching, but how does one do that without medical insurance? Oh, and I can't get my blasted brain to shut up, so it just goes over all these thoughts over and over and over.

I didn't say a word about what I was struggling with—they were my struggles, not hers. I listened as she threw her list at me, and when she was done, I said, "Wendy, I just want to talk about this." I wanted to explain to her what life post-chemo was like. I wanted her to understand how a great many things weren't okay, even though the chemo was no longer going into my body. I wanted to better understand where she was coming from, without the yelling and throwing blame at one another.

"No," she said. "You obviously are too busy, so I'll do it. Don't even bother." And she hung up the phone.

***

A couple of weeks later, at the beginning of July, I saw Dr. N. At that point, I was seeing her every three months. When she joined my dad, my mom, and me in the examination room, she smiled and said my test results were fine. She then asked how I was doing.

"I have diagnosed myself with PTSD," I said. I'd read through the list in the latest *Diagnostic and Statistical Manual of Mental Disorders* (DSM-TR-IV), which is published by the American Psychiatric Association and is used as the standard for classifying people's struggles. Looking through the criteria for diagnosis, I was certain I qualified.

Mom jumped in and said, "Actually we're calling it post-cancer trauma syndrome."

Dr. N smiled at Mom and said, "That's exactly what it is." She turned to me and said, "What are you doing about that?"

"I'm on twenty milligrams of Prozac," I replied.

"What are you doing about breakthrough anxiety?" she asked.

I looked at her, surprised. "How do you know about breakthrough anxiety?"

Breakthrough anxiety was just that. It was anxiety that came up and over the general sense of okay the Prozac created. Breakthrough anxiety came during extreme moments, like going to the oncologist, an anxiety-producing event for anyone.

She made a phish sound. "How could I not know about it? What are you doing about it?"

"One milligram of Klonopin,"[18] I replied.

"That works," she said.

I said, "My nurse practitioner said that I might be on Prozac for the rest of my life."

Dr. N nodded. "That happens. When you come to see me, be sure to take the Klonopin. I have one woman who has been out of treatment for eight years, but when she's coming up the elevator to come here, she still throws up."

"After eight years?" I asked.

Dr. N nodded her head and said, "Every time. Take the Klonopin."

---

[18] I took Klonopin as infrequently as possible those first couple of years out of treatment. It was only one milligram, but it still made me loopy and made me feel a little drunk. I took it in extreme situations, like when I was in airports or when family members told me I was flipping out and I just needed to chill. I now have a primary-care physician I adore. He's the greatest guy, and when we get together, we just get silly goofy. I told him about my issues with Klonopin, and he put me on a small dose of BuSpar when I need it for breakthrough anxiety. It's so much better. I don't feel drunk or loopy on it, and it just takes the edge off; however, I think it gives me ringing headaches. I would rather be anxious than headachey. I will say, being on Prozac long-term has messed with my libido. My primary-care physician hopes that Wellbutrin will fix that problem. It's really bad when you are taking medication to fix a side effect from a previous medication. It's sort of like what chemotherapy is all about: take all of these other side pills to help you cope with the poison they keep shoving into your system.

Vein Pain

Months after treatment was over, I might be sitting in a faculty meeting, in professional training, at a family dinner or walking down the hallway at school when my arm would start to ache. It was not my whole arm, just one small inch or sometimes a whole line going up the inside of my arm. It was a deep, deep ache that could only be one thing.

My veins.

One time, I sat with my hand just resting on my lap, and the vein near my wrist, on the side of my hand—one that is near the surface and was used a whole lot in the beginning—started to throb. It was just a small part of it. I could see the vein; it was raised a little and extended and hurting in a way I had never felt before, at least not before chemotherapy. I knew what it was and why it was, and I wanted to apologize to it:

> I'm sorry you are still grieving. I'm sorry you are still hurt. I expect you to be like my psyche—fine about everything that happened—but how can you be? You've been through trauma, like the rest of me. There isn't any Prozac that will make you feel better. I don't know what will. But in time, you too will forget what you've been through.

I hope all of me does.

Toilet Paper

I wasn't completely aware of all of the ways the medication that turned off my period had affected me. One day, after I was better, my uncle and aunt came down to Delaware to go to the Apple Store in the Christiana Mall. My uncle was talking to a Genius about how DOS would work on one of their machines. My aunt had finished what she needed to do there, so she and I went off to the bathroom.

My aunt was talking about a hot flash as we were leaving the bathroom, and I said, "Can I ask you a question? Only because of what was going on with me last summer."

"Sure," she said slowly. She's a very private person and doesn't discuss things like menopause symptoms easily.

"Do you ever find yourself shredding toilet paper?" I asked.

"What do you mean?" she asked.

"Well, when I was in the throes of menopause last summer, whenever I peed and wiped, I would shred toilet paper."

She swore and said, "I thought that was happening to me because your uncle was buying the cheap toilet paper at Costco."

Serge, Part 2

After my treatment was over and I was okay again and back at work, I went to a Friday night gathering at my church. I was standing by myself and worshipping when a tall white woman with blond hair came up and said, "You're Kim?"

I nodded.

She said, "I'm Serge's wife, Simone." Then she paused before adding, "Serge's not doing so well."

And I wept.

It was a Sunday in the spring, and Serge was up on the sixth floor of the Hospital of UBF.

When the elevator doors opened, and I stepped out, the smell was the same. But this time, it wasn't coming from me or my hospital room. I was just visiting.

I walked down the glass-lined hallway, and all of my memories assailed me. The last time I had been in that hallway, I was in a wheelchair being pushed by my mom. I'd lacked the strength to face the bright sunlight coming in the windows.

The day I went to see Serge, I walked directly in the sun, allowed its glare into my eyes, and my heart broke for the people in wheelchairs who were shading their eyes from the brightness. I walked past the nurse's station. Serge's wife was on the phone, and though I didn't fully recognize her, I knew it was she, because she teared up when she saw me and pointed me to Serge's room. I walked in.

The smell of urine hit me first. I paused and took in the number of family members present. But what I focused on, what I couldn't drag my eyes away from, was the yellow-skinned, shrunken-cheeked, spindle-limbed man with haunted eyes who sat on a reclining chair next to the hospital bed.

He stared at me a moment, as I did at him. The two of us did not recognize each other, and then he smiled and whispered, "You're Kim."

I nodded, and he started to cry. I tried to stop my own tears, but that wasn't possible. My throat tightened, and I had to force the words out in a whisper, "Here's the CD of the words from that night."

He tried to explain who I was to his family—the weird circumstances of our meeting—and somehow I was let into the family circle.

But what I felt the whole time was that I was pink-cheeked, and muscles were back on my bones. I had walked down the hallway and rode the elevator standing up. I had survived; I would live.

That was Serge's question. "Are you well? Is it all over for you?"

Four months, and I was done. Four months, and there was no more sickness, no more suffering.

I had time to go out into the hallway and talk to Simone. She was crying, but wouldn't let herself weep, although she wanted to. She needed to. She had just been informed that Serge had cancer in his brain, but she hadn't told him and didn't want him to know yet how wrong things still were. In fact, everyone in that room knew Serge had brain cancer, except Serge. While we were talking, one of his daughters came out and said, "Mom, he just peed."

"I'll clean him up," she replied and walked back into his hospital room.

When I prayed for him before I left, I knew in my heart that he had dignity, but I lacked faith that he would get well. When I hugged him, all I could feel were bones.

Serge died on Friday, June 3, 2011. His funeral and viewing were on a weekday morning. I had to teach, and since I'd had the year I had, if I were not at work for even one day without a good excuse, I wouldn't get paid.[19] It was with a sad heart I missed his funeral.

After his death, I felt like something was wrong. I was alive. I had air going in and out of my lungs. I loved the sound of the leaves as they

---

[19] Finances at this point were tight because I was about to start classes for a master's in counseling and the payment for classes was steep. If I missed a day of work, I would be docked about $200. Friends said they would give me one of their sick days to go to the funeral, but the main office said it didn't work like that.

danced in the breeze. In my heart I knew Serge was in heaven, and the lucky guy got to experience eternity before all of us.

We had been diagnosed at the same time, and I survived. I was a survivor. I would continue to take big risks in life. Serge would not have the opportunity to see his kids graduate, get married, or take risks with the lives he helped give them.

July 4

It was a year after my diagnosis and treatment. I was at Mom's. She was dating a man I really didn't like for a number of reasons. Only, I knew she was happy with him, and I wanted her to be happy.

I was still going for tests every three months, and I am never happy before CT or PET scans. I get cranky and miserable. This day was no exception.

I was upstairs, freaking out. Mom told Aunt Maureen to come up and talk to me. I was in the middle of a full-blown anxiety attack when she walked in. I was pacing around, flapping my hands about, trying to lose some of the excess energy. I was crying and hysterical. My body might have been freaking out, but I could understand some things quite rationally.

Aunt Maureen watched this for about fifteen seconds and said, "Is there something you can take?"

I said, "Yeah, but it makes me feel drunk, and I don't really like it."

"What is it for?" she asked.

"It's for when I have breakthrough anxiety, like now."

I continued to pace and flap my hands back and forth. Aunt Maureen watched for about ten seconds, and then she said, "I think you should take it."

I looked at her, "You do?"

"Will it make you feel better?"

"Yeah," I replied.

"Then take it," she said.

I agreed, went over to my stuff, found the bottle of Klonopin, and took one using the paper cup in the bathroom. I came back, still wigging out, and waited for the medication to kick in. I said to Aunt Maureen, "I really don't like Mom's boyfriend."

She replied, "You're all keyed up right now. You aren't thinking clearly. Don't form an opinion yet. Wait, and form an opinion later."

I wanted to get mad at her, but I knew there was no point in arguing. Having an anxiety attack makes you look irrational. It wasn't a spur of the moment thing. My brain flew through my reasons for not liking him, but I couldn't articulate them with my body acting that way. I could only nod in agreement, even though I didn't agree at all.

***

Back downstairs, I announced that I wasn't going to the fireworks. I was already keyed up. Why did I need to put myself into large crowds and listen to big booming noises for a couple of bright lights? I was content to sit on the pink couch in the back sunroom and enjoy the dark and quiet after the noise of having people over for the July 4 celebration.

I curled up on the sofa and bid people good-bye from there. Most of them were going to the fireworks. One neighbor, the husband of my mom's friend, decided not to go. He sat with me in the darkness of the den. He sat on the ottoman, as I curled on one couch cushion. He sat close, knowing that I was freaking out about the tests the next day and the meeting with the oncologist the day after. He looked at me and said, "You know what you are?"

"Weak?" I replied.

"You're not weak," he said. "Your body is reacting to outside stress. Your body is remembering what it's been through, and it's reacting. You, your spirit, and your soul are not reacting this way. You are a warrior. You have been through battle. You know what battle means, and you have come out the other side, victorious. You are a warrior. True warriors fear the battle, but they face it anyway. Tomorrow, you will face the tests. The day after, you will go into the BFU's Cancer Center. You will go in with your head high, because you are a warrior."

As he spoke, my throat got tight, and tears streamed down my cheeks. I wanted to argue with him, but what he was saying resonated deep inside and made sense. And when the time came, I took the CT scan and went into Dr. N's office with my head up even though my insides were jelly.

POST-RECOVERY

The Ways I Changed

When I was getting close to the end of treatment, my stepmom asked me, how I had changed.

I replied, "I don't know. But I do know I'm different."

"What does that look like?" she asked.

I said, "I guess we'll find out as we go along."

She agreed to take that journey of change with me and be flexible about the person I'd become.

***

It took me a couple of months to figure out where I was headed after chemotherapy. When I first returned to teaching, I was … not ready to be there. I was exhausted and couldn't really handle the energy of the students. The first couple of weeks back showed me some truths very quickly:

- I was tired of caring more than my students.
- I was tired of trying to motivate my kids to do work, tired of finding ways to help them be successful when they weren't willing to even do the minimum effort.
- I was tired of reading *To Kill a Mockingbird* out loud because they wouldn't read it on their own.
- I was done with the discipline and the shenanigans, knowing that most of the behaviors in the classroom had very little to do with me and more to do with their lives outside of school.

As an English teacher I was supposed to focus on curriculum and not my students' personal needs and problems. That stuff doesn't get measured in the standardized tests and the data one of the assistant principals is paid to track. Emotional health is not something education administrators care about. They care about test scores, attendance rates, and graduation rates. The data collectors, assessors, and teacher evaluators aren't concerned about whether a kid was beat up by his father, or if she didn't have breakfast, or if his mom is being abused by her boyfriend. Those things are not factored in any of the testing data.

When I compared my students to the patients in any waiting room, I realized my compassion had switched. I cared more about people as people than as students. Maybe I just realized I could be a different person in a different job. Maybe I would make more of a difference in a different profession.

***

It took me some time, but I eventually went back to school. I hit a bump in the road, trying to figure out where and what I wanted to study. I started with a master's in counseling, but I had second thoughts.

One day, I called Dad and said, "I'm thinking of switching to a master's in social work."

Dad didn't even pause before he said, "I think that's a good idea. What made you make the change?"

"The amount of doors an MSW would open to me as a social worker."

I could work in hospitals, hospices, residential facilities, community behavioral health facilities and endless other possibilities, including politics. A master's in counseling didn't offer such options.

As the school year grew closer and closer to the end, Josephine, the lead English teacher, came to me a couple of times and said, "What are your plans for next year?"

I said, "I've got all my ducks in the pen at least. I just need to get them to line up."

She asked for specifics, and the biggest issue was how I would pay for medical insurance. I couldn't just take the graduate-level medical insurance. Because I was a cancer survivor, I needed amazing medical insurance.

I found out that if I took a leave of absence from Boon Win, I could pay for my medical insurance through the high-school's group plan. When that was up and no longer available to me, the Affordable Healthcare Act would be in place, and I would be able to get insurance through the marketplace.

I figured this all out within moments of needing to write the letter requesting the leave of absence. Mr. Trebuchet said I had to give him the letter that afternoon if it were to be read at the next board meeting, which was to be held a few nights later.

It all went through, and I entered West Chester's master's in social work program.

***

To say that having Hodgkin's changed my trajectory would be an understatement.

If it weren't for my waiting-room companions, I never would have realized how much I like working with sick people. I never would have learned how to have compassion for anyone in traumatic situations.

However, I wasn't ready to face the hospital just yet. My first-year internship was at the Victim Services Center in Norristown. One time in this internship, I worked in a hospital emergency room, helping a rape victim get through a rape exam. I had to take deep breaths much of the time. I also counseled many people who were dealing with traumatic deaths, molestations, and violence. I learned that their trauma-related symptoms were not that different from my own. I learned that I had to take care of myself before I could really help others get past their trauma.

My internship supervisor rocked. She and I connected at such a fantastic level. She would challenge my ways of thinking. She pushed me when I was insecure, supported me when I screwed up, and laughed with me when I was laughing at myself. This internship helped shape the kind of clinician I wanted to be.

My second-year internship was challenging in very different ways. I worked in a community behavioral health setting. I had been thinking about working in a hospital, but I had a couple of key conversations that helped me put my decision in a different perspective. I needed more time to let myself heal psychologically from my own medical experiences before I could help others cope with being in the medical system. I wanted to hone skills that would be transferable to the medical setting: anger management, mindfulness, emotional regulation and how to cope in challenging, even overwhelming, situations.

I had lived through hospital trauma, and I wanted to give myself more space to heal before I served in that capacity.

***

Right now, I work with youth living in a residential facility, some of whom want to work through their trauma experiences. I have been applying to hospital social work openings as well as social work opportunities in hospice. However, I haven't been called to any interviews. I didn't do medical social work in my internships and the skills I do have are not what people are looking for in their medical social workers. I have started to volunteer at the Hospital of UBF in the hopes that making connections will help me work my way into the system. But as it stands, I wish I had received other advice from advisors regarding where I should have done my second year internship.

***

I changed in other ways as well.

I made a mental list of all of the ways I'd put off living before I got sick, ways I'd protected myself from pain and rejection. I actively worked toward making changes in those areas.

After cancer, when I had something important and burning to say, I said it. I let more people into my head and heart. I wasn't so afraid of conflict. I decided I would rather be authentic than let people think everything was okay, when it really wasn't.

I stood up for myself and protected myself from hurtful people. I chose whom I wanted to spend time with rather than with those I was expected to spend time with. I made changes about where and with whom I spent holidays.

I also stood up for people when I heard about unjust situations and there was something I could do about it. When I heard students were being treated unfairly at Boon Win, I e-mailed Mr. Trebuchet, even though he was no longer principal but had been promoted up to the head office. I wrote him and gave him my opinion.

Here was something else I learned as a result of having cancer. Being real and authentic in all areas meant sharing your thoughts and feelings and taking responsibility when you made a mistake. I screwed up. It happened. I said things that didn't come out as I meant them. I made decisions that I should have looked into a bit more before making. I took responsibility where I messed up. What I still needed to learn, however, was how to take credit when I was doing something well.

Faith

Some parts of this section, if not all of them, are hard to write.

I took a writing class when I was a graduate assistant at West Chester University's Writing Center. The professor—a white woman with a lovely southern drawl whom I came to adore, and we now get together whenever we can—was describing a writing assignment. She wanted us to be "personal" but not necessarily "private." The thing is, in this book, I'm personal and private. This book takes the reader into some pretty intimate moments and, at times, I wonder if I am comfortable with that. But cancer changes everything, from whether you can hover over a toilet to pee to the way you deal with family dynamics. Doctors don't tell you that, either. They also don't tell you, "Your faith is really important and will help you, but cancer can turn the most faithful person into a doubter."

Or even an atheist.

By the time I had cancer, I had read the Bible all the way through three times. At seventeen or so, I promised God I wouldn't have sex until I was married, and at twenty-two or so I decided oral sex was sex and stopped having that as well. I didn't change jobs until I felt He had said, "Go." I was actively involved in a church, and I was waiting on God for two major things: my husband and being able to make a living off of my writing.

At the end of my cancer ordeal, I didn't trust God. I didn't trust Him to take care of me, and when people said he was good, I wondered about the validity of such statements. I always thought that if God treated me as He'd treated Job, I would be as successful as Job was. But I wasn't. And I took it personally.

If a best friend had the wherewithal to help me financially but that friend chose not to help, I would wonder about the friendship. I would see her lack of help as a lack of support. Yes, it was her money, but if she had endless reserves that would never dry up and didn't use them,

I would be disappointed. If I had sacrificed over and over and over for the sake of that friendship, I would be more than disappointed. I would feel betrayed.

God, according to the Bible, had the ability to heal me. He had the ability to make it all better with a single laying on of hands. He didn't. I took that personally.

One day in church—I was better, but still recovering—a friend said, "I heard a word for you in the service. It's not a very nice word though."

"I'll take it," I said, sincere, open, and listening.

He said, "Entitled."

I thought for a moment and then said, "Yup. I do. I feel like God owes me something and that He's holding out."

"You need to work on that," was his response.

The truth is, I now wonder about the kind of God who is in heaven.

***

One night after class, I was talking to one of my Masters in Social Work compatriots, Jena. I said to her, "I just need to pray about something that's really bothering me. Do you mind?"

"Nope," she said. "Go for it."

I prayed aloud, and when I was done she said, "Do you realize that you told God you don't trust Him?"

"What?" I said.

"In your prayer just now, you said you really wanted this thing to work out, but you didn't trust Him to do it."

I paused and then said, "Yeah, I believe that's true."

"How can you pray to a God you don't trust?"

"I guess it's the same thing as praying to a God I'm not sure is real," I replied.

I hopped into her Jeep, and she drove me to my car, which was parked on the other side of campus. We sat in the car and talked for about two hours. I told her a bit of my history: raised Jewish, converted to Christianity when I was fifteen, went to a Christian college, got an MFA from Goddard College, taught in Massachusetts and Maryland, diagnosed with Hodgkin's, and now in school for an MSW. I also told her that I hadn't had sex yet and that I was holding out for God's man. I told her I was God's bride.

I thought she would lose it when she heard that. "You haven't had sex?!?"

I laughed, feeling a little embarrassed and a little proud. "Nope."

"How do you live?" she asked in all seriousness.

I grinned. "Creatively."

She laughed. "Let's just see where you are at graduation," she said.

She was right. By graduation, I had intentionally lost my virginity, was practicing meditation and mindfulness, and had stopped going to church.

***

My last night at church I'd felt like I didn't want to go. I had been attending a truly unique congregation that met at a local church on Sunday nights. I walked in, found a seat, and thought, *I'm here to hear from God and see what He's up to.* I had a hard time with the worship songs and didn't sing many of them. I couldn't pour my heart into the words about surrendering to Him or trusting Him or singing about His goodness. Those were things I didn't feel or see.

I looked forward to what the pastor had to say. I wanted to hear what was in his heart for the people. But he got up and said, "My concerns tonight are what is in your heart. I want you to get into small groups, and pray about whatever concerns you tonight."

I wound up in some group, though a huge part of me just wanted to walk out. I hate groups for so many reasons, and that night reinforced my feelings. We went around and talked about our struggles. I said that I was struggling with my faith and where I stood with God. When it was time to pray for each other, I was told not to pray, since where I was coming from might not be from God. After fifteen years of faith, I was told not to pray.

I talked to someone I considered a friend, and she said, "That's what you get when you aren't sure of your faith."

But she encouraged me to come back and keep seeking.

***

During my conversation with Jena in her Jeep that night, she pressured me to state that I wasn't going to shelter myself off from life. What kind of God asks His people to do such things? Though I agreed with her, I wasn't willing to say it.

I wasn't willing to say, *I'm done waiting on God.* I wasn't willing to say, *I'm done holding out for what might just be a myth.*

I started to pay attention to my breath on a regular basis and found peace in a way I never had with prayer. I no longer judged myself so harshly. I gave myself room to make mistakes. I gave myself the ability to be flawed.

I gave myself grace in ways I never had as a Christian.

As a Christian, I embraced Bonhoeffer's idea of "cheap grace"— meaning that it would be for nothing if Jesus died but we continued to live as we wanted, doing whatever and expecting forgiveness. Bonhoeffer's words fed my perfectionist tendencies. But by releasing my grip on Christianity and seeing the good in Buddhism and Judaism as well, I allowed myself the ability to be human and be okay with that.

If you had told me before cancer that I would turn my back on God, I never would have believed it. I would have told you there wasn't any way. But now, yes. There is a way. It comes from feeling betrayed.

***

It was five years out of cancer, and I didn't believe in God. In fact, I felt like I was a better version of myself without God. Erin said I was still on a spiritual journey—it started with Judaism in my childhood, Christianity in my adolescence and young adulthood, and as I approached my forties? I was not sure.

I was now more content with where my life was. I didn't judge others or myself harshly, the need to be perfect dropped off, the ability to be compassionate and loving grew, and my happiness increased. I was no longer fighting my nature and my natural self by trying to live up to some biblical standard of what life should be like. I no longer thought it possible God wrote the Bible. I no longer believed all the Bible and church folk had to say. I had a bigger view of God than the Bible offered, and the idea of eternity without heaven no longer scared me shitless. Living and experiencing all aspects of life became important, but discipline also mattered—I kept my room clean because I liked living in a clean space. I watched what I ate because I wanted a fit body and I didn't want to put too many harsh and toxic chemicals into it— chemo was plenty of harsh chemicals. I traveled to visit friends because relationships are important to me. Without using a God perspective, I identified my values and started to live by what was most valuable to me in my own core. I started to say how I was feeling, started to date, started to stand up for myself, and started to identify what kind of work I wanted to do professionally. I invested in those decisions. Waters rippled into tidal waves at times, as I confronted those who hurt me, instead of turning the other cheek as Jesus instructed and allowing myself to be hurt over and over. I found myself in new conflicts as a result and embraced the idea that conflict is an opportunity for growth and change, for me and for the relationship.

Without God, I no longer hid behind faith, waiting for Him to sculpt my life into something I wanted it to be. I embraced life and living—which meant risks, boldness, and authentic honesty and vulnerability. These were new values I embraced.

An Update on My Side Effects

During one of my first meetings with Dr. N after chemotherapy, she kept telling me that she wanted me to exercise. I had to go to physical therapy for the neuropathy in my right leg, but with that and teaching, I was wiped out.

I still didn't exercise very much, even five years out of treatment. I climbed a ton of stairs at work. I also liked to walk the dog. Those things were not intentional exercise, however.

It wasn't until I was about to start graduate school that Dr. N handed me a report and said, "Read this."

It was an update on my latest scan. It said that one of my lungs had partially collapsed because I'd been spending so much time on the couch, and exercise was recommended to make it fully inflate again.

I had a 9:00 a.m. class on Mondays, for which I was regularly late. I would text the professor and complain about traffic on the expressway. There was rarely anything express about the expressway; it was a complete misnomer.

I'd hoof my ass to class as quickly as I could, usually carrying a ridiculously heavy bag, weighing between fifteen and twenty pounds, slung over one shoulder. The walk from the music building to my class was one full block, up a set of stairs, past the library, down a walkway, through the heart of campus to the other side of the quad, down another walkway, down a set of stairs, and about another half a block to the front of the building where class was held. I would get to class winded and exhausted. Many days, I would drop my bag quietly, slip into my seat, and flop my arms over the desk so my hands were hanging off the front end. Then I would put my head down between my arms and pull air into my lungs, exhale, and pull it in again. My body expelled the breath without me trying. It was so hard to get the air in. I would sit and puff like that for a while before I could pick up my head and join the rest of class in the discussion.

I didn't tell the professor until much later that I'd had a partially collapsed lung at the beginning of the first semester.

He said, "Why didn't you tell me?"

I shrugged. "I didn't think you needed to know. It was just something I was coping with."

You don't get something for nothing.

***

The weird yellowing of my fingers was less prevalent the second winter after chemo. Dr. N asked about it while I was still teaching, and I said, "I haven't had a problem with it. But it was a mild winter."

She nodded.

The winter after that, however, was not mild. The winter of 2013 to 2014 was bitterly cold, with snowstorms almost every weekend, which affected most Mondays. I always wore fingerless gloves that winter. I wanted to experience winter in all of its coldness to see what my fingers would do. They never yellowed or became numb or wonky.

When I told Dr. N later, she said, "I'm glad. That's one less thing we have to worry about into the future."

However, in the not so cold parts of late 2015 and early 2016, the index finger on my right hand would turn faintly yellow and started to hurt. Clearly, "could be for the rest of your life" was my reality.

My right leg, however, was another story.

***

The toes on my right foot couldn't curl for a long time after chemo, perhaps a year and a half to two years. At the start of my second year in graduate school, I was standing outside curling my toes in my flip-flops, and my toes started to curl for real. They curled so tightly, they pulled on my Achilles tendon and made both my toes and ankle cramp up in pain. I was so excited by the pain and the curling, I kept doing it. Curl, cramping toes, then cramping ankle, which I wouldn't release until I couldn't handle the pain any longer.

I found myself scratching itches in my right thigh every now and then. I wouldn't realize I was doing it. I would be holding a pen, a pencil, a knitting needle, sometimes it was just my fingers, and probe into my thigh looking for the itch. It was only when I found the spot and gave it a good poke, which caused ripples of pain throughout my thigh, that I would realize I was scratching.

My thigh seemed to be in a constant state of electricity. It always felt charged. At times, I had tingles in my knee. Or I had a thickness in the thigh itself. It would feel a bit achy, a bit tingly. It was the sensations before the painful itching started.

I recently went to buy a pair of jogging shoes (as if I would ever jog).[20] I tried on two different pairs, and one pair pushed on my right toes in such a way that they got cramps and hurt. It wasn't a bad pressure either; in fact, my left foot rather liked it. But it was too much for my right foot.

At one job, we had to practice restraint holds. Once we were practicing how to take a person down to the floor. We had to rely on our legs to support us as we held the individual with our arms. I took one of my colleagues around her waist, held her arms, practiced taking her down, and I realized that if I did that with her in my arms, we would both fall and maybe get very hurt. She tried to get me to try again, but there was no way, no way, I was going to put her at risk because my right leg was messed up.

The trainer looked at me after my partner had successfully taken me down a couple of times and said, "What's up with your leg?"

"My right leg is fucked up from chemotherapy." And it might be for the rest of my life.

---

[20] I recently learned that I have exercise-induced asthma. I knew that I had hated to run since I was in high school, because I couldn't breathe when I did. This new diagnosis gives me additional knowledge about my body and how it works. This new information makes me wonder what I can do to support my lungs if I am interested in cardio exercise in the future.

Final Words on What the Doctors Don't Tell You

When I told Dr. N I was writing a book titled *What the Doctors Don't Tell You*, she said, "We don't tell you much. We don't, because we want you to go through treatment. Treatment can save your life. If you know too much, you won't do it." She paused, then said, "Who would?"

***

Everyone told me that when my hair came back after chemotherapy, it would come back thicker and curlier. They were right. The hair on my head was full of cute curls.

What the doctors didn't tell me was that it would grow back thicker and curlier *everywhere*. I had hair in places I'd never had it before. Hair grew on my lower back, and it was inches long and curly. The second Thanksgiving after cancer was hosted by Wendy. Some of my family members talked about having their body hair lasered. I reached around to my back, grabbed one of the hairs that was growing where a tramp stamp would have been if I had one, and pulled it out. We all decided that this was not acceptable.

I'd felt ugly enough during cancer. I wasn't going to be ugly after cancer by having man hairs growing above my upper lip and from my chin. I went to a laser treatment center and paid to have it all removed.

***

The doctors also didn't tell me that I would become more of a makeup hound, nor that I would become a person who was worried about my appearance after cancer. One might think the opposite would be true; after all, I'd been okay about not having any hair, but I now love having sparkly doo-dads in my hair. Even if it's short, I have bobby pins with bling.

I also became a glitter eye shadow fiend; the more glitter, the better.

At my twentieth high-school reunion, I wore sparkly eye shadow and silver glitter eyeliner. One of the people I used to walk the hallways with at Lenape Valley Regional, a beautiful, tall, and striking woman, stopped me and said, "I love your glitter eyes."

I replied, "You can never have too much."

That's not exactly true. But after cancer, I really don't care what people think. I like glitter eye shadow. It makes me happy, brings me joy, and makes me smile. I want way more of that in my life—things that make me smile and bring me joy.

***

I went to the gynecologist shortly before I graduated from the Masters in Social Work program. I went in with a list of concerns, and one of them was I thought I was perimenopausal. That was what my knitting friends told me when I described my symptoms, many of whom had already gone through menopause. When I sat down with the gynecologist, I said, "I think I'm perimenopausal."

She said, "Why do you think that?"

I listed my symptoms. "I'm beginning to have spotting between my periods. I have incredible vaginal dryness, so much so that I shred toilet paper. I have itching before my period arrives. I'm having horrible night sweats."

Before replying, she thought for a few moments and said, "You're making a really good case about why you think you are perimenopausal. But your age … you're 37. That's too young for you to be perimenopausal."

"And I'm a cancer survivor. I had Hodgkin's and was treated with chemotherapy," I replied.

"You're perimenopausal," she decided. Then she said, "We will give you a blood test, but it might come back with a false negative. It has to be taken at just the right moment of your cycle to really register."

When I told this to Dr. N, she said, "That makes me really glad I didn't give you six rounds, like I was thinking."

My snarky response was "I probably wouldn't have done them."

I'd learned something else. Not only does chemotherapy affect the ovaries and the potential of getting pregnant; it can also kick-start menopause in relatively young women.

***

Another thing the doctors didn't tell me is that my personality would change and make me a pariah among my family members, who were used to me acting in some very specific ways. The doctors also didn't tell me that what I had tolerated before would become things that I wouldn't just accept.

I used to make excuses for bad behavior, saying, "That's just who they are," or "She's just like that." Now, those excuses aren't enough. There's no reason for a person to be rude or judgmental. There's no reason for a person to put others down all the time, even if it's a sign of how badly they feel about themselves. I used to be the brunt of family jokes and accepted being called the crazy one or the unwise one. Now, I speak up for myself. I fight back and say, "I'm sure that not all of your decisions were wise, but I certainly hope that they added to your happiness."

I also recognize my flaws and admit them. As a result of cancer, I am learning to be authentic with everyone. And that weirds some people out.

A Carolyn Update

Carolyn, whom I also called Sunny, got married in January 2014. She married a man she'd been seeing for years, and he finally asked. The wedding was a delightfully beautiful affair in Whistler, British Columbia.

It was cold in Canada in January. Sunny had all her bridesmaids wear little black dresses and gave us light blue pashminas to wear. Jennifer, Sunny's sister, and I went upstairs during the cocktail hour to change into more comfortable little black dresses. Her wedding was the night the Seahawks won their championship.

Seattlites, Canadians, and Sunny's friends and family were celebrating all over the lodge.

Sunny gave birth in August 2014. She was a mom, something she had always dreamed of being. She saw her baby as a miracle and a dream fulfilled, which filled me with joy as well.

The tumor in Sunny's head had started to grow about two years before her wedding. She took the chemo pill for a year, but it was not very effective. Although the tumor didn't grow anymore, it didn't shrink either—meaning chemotherapy was not effective in her situation. At least, not that type of chemo.

If (or really when) it would start growing again, radiation and surgery would be the most likely treatments, unless one of the miracle pills one hears rumors about[21] works for Sunny.

---

[21] Doctors in England and the University of Pennsylvania are working to refine a miracle pill. Once the pill is swallowed, it attacks and destroys cancer cells. The agents in the pill stick around and then attack any future cancer cells as well. The validity of such statements is still under question, and much research is going into these little miracle capsules.

***

One Thursday morning in late March 2015, I received news that Sunny's tumor was growing again. She had gone in for her six-month checkup scan and found out that not only was it growing; part of it was "enhanced."

I questioned what "enhanced" meant; both Sunny and her husband were unable to give more information than the tumor was taking in more of the sugar dye than another part of her tumor.

Lots of texts flew on Thursday from Seattle to my phone and back again. Sunny stated she was going to take another leave of absence from work. She would know more in a couple of days, but the doctors wanted to try both proton therapy and chemotherapy. The schedule for proton therapy would be daily for six days a week, making her progressively exhausted as time went on.

My heart broke for Sunny, her husband, and their daughter—their little baby-bear.

To be honest, my heart is broken in general. When I received the news, my heart was already pricked by heartache. There are times I don't know that I'm doing well handling this Sunny update. If I even start talking about it, my eyes well up, my breath becomes ragged, my throat tightens, and I get slightly nauseated.

Her news also changes some of my beliefs about the world. Perhaps "happily ever after" doesn't exist. Perhaps in this life you only get pockets of peace, joy, and contentment. When those times arrive, you should hug them tightly, swallow them whole, and enjoy them with everything you have, because you don't know how long they are going to last.

Thinking about my own cancer situation and Sunny's cancer situation, I want to live without regrets.

My Soapbox

I moved back to my mom's when I enrolled at West Chester University. I wanted to be a person who supported people emotionally in the same way doctors and nurses worried about a patient's physical frame. During treatment, while I was receiving my doses, or afterward when I was recouping at home, no one talked to my family and me about how our souls and psyches were handling the chemotherapy. People were concerned about blood counts, blood clots, and lymph nodes, but not about the effect being sick had on me as a person.

I decided I wanted to support patients and families through sickness. Then I found out, only children's hospitals hire people to do that kind of work. I was told adult hospitals have social workers but only for discharge planning and bed finding. The social workers are not paid and do not have time to worry about the spirits, souls, or psyches of patients and their families. Hospital social workers are not there to make sure that patients and families are coping with what is going on at the hospital, unlike social workers who work in hospice care. Instead, social workers at hospitals do behind the scenes work of discharge planning and coping with insurance companies.

One can make the case that hospitals, insurance companies, and the US government do not care about how a patient copes with the diagnosis of a disease and its appropriately administered treatment. If they did care, they would fund and hire social workers to do the work that helps patients and their families cope with mortality, death, and the mental-health side effects that accompany grief, loss, treatment, and the reality of one's mortality.

Despite what I have heard about what hospital social work is, my dream is to work with patients and their families. My dream still is to support sick people in the way my family and I were not supported. I want to be in the medical system. Maybe from within I will be able to help change the medical model. But more than that, I got into social work to make patients lives and their family's lives better. However that looks – creating a discharge plan, sitting on the phone with insurance companies – taking some of the burden off of the family is my ultimate desire.

ABOUT THE AUTHOR

Kimberly Beam holds a master's of fine arts in creative writing from Goddard College and a master's in social work from West Chester University. She currently works as a clinical therapist in the Philadelphia suburbs. Beam knits floppy hats and fingerless gloves. She dreams of finding her soul mate and one day moving back to the coast.

Printed in the United States
By Bookmasters